Daycare Institutions and Children's Development

ARNE SJØLUND
*Danish National Institute
of Social Research*

Translated from the Danish by
W. GLYN JONES

SAXON 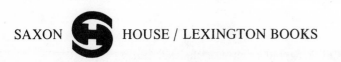 HOUSE / LEXINGTON BOOKS

Published by

SAXON HOUSE, D. C. Heath Ltd.
Westmead, Farnborough, Hants, England

Jointly with

LEXINGTON BOOKS, D. C. Heath & Co.
Lexington Mass. U.S.A.

First published in Danish as
*Børnehavens og vuggestuens betydning
for barnets udvikling*

☺ Danish National Institute of Social Research,
1969

ISBN 0 347 01021 0
LC No. 73-10635
Printed in Great Britain by Kingprint Limited, Richmond, Surrey

Contents

PART I

The Object and Method of the Study

1 The Aim and Background of the Study

The position of daycare institutions

In 1968 there were rather more than 7,000 children in day nurseries and more than 45,000 children in nursery school in Denmark. These figures show a rapid increase. Ten years ago there were just over 4,000 and 29,000 children respectively in these institutions, and twenty years ago fewer than 2,500 and 18,000. Today there are very long waiting lists, in addition to which there is a considerable but unregistered demand for places.

The demand for day care for children under school age comes from various groups with widely varying motivations for their wishes.

Lone parents, which in most cases means mothers on their own, are in great need of having their children looked after during the daytime, while they themselves are out at work. Their needs have always been at the heart of the daycare institution's social function. This group has been on the increase, and the job possibilities for mothers on their own have certainly changed in such a way that fewer and fewer can look after their children at the same time as they go out to work, but it seems likely that this group only accounts for a modest proportion of the increased demand for places in daycare institutions.

Married women taking work because of the low wages earned by their husbands also represent a notable proportion of those seeking places in institutions. It is not possible to say how far this group contributes to the increase in demand, however; neither is it clear when the wife's income should be looked on as a necessary supplement to the family income, and when it is a question of raising the family standard of living above the necessary minimum.

Other women wish to undergo training or to make use of the training they already have, and they look on daycare institutions as a means of avoiding putting an end to their career because of the need to look after their children.

Others, again, do not consider taking work outside the home, but wish to see their children admitted to a day nursery or nursery school for at least some hours each day in order to reduce the burden of work in the home.

Finally, an ever increasing number of mothers wish to place their children in nursery school, because they believe the children will benefit from it. The institutions are seen as a supplement to the home, offering possibilities for development which the limited opportunities found in the home cannot equal.

Alongside these motives it is to be supposed that the general trend in the direction of greater liberty and equality for women plays its part. Women's desire for financial independence, their desire for equality in training, in employment and careers, and their desire to be relieved of menial household duties and freed from the narrow milieu of the home, also seems to contribute to the trend.

In most instances there is presumably a mixture of motives, and the divisions between the groups are not sharply defined. Thus many mothers will have given consideration to the question of whether periods spent in institutions have a good or bad effect on their children; among these there will be many of the mothers who are compelled to make use of them.

Apart from some minor and insufficiently documented reports, no actual examination has been made in Denmark of the motives prompting families to seek to place their children in daycare institutions (though on the other hand there have been some short studies of the employment situation of mothers who have children in nursery schools). It is therefore impossible to know whether other motives than those listed are of significance. Nor is it possible to know what importance can be attributed to each individual motive in the overall picture. On the other hand it can be documented that even women with small children are to an increasing extent undertaking paid employment. There are signs of a change of attitude towards daycare institutions, in particular towards nursery schools. While many formerly considered them a reasonable way out, though less good than a home upbringing, it now seems that there is an increasing confidence in the nursery school's beneficial influence on the children. This clearly emerges from the demand for nursery school places from mothers who have not and do not intend to take paid employment. Some regard the nursery schools as a social service which should be available to all.

The point of view that nursery school places should be available for everyone wanting one is the conclusion reached in the section entitled 'Long term views in principle' in the report on nursery school problems published by the Educational Committee for the Care of Children and Young People, (337, 1963). The report states:

4

Concerning long term developments in principle the committee considers that it would be reasonable to build sufficient nursery schools for all parents so wishing to have the possibility of sending their children to a nursery school without payment.

The committee agrees that it seems reasonable that society, which feels it a duty to provide schools and training institutions free of charge for all children of seven and over, should feel the same duty to provide a basic education for children of nursery school age.

The justification for this must first and foremost be consideration for the education and development of each individual child, that is to say, the educational principle, and in the longer term the development to be aimed at should be half-day nursery schools rather than full-time institutions.

Present estimates of the demand for places in daycare institutions vary greatly, depending partly on the kind of needs considered. In Study number 10 of the Danish National Institute of Social Research, *The care of married women's young children* (Bentsen, 1968), there is an extensive discussion of these problems. Among other things, emphasis is laid on the uncertainty felt in estimating the desire of women at home to send their children to nursery schools. Likewise it is stressed that the demand depends, among other things, on the existence of other possibilities for having the child looked after, on the location of the nursery schools, their price and their quality. If sufficient nursery schools are to be created for all parents so wishing to be offered free places for their children, it is to be foreseen that the number of places available today will have to be increased very greatly indeed.

Traditionally the objectives of daycare institutions are categorised as social or educational. The first of these should coincide with the needs of mothers forced to work outside the home, while the second is intended to meet the children's need for greater opportunities for personal development and for playing in groups with others of their own age. The division of these two objectives is historically the result of the present-day nursery school's development from, on the one hand, institutions built with the social objective of providing for the children of mothers at work, and, on the other, from the nursery schools based on the educational theories of Fröbel and others.

In many countries the division into half-day and whole-day institutions has coincided with the division between educational and social institutions, in the sense that the latter were rather 'somewhere to go', while the former were 'somewhere to learn'. This is the case, for instance, in the

United States and Sweden, where 'nursery school' and *lekskola* are half-day institutions with an educational objective, and 'daycare' and *daghem* are whole-day institutions with a social purpose. The former are principally intended for the children of parents at home, the latter for children whose mothers go out to work.

In Denmark there are also characteristic differences: only 13 per cent of children attending nursery school in Copenhagen are registered as half-day children, while the corresponding number for Gentofte is 49 per cent.

This division into two categories is, however, scarcely suited to present day conditions. To begin with there is a general tendency to lay greater and greater emphasis on the educational responsibilities which the institutions have towards children from the lowest social strata. In other words there is a greater realisation of the possibilities which the institutions have of stimulating and developing the very children who were once seen as predominently social responsibilities. Secondly, a great deal of the increased demand for institution places is of a completely new kind, being the result of far-reaching social movements and changes in social attitudes and family life. Thirdly, it is contrary to current ideas in Denmark that the quality and the services offered by the institutions should be inferior for children from less fortunate social surroundings. In the face of these new demands the tasks of the institutions can be classified neither as social in a narrow sense nor as purely educational.

The growing concentration of the population in urban areas, with less room to move around or to play, the possibility for more women to take employment, the willingness of women to go out to work, the changed concept of the mother's role in bringing up her children, and the growing realisation that early educational stimulation is of importance for normal and socially-advantaged children as well as to the handicapped and socially less fortunate, have all contributed to a development pattern which has entrusted daycare institutions in modern society with a host of different tasks.

Suspicion of daycare institutions

As has already been indicated, it is a general feeling that small children are not looked after as well in institutions as by their mothers. This feeling is still very widespread, especially where very small children are concerned. The same scepticism towards the institutions is to be found among experts in the field; it is directed especially at day nurseries, but also at very long periods spent daily in nursery school. The risk of infection in large groups has played its part, but in particular the feeling has been that the mother would be best equipped to give the child the love and individual attention it requires, and that the small child needs stable conditions and tender care by a single adult, and only later is sufficiently mature to be able to take part in the life of a larger group.

In the case of day nurseries the alarming results of research into the harmful effects of residential institutions on very small children's physical and mental development (Bowlby, 1951) have given rise to some—not entirely justified—concern. The question of the extent to which these results can be applied to daycare institutions will be discussed in more detail in the chapter on day nurseries, but even at this point it can be stated that one cannot, without reservation, draw parallels between the effects of a complete loss of the mother in residential institutions and the fact that a child in a daycare institution will miss its mother for part of the day.

This does not, however, resolve the problem. Even though the effects of periods spent in daycare institutions are nothing like as serious as can be the case of periods spend in residential institutions, there can still be some doubt as to whether children benefit from being in daycare institutions.

Experts consider that the conditions in which a child grows up before reaching school age are of the greatest importance for the development of character, but the question of the influence of daycare institutions still remains unresolved, and no Danish investigations of the subject have yet been published.

In view of the fact that the institutions play an essential role in looking after small children, and that the authorities are by and large favourably disposed towards the institutions, the question of their effect on the development of children has become of immediate importance.

The object of the study

This study takes the form of a review of research already carried out, and its object is to provide a critical evaluation of methods and results and a summary of international knowledge in this field. Investigations into the influence of daycare institutions on children's development must in the first instance effect a comparison with children who are looked after in other ways. The comparison has often been with children who are looked after at home by their mothers. Such comparisons are of great interest to mothers whose situation is such that they can make a more or less free choice and, without incurring any great sacrifice, elect to stay at home while their children are small. But the comparison is of less significance for mothers who for financial reasons are obliged to go out to work or for other reasons are under pressure to do so. In cases such as these a comparison with other methods of looking after children, e.g. private child minding or care at home by a domestic help or older brothers and sisters will be more relevant. Available studies only deal with alternative methods to a very limited extent, whether they are hypothetical or experimental or whether they are methods which mothers do in fact use. This is unfortunate, as the question is relevant to the situation in Denmark.

A few studies have been made of the effect of residential care in comparison with a home upbringing supplemented by daycare institutions. This aspect is relevant in areas where there are no daycare institutions and where, for example, unsupported mothers are obliged to put their children into residential institutions in order to support themselves. All available studies of this question are unfavourable to residential institutions and might well give a stimulus to the establishment of suitable opportunities for daytime care in areas where mothers might be forced into a choice between applying for supplementary benefit or sending their children to a children's home.

In general, however, it must be pointed out that investigations so far only indirectly and to a limited extent throw new light on the problem of daycare institutions versus private daytime care. The two methods have in common the fact that the child must do without its mother for part of the day. In daycare institutions the child has the advantage of excellent opportunities for play, for educational stimulus and for learning to take its place in a group; if cared for privately it has the advantage of a quieter milieu akin to that with which it is familiar, together with more individualised care, that is to say advantages comparable with those which the mother herself can offer. To the extent to which it is possible to observe that children in daycare institutions develop more rapidly than children who stay at home with their mother, it is perhaps justifiable to assume that the same differences will occur when compared with privately organised individual care. But in cases where the effects of periods spent in institutions are doubtful or even negative compared with those of being brought up at home, it is impossible to say whether the provision of private care would have been better for a child than institutional care.

As has already been mentioned, suspicion of institutional care is most widespread where very young children are concerned, and where the expense per child incurred is the greatest. This study deals with much valuable research in this field. It has been suggested that it might be as well to make a direct payment to the mother to enable her to stay at home and look after her child without any great financial sacrifice. How the criteria for deciding payment should be worked out is not relevant to this study; on the other hand it would be extremely valuable if it could establish the results of comparisons between children who have spent much time in day nurseries and those who have been brought up at home by mothers who have been given a sufficiently large grant to enable them to stay at home without intolerable sacrifice. This question, however, does not seem to have attracted the attention of foreign researchers.

Meanwhile research has been carried out on the effect of institutional care on various groups of handicapped children. Examples are mentally subnormal children, physically handicapped children, children with sense defects and children from poor and so-called culturally deprived homes. This last category has attracted much attention in recent years, as such homes, with their very narrow horizons, give their children an extremely poor start in the educational system. The groups mentioned have not all been studied with equal thoroughness, but in some instances it is possible for this investigation to refer to a large volume of important literature. In so doing we shall be able to break down the far too general question of the beneficial or detrimental effect of daycare institutions into a series of more closely defined questions of which children in which situations can derive benefit from daycare institutions.

Similarly the question of the best means of equipping the institutions, the optimal length of stay there each day, and even the educational aims and methods have been the subjects of research in both ordinary and experimental institutions.

Teachers, architects and administrators will be able to ask far more questions on these points than the available research can answer, but the study can nevertheless present an up to date summary preliminary report on these problems. This is particularly true of the daycare institutions' possibilities for establishing a milieu conducive to emotional, intellectual and social development.

This examination and evaluation of the large number of investigations has necessitated a critical appraisal of the methods used. The experience gained from this has led to the formulation of a theoretical framework for such investigations, as will be seen in Part II of this book. In the examination of the individual studies in the later sections in the book, some critical and methodological comments are made which refer back to the considerations contained in Part II. This theoretical work has been necessary for the evaluation of the results of the various research projects, and it emerges that hardly any of the projects are ideal. But this examination of the methodological problems can have value in itself if ever it is decided to carry out an investigation into the significance of Danish daycare institutions for children's development.

The object of the present work is, by means of a study of international research, to discover the effects of time spent in daycare institutions on children's development, especially on their psychological and social development.

As has been said already, no Danish studies on this subject have yet been published, and the possibility of applying the results to Danish conditions is limited by the fact that there are relatively few studies from adjacent countries, while the many carried out elsewhere refer to conditions different from those in Denmark. Moreover, it is a disadvantage that a number of the questions which are current in Denmark have not been treated in depth anywhere else. Finally, the methodological problems in investigations of this sort are enormous and few projects entirely overcome them.

The examination of a great number of studies can, however, present an up to date account of available knowledge and establish contact with modern educational thought and experiment in this field from countries outside Denmark. The very concrete questions which gave impetus to the investigation, i.e. whether any significant research has been carried out which throws light on the urban child's upbringing in day nurseries and nursery schools as opposed to an upbringing at home with the mother, can be answered in the affirmative. But on many points the results of this research can only be seen as points of departure for further studies of the situation in Denmark.

2 Collecting and Preparing the Material

Earlier reviews

No comprehensive critical evaluation of the effects of pre-school institutions on the child's development has been published anywhere before.

There are in existence a small number of partial reviews of certain aspects of the question, e.g. the effect of nursery school on a child's social development (Jersild and Fite, 1939), on the child's intellectual development (Wellmann, 1945; Hunt, 1961), on the emotional and intellectual development (Moustakas, 1952) and its significance for subsequent progress at school (Gardner, 1967 a and b).

A common factor in these reviews is the fact that they cover a specific area of a child's development, but only two (Wellman, 1945, and Hunt, 1961) attempt a critical analysis of the results contained in them.

In addition there are a few reviews which cover more than one aspect of the effect of nursery school and seek to consider the child's development as a whole (Sears and Dowley, 1963; Swift, 1964; Stukat, 1966). However, these merely recapitulate the results of previous research without seeking to evaluate them critically.

All these reviews have in common the fact that they only take into consideration a small selection, mainly American, of the available research results.

A new Danish review of the influence of pre-school institutions on the child's development in relation to its readiness for school (Schultz Jørgensen, 1968) is distinguished partly by covering more than one aspect of development and partly by carrying out a systematic criticism of the validity of the studies concerned. However, the analysis includes 39 studies only, almost all of which are American, dealing with all aspects of the child's development. In addition it is limited to an examination of whether nursery school has a given effect or not, but it does not look at the preconditions necessary for producing or not producing this effect.

The studies summarised in the reviews are all included in the present analysis, and their conclusions are taken into consideration in the methodological discussion.

The collection of available material

The available material on completed research and work still in progress was registered in two ways, on the one hand by going through specialist literature and tracking down published results, and on the other by means of a questionnaire on social research circularised by the United Nations office in Geneva to correspondents in member countries.

This questionnaire brought in information on something approaching 100 studies which either had not yet been published or else were of such recent date that they had not yet been included in international registers.

As for the USA, which was not included in the questionnaire, research in progress, and recently completed research projects were traced, as far as possible, mainly through Science Information Exchange: Children's Bureau, Division of Research, Department of Health, Education and Welfare and through Research Relating to Children, vols. 1-18. (US Children's Bureau, 1953).

Published investigations were traced through the subject index of Psychological Abstracts 1927-1960, Psychological Index. From the references here summaries in Psychological Abstracts were examined, and relevant summaries transferred to card indexes. The volumes of Psychological Abstracts after 1960 were examined for relevant articles, which were also transferred to card indexes.

Then an examination was made of Child Development Abstracts and Bibliography for the years 1927-1966, and relevant summaries not already registered were transferred to card indexes.

The Education Index was then examined; this covers some 200 educational journals, and the references found here were looked up in the Educational Abstract, from which relevant summaries which had not already been registered were transferred to card indexes.

Finally the French *Bulletin Signalétique*, Sect. 19, *Sciences Humaines* and *l'Année Psychologique* were examined. By this means a number of eastern European investigations which were not contained in the American abstracts were discovered. These investigations were likewise transferred to card indexes.

This systematic examination of registers led in fact only to about two-thirds of the articles listed in this investigation. The remainder was found in more or less haphazard fashion through references in specialist literature, e.g. through the reviews mentioned above and through a close examination of particularly relevant periodicals which theoretically should have been covered by the registration systems referred to above. Since so many investigations are missed by the registration system there can be no guarantee that all available research has been taken into consideration in this study.

Consideration of the abstracts collected and selection for closer analysis

After articles were registered, an examination was made of the summaries; in some cases, however, it was first necessary to write a résumé. Of the approximately 1200 summaries thus collected, some 700 could on this basis be left out of further consideration as, although they were concerned with children of nursery school age and, in the main, with children actually attending nursery school, they only touched on general psychological problems and did not deal with the specific question of the effect which periods spent in nursery school had on them. The remaining 486 articles can be divided into the following three categories:

(1) investigations directly concerned with the effect of the institution on a child's development, including theoretical analyses of these investigations; there are 291 investigations in this category which are mainly dealt with in Part III;
(2) investigations indirectly concerned with the effect of the institutions and including, on the one hand, various aspects of the institution which might be thought to be of significance, and on the other examining the backgrounds of the different children at the start of their nursery school careers; there are 150 investigations in this category, including theoretical analyses of such investigations. These are mainly dealt with in Part V and Part IV.13 respectively;
(3) theoretical considerations of the problem of nursery schools which, while not in the true sense of the word being studies, nevertheless put forward relevant points of view. In this category are included statistical information on the extent to which use is made of nursery schools, the number of places, the need for places etc. There are 45 reports in this category, most of which are dealt with in Parts II and I.

All the reports in the first category, examinations of the effect of nursery schools, have been subjected to further analysis, cf. the following section.

In the case of the second category, various personal and institutional aspects, all have been included for the sake of the results they produce, but they have not been subjected to a systematic analysis, since on the one hand the material must be considered insufficient for final conclusions to be based on it, while on the other it appears to contain perspectives for future research on the basis of what turned out to be the principal conclusion of this investigation: that the question of whether nursery school is beneficial or not should be changed to the question of under which conditions a nursery school can have positive effects and under which conditions negative results can arise.

The investigations in the third category, the theoretical considerations, which are included, are such as can contribute to a deeper understanding of the points of view in the empirical investigations.

Analysis of the studies of the effects of nursery school attendance

The studies of the effects were all read and analysed, and the index cards were supplemented with other necessary information which was available: cf. the sample index card illustrated.

The reason for including this information will become apparent from the later section on the analysis of the scientific standard of the investigations.

The index cards were divided by means of a colour system so that the subject of an investigation could be clearly seen: the sort of effect; categories of children; variables in the nursery school. Moreover it could easily be seen whether each card contained statistical information, a discussion of aims or an investigation of methods. Finally the cards were divided according to the countries concerned.

Distibution according to country, year and subject

Apart from this division of the collected summaries into the three main categories described, summaries were also divided according to the country (or culture) from which the study stemmed, the time of the study and the subject with which it is concerned. These divisions are the subject of this section. Connections between these data and the results of the studies will be pointed out in the respective chapters.

Distribution according to country and study category

The material included in the study is divided according to the country of origin and sub-divided into three main categories as in Table 1.

INDEX CARD

Author: Title: Journal:
Setting: (field vs. lab., nat. vs. exp.) Subjects: (normal vs. special group, sex, age) Control group: (matching) Time span: Follow up: Methods:
Study:
Author's findings and interpretation: Our comments (on back):

It emerges from the table that the USA accounts for two-thirds of all studies. Apart from this there is in the main only research into nursery schools in Scandinavia, Great Britain, France and the Soviet Union (only reports in translation have been taken into account in this case), together with research into the kibbutz system in Israel.

American and British research belongs especially to category (1): 'What is the effect of nursery schools?'; while Russian and French reports figure in category (2): 'What should the nursery school be like in order to

TABLE I

The studies divided according to country and category: (1) studies of effects; (2) institutional and personal variables; (3) theoretical studies

Country of origin (cultural area)	Category				
	1 1	2 (figures in parenthesis also contained in (1)		3	Total
USA	213	137	(22)	13	341
Scandinavia	15	17	(4)	11	39
Great Britain	25	12	(11)	6	32
Soviet Union and Eastern Europe	9	20	(6)	7	30
France	10	13	(7)	3	19
Israel	10	1	(1)	0	10
Italy	3	1	(1)	0	3
Germany	1	2	(1)	1	3
India	1	0		0	1
Japan	1	0		0	1
Philippines	1	0		0	1
International	2	0		4	6
Total	291	(203−53)= 150		45	486

achieve such and such an effect?'; Scandinavia is equally divided between the two categories. While most American and British research is only concerned with the question in category 1, this question is the exception in French and Russian work. The question in category 2 is present in almost all these reports.

Category 3, which does not include all the available work in this field, does not give an accurate picture of the distribution by country because of the selection which has been made of work in this category. For instance the USA could in the 1960s be represented by a large number of theoretical dissertations centred on 'Operation Head Start'. West Germany, represented by one report in category 1 and two in category 2, could, according to information passed on by the UN, be represented by forty dissertations in category 3, mainly in the form of arguments for and against nursery schools, but without any empirical foundation.

Divided according to date of publication, divided into ten-year periods, and according to the three categories, the material is distributed as in Table 2.

TABLE 2

The studies divided according to the decade in
which published and the established categories:
(1) studies of effects; (2) institutional material;
and (3) theoretical studies

	Category			
	1	2	3	Total
Before 1930	13	2	0	15
1930–39	62	31	0	93
1940–49	57	34	1	92
1950–59	46	32	17	95
1960–68	113	51	27	191
Total	291	150	45	486

It appears from the table that the progressive rise in the number of studies is not maintained in the 1940s and 1950s in the case of category 1 or in the 1950s in the case of category 2.

A division according to different intervals indicates the following distribution for Category 1: 1925-34: 37; 1935-44: 71; 1945-54: 39; 1955-64: 101. This indicates that the fall in numbers is to be sought in the years from 1945-54, which is perhaps not surprising but may well be of significance in evaluating the results.

A corresponding reduction in the number of studies in category 2 is to be found in the years 1945-54, when 20 studies were published, while there were 44 in this category between 1935 and 1944 and 61 in the years from 1955-64.

Distribution according to year, country of origin and study category

Of studies carried out before 1930, 13 are American and 2 British. Of the

93 published between 1930 and 1939, 91 are American; of these, 62 are in category 1 and 29 in category 2.

Of the 92 studies carried out between 1940 and 1949, 84 are American, of which 51 are in category 1 and 33 in category 2; 5 are British, of which 4 belong to category 1 and 1 to category 3.

Of the 95 studies carried out between 1950 and 1959, 54 are American, of which 21 belong to category 1, 25 to category 2 and 8 to category 3; 13 are British, of which 9 belong to category 1 and 4 to category 3; 8 are Israeli, all in category 1. From the Nordic countries there are 6, 2 in each category.

Of the 191 studies carried out between 1960 and 1968, 100 are American, of which 66 belong to category 1, 29 to category 2 and 5 to category 3; 12 are British, of which 11 belong to category 1 and 1 to category 3; 26 are Russian, with 9 in category 1, 10 in category 2, and 7 in category 3. There are 31 Scandinavian studies, 12 being in category 1, 11 in category 2, and 8 in category 3. There are 12 French studies, 9 in category 1, 2 in category 2, and 1 in category 3.

This shows a rapid increase in the proportion of the studies carried out outside the USA. While in the 1920s these only accounted for 2 of 15 studies, in the 1930s 2 of 93, and in the 1940s 8 of 92, in the 1950s they accounted for 41 of 95 studies and in the 1960s for 91 of 191.

Distribution of effect studies according to the effect area studied and the time of the study

Divided partly according to which effect is studied and partly according to when the study was carried out, certain tendencies appear.

In general most studies of the nursery school's significance for a child's physical development are from the 1930s; of the intellectual development from the 1940s and for the start at school and culturally deprived children in the 1960s. Social development was studied most in the 1930s but again in the 1960s. Studies of day nurseries are in general of recent date.

The distribution of effect studies according to the area concerned, the date of the study and the relevant country

On dividing the previous distribution table, Table 3, according to the country in which the studies were carried out, further specific tendencies appear.

TABLE 3
The studies divided according to subject and decade of publication

	1920s	1930s	1940s	1950s	1960s	Total
Day nursery children	0	0	7	12	*25*	44
Social development	3	*23*	9	12	22	69
Physical health	3	*8*	4	5	*13*	33
Intellectual development	5	26	*35*	6	33	105
Start at school	6	13	7	8	*22*	56
Culturally deprived	0	0	0	1	*33*	34
Handicapped	0	7	4	9	5	25
Total	17	77	66	53	153	366
Dealing with more than one effect area	2	12	11	7	26	58

The studies of day nurseries proper have in the main only been carried out in France and eastern Europe, and most of these in the 1960s. A number of Israeli kibbutz studies are included in this category, dating from the 1950s. A number of studies taking the problem of deprivation as their point of departure were published in the 1940s in the USA and in the 1950s in Great Britain.

Studies of the health of children in nursery schools in the 1930s were for the most part carried out in the USA and Great Britain, while the number of such studies from other European countries rose in the 1960s.

Social development was studied especially in the 1930s in the USA and in the 1950s and 1960s in Great Britain and other European countries.

By and large, intellectual development was studied only in the USA from the end of the 1930s to the middle of the 1940s. In the 1960s studies of this nature were usually British, Russian and Swedish.

The culturally deprived were first studied in Israel, the first being in the 1950s. Since the 1960s the USA has been the main source of such studies.

All studies of the start at school were American until the 1960s, when 8 European reports were published.

The discussion and order of the studies

The space devoted to the discussion of the individual studies in this publication has not been dictated solely by their scientific validity. The point of view has been rather that, irrespective of the scientific value of the individual studies, they are not all equally interesting in the larger context. For instance a study of the skills of children attending nursery school and those brought up at home to fasten and unfasten buttons, which from a formal point of view is beyond criticism, has only received a brief mention. Other studies, for instance of the development of a child's personality or the way in which nursery schools are equipped, have, despite methodological weaknesses, been dealt with at greater length because of the perspectives which they open up, though methodological short-comings are pointed out.

Many studies are mentioned in several chapters. The main reference in this case is usually the first. In some cases, however, the principal reference will be found in the chapter to which it makes the greatest contribution.

In principal, the studies are arranged chronologically, though sometimes only after a sub-division, e.g. according to cultural sphere or country, if it is considered that this will be of benefit to the analysis. On occasion, for instance, American and European studies are treated separately.

However, the chronological order is frequently dispensed with, for instance when studies leading to different conclusions are compared with each other in the discussion, or when others are grouped together on the basis of methodological points of view, as for instance studies with and without control groups, etc. The order used should in these cases become apparent from the context.

PART II

The Problem of Effect

3 Expected effects

Types of effect

In studying the effect of nursery school on the child's development, various questions immediately arise as to which effects are to be considered, what they are to be compared with, how and when they should be measured. Should one try to discover whether nursery school has the effect which nursery school teachers maintain it has, or should one seek to ascertain whether nursery school has other effects which the teachers concerned have not noted? Should one look for a positive effect in the sense that time spent by a child in a nursery school should have a better effect than a purely home upbringing, or should one be content with the absence of a negative effect in the sense that the child's development is not retarded more by going to nursery school than it would be by remaining at home? It may be that the effect should not be compared with that of home upbringing, but rather with other available methods of looking after a child if the child were not attending nursery school and could not be at home because of the mother's need to go out to work. Furthermore, the question must be asked whether any positive effect from the nursery school can be traced beyond the commencement of school attendance, or whether it is sufficient that nursery school should have a positive effect as long as the child is there.

Parents' wishes

One obvious question is whether the effect of nursery school corresponds to the parents' expectations, whether these expectations be positive or negative, in order on the one hand to discover what the parents fear, and on the other to learn whether their wishes are fulfilled. Although it would seem reasonable to take the consumers' expectations as a point of departure, they are not the only thing to be taken into consideration. It is possible that nursery school has an educational influence which is of more significance for the child than the fulfilment of the parents' original expectations.

Nevertheless, this point of departure can throw light on some aspects of the problem. Among other things it would be important to discover differences between the expectations of parents and those of teachers.

Most parents whose children attend nursery school may be presumed to have positive expectations. But among those who are compelled to make use of nursery schools there may well be differences between the parents' and the teachers' expectations.

Negative expectations of the effect of nursery school are more likely to be found among parents who do not send their children. Some mothers stay at home to look after their children instead of going out to work. Others prefer private arrangements rather than sending their children to nursery school. This latter category does not, however, comprise large numbers; a Swedish study (Thorsell, 1966) shows that the great majority of working mothers prefer nursery school to private arrangements for home care.

Some mothers who do not make use of nursery school are presumably of the opinion that nursery school has an unfortunate effect on certain aspects of a child's development. A study of parents who have taken their children out of nursery schools would be of special interest as it would indicate some of the expectations which were not fulfilled.

Parents wishing to place their children in nursery schools have given various reasons for wanting to do so and have expressed different expectations of what a nursery school can achieve.

It is useful to distinguish between the categories of parents who have provided this information: (1) those with children in nursery schools; (2) those seeking places (perhaps with a child on a waiting list); (3) others who might be expected to make use of nursery school.

Unfortunately what is probably the most important category is not represented: the expectations of parents who have had their children at nursery school for some time. From studies of other social systems, i.e. groups, organisations, institutions etc., it is known that motives for seeking access to the system and for remaining in it can be different.

All these categories of people may well expect different things of nursery school. Neither in Denmark nor elsewhere is there one single study including all these categories, but some impressions can be derived from a comparison of various studies. Danish reports on the number of women at home who make use of nursery schools give some idea of how many in category 1 (those with children in nursery school) expect the nursery school to have a positive influence on their children. An English report has asked a group of mothers on waiting lists (i.e. category 2) about the motives prompting them to apply for nursery school places for their children, and some Norwegian investigations have undertaken broadly based analyses of needs among all mothers with children of nursery school age, i.e. category 3.

These reports are discussed below and indicate that the proportion of mothers wanting their children to attend nursery school out of consideration for the child's development increases from category 1 to 3. This tendency must be regarded with certain reservations as the reports come from three different countries, but it does tend to substantiate the widespread feeling that the scarcity of nursery school places gives the children of mothers with the most urgent social needs priority for places in nursery schools or on waiting lists.

Although Danish nursery schools are intended mainly to provide for the children of mothers who go out to work, a number of random inquiries indicates that the percentage of children placed in nursery schools for educational reasons is probably significantly greater than is generally assumed.

In the one year courses for nursery school teachers at the Danish Teachers' High School studies have been made over the past five years of children in nursery schools where the distinction has been made between the children of mothers at home and those whose mothers go out to work. Of the 60-100 children who are chosen each year at random for this study the percentage whose mothers are at home has varied between 30 and 39.

In a report on the position of married women in the home and at work the Institute for Social Research was able to state a few years ago that of married women with children in nursery school 44 per cent were at home, while 56 per cent went out to work (Bentsen, 1968). A report published in *Forebyggende Børneværn* (Fredsted, 1967) concluded that only about 25 per cent of married women with children in nursery schools were at home. The explanation of these different figures is presumably to be found in the fact that the last figures are based on registrations, since the mothers either had or professed to have a job at the time of registration, while the figures provided by the institute are based on whether the mothers in fact did go out to work or not.

The study carried out by the Institute for Social Research of precisely which married women make use of nursery schools in no way indicated that nursery schools are an institution particularly used by mothers in difficult social or financial situations.

Apart from in rural areas, where nursery schools are almost unknown, it appears that married women with larger incomes tend to make relatively more use of nursery schools. Only 7 per cent of the lowest income group had children in nursery school. In the middle income bracket there were 17 per cent, while in the higher income bracket 30 per cent had their

25

children in nursery schools. The tendency is even more pronounced in the case of mothers at home, taken as a single group. In the higher income bracket six times as many sent their children to nursery school as did those in the lowest income bracket (23 per cent as opposed to 4 per cent).

Similar tendencies will be found by division into social status. In families in the highest social strata (cf. Kaare Svalastoga, 1959) mothers at home make just as much use of nursery schools as mothers out at work. In the strata below these, i.e. minor officials and shopworkers, skilled workers and unskilled labourers, however, mothers at home do not make nearly so much use of nursery schools as mothers who go out to work.

This indicates that the higher the income, the higher the social status and the higher the standard of education, the greater will be the tendency amongst mothers at home to send their children to nursery school; in fact they do so as often as do mothers going out to work. This undoubtedly indicates that motives other than the traditional social ones are beginning to make themselves felt.

A British investigation (Gardner, 1957) asked 438 mothers on the waiting lists for eight nursery schools what were their reasons for wishing to send their children. The reasons given were as in Table 4.

TABLE 4

Mother out at work	224
More room to play	154
Getting used to children of their own age	151
Relieving burden on parents on account of housework, night work, illness and pregnancy	108
For the child's health or recommended by doctor	94
Unsatisfactory living conditions	84
Adjustment difficulties; difficult to bring up	73
Learning routine actions	50
Brothers and sisters in nursery school	40
Preparation for school	26
Total	1004

Of these, half the reasons given (510) can be classified as social: mother out at work, bad housing conditions, reasons of health and relief for parents; the remainder, 494, are classified as educational: room to play, getting used to other children, brothers and sisters, learning routines, difficult to bring up, preparation for school.

In two Norwegian reports from Oslo (Lie and Egge, 1965) and Bergen (Ås, 1966) people with children of nursery school age were asked whether they would like their children to attend nursery school if they could get a place. A good two-thirds of those asked would have liked a place. 19 per cent of these mothers already had a job, while 81 per cent were at home. Of the 81 per cent at home, 33 per cent replied that they would take a job if their child was admitted to a nursery school, but 48 per cent answered this question in the negative, stating that they would prefer to remain at home.

The first report dealing specifically with the relationship between the desire to have a child in a nursery school and the mother's work situation comes to the conclusion that in the majority of families parents wish to see the child in a nursery school for the child's own sake. Families interviewed who had found places for their children in nursery schools laid particular emphasis on the positive effect which the nursery school had had on the child and its development.

Thus it is important to appreciate the fact that a very large proportion of parents seeking nursery school places for their children—certainly a third, and perhaps as many as a half—do not merely wish to have the child looked after while they themselves go out to work, but want their children to attend nursery school for educational reasons. Both the British and the Norwegian studies indicate that the same motivation is more pronounced among mothers with children on the waiting lists, and still more so amongst all mothers with children of nursery school age.

This situation stresses the importance of the question of the educational aims of the nursery school and the educational effect it will have.

The nursery school's own objectives

It might seem more reasonable to relate the problem of effect to the objective of the individual nursery school, that is to say the aim which it maintains it has. The question of whether the nursery school does in fact achieve what it theoretically sets out to do, however, produces a number of problems. To begin with, it is difficult to be precise as to what the objective of the nursery school is. Public authorities are often very imprecise when talking on this subject. On the other hand, nursery school teachers are much more precise in their statement of aims, but such studies as there are, for instance questionnaires sent to nursery school staff, show great differences of views as to what the aims should be. Should a study then be based on the aims which 'most' or 'the best' claim to have?

A Swedish study (Stukat, 1966), with the object of examining the extent to which nursery schools fulfil their aims, formulated a theoretical aim on the basis of interviews with 31 nursery school teachers. They were asked to indicate what in their views were the primary objectives of a nursery school. The replies could be divided into 13 categories, as is indicated in Table 5.

TABLE 5

Teachers' views on Swedish nursery school's aims (31 replies)

	Categories of objectives	No. of teachers	%
1	To teach the children to associate with each other and work in groups, learn consideration for others, reduce exaggerated aggressiveness	31	100
2	To encourage the children to behave spontaneously and with confidence, remove shyness, inhibitions and nervous difficulties	26	84
3	To teach the children good habits, to keep their things in order, to manage dressing and undressing, keep to time, to be polite	26	84
4	To accustom children to tell the truth and to teach them the difference between right and wrong	25	81
5	To teach the children to respect rules and prohibitions	24	77
6	To train the children to sit quietly and listen, to develop their ability to concentrate	23	74
7	To develop (manual) dexterity	20	65
8	To give speech training and remove speech difficulties	19	61
9	To develop the children's desire to learn, create healthy and constructive interests and to stimulate aesthetic interests	16	52
10	To teach children physical control	14	45
11	To carry out regular health checks and to teach the children personal hygiene	14	45
12	To instruct the children about nature and society	14	45
13	To prepare the children for school	12	39

(From: Stukat, 1966).

A questionnaire sent to a group of 40 experienced Danish nursery school teachers in connection with this publication asked what the teachers considered to be the most important aspect of the nursery schools' work with children, and to arrange them in order of importance; the replies could include as many or as few points as the individual desired. The replies received could be divided into 12 categories, in the main corresponding to the Swedish analysis with the exception of point no. 13, preparation for school, of which no mention at all is made by the Danish teachers. This might be explained by the fact that the Swedish teachers were from half-day nursery schools (*lekskolor*).

When the Danish teachers concerned had been given a further opportunity of arranging in order of importance the objectives for nursery school which they had originally mentioned, this being done in order to discover each individual's attitude towards aims which she had not mentioned in the original, spontaneous questionnaire, the order was as follows, in order of importance:

(1)   Learning to adapt to society, development in a social context;
(2)   Personal development, independence etc.;
(3)   Linguistic development;
(4)   The ability to play;
(5)   Motor development, physical and rhythmical sense;
(6)   Development of the imagination;
(7)   Development of creative and constructive abilities;
(8)   Intellectual development;
(9)   Natural and spontaneous behaviour;
(10) Cooperation between nursery school and home on upbringing;
(11) Widening of the child's horizon, learning about the world;
(12) Good habits.

Although the two tables on the whole contain the same categories, there are nevertheless some striking differences in the suggested order of importance. The development of good habits, which takes third place in the Swedish report, comes last on the Danish one. In the Swedish report the first half includes such things as teaching the children to tell the truth and to distinguish between right and wrong, teaching them to respect rules and prohibitions, and training them to sit still and listen, none of which are mentioned in the Danish report. The Danes, on the other hand, include among the most important objectives play and occupation, the development of the imagination, the development of a child's creative talents and musical instincts. These are not mentioned in the Swedish survey.

It is difficult to decide whether these differences are only apparent, due to differences in language, or whether they indicate real differences in the objectives of nursery schools. They do, however, emphasise the fact that research into the effect of time spent at nursery school cannot exclusively be based on the objectives claimed by the individual teachers.

In addition it must be pointed out that general educational objectives are often normative in content, following some way behind the actual social developments and tendencies. For this reason the objectives do not always correspond to the aims of the teachers themselves. An investigation of effect basing itself on objectives thus risks being out of date.

Meanwhile a study of the effects of nursery school in relation to the stated objectives of nursery school teachers is not without interest. Such a study, especially of it does not lead to a positive result, can either help to change the objectives or, if no change is desirable, can lead to a consideration of more suitable means of attaining the desired objective. One objective of nursery school which is often emphasised, helping the child's motor development, is not, according to available research, in fact achieved. There is no difference in this field between a child attending nursery school and a child kept at home. As the nursery school provides everything needed to attain this objective, the explanation can scarcely be that there is anything wrong with the methods, but rather that children kept at home will themselves discover means of developing themselves in this way. It seems, therefore, that the objectives of the nursery school in this area need to be revised. It may not lead to any better result than normal, but of course it must provide an equally good means of encouraging motor development as the home. The child's development of linguistic skills which is also often mentioned as one of the objectives of nursery school is another in which results are difficult to determine, especially for older children. According to available research, however, there is even a tendency for children in nursery school to be retarded in comparison with children brought up at home. Here it is hardly the objectives of the nursery school which need changing, but rather some of its activities, so that the objectives can actually be attained.

One objective which nursery schools often hesitate to mention, the intellectual development of the child, is on the other hand one in which research indicates positive results. This area would be low on the list of subjects for research if the professed objectives of nursery schools were taken as the sole guide.

In addition, it must be mentioned that objectives obviously undergo changes in the course of time. A study of registered research projects divided partly according to date and partly on the basis of the effect being studied, indicates that educational objectives change in accord with social needs. Reports from the 1920s are particularly concerned with the effect of nursery school on a child's health; in the 1930s the social effects predominated, and now, in the 1960s, interest is particularly concentrated on the effects of nursery school as a preparation for school.

The weightiest objection to using the nursery schools' objectives as a point of departure for research into effect is the fact that the research is automatically prevented from looking for other effects which are not included in the objectives. It might well be in this unstudied area that negative effects would be discovered.

The child's developmental needs

Instead of taking the needs and expectations of others as a point of departure, it could be worthwhile to consider the extent to which nursery school fulfils the child's own developmental needs. Reports on day nurseries indicate that if the original objectives of the day nurseries are taken as a starting point (physical care and feeding), it is possible to trace a positive benefit ensuing from time spent in a day nursery. On the other hand, if the child's physical need is taken as the starting point—and this is the most important aspect at this age—then research in many countries suggests time spent in day nurseries has a negative effect on this.

Child psychologists have produced various developmental theories based on a number of essential needs in the child of pre-school age. If the child is to undergo its optimal development these needs must be satisfied at the right time and in the right manner, and the question is to what extent daycare institutions contribute to this or, perhaps, even hinder development.

The British psychologist Susan Isaacs has in an article (Isaacs, 1949) and a book, *The educational value of the nursery school* (Isaacs, 1952) summarised the needs which nursery school can help to fulfil as follows: (1) warm human relationships; (2) confidence and security; (3) active experience based on reality; (4) the opportunity to develop as an independent individual; (5) play with other children. Isaacs sees this last point as being the most fundamental need of a child of nursery school age.

Two American psychologists, Sears and Dowley (1963) have summarised the needs in children to which nursery school can make the greatest contribution as follows: (1) to fulfil the child's organic needs and help it form good habits in regard to eating, cleanliness, sleep, washing and dressing; (2) to contribute towards physical achievements such as climbing, running, jumping, balancing, learning to use the body effectively and reducing fear of trying strength or exercising other abilities; (3) developing the ability to manipulate small things as, for instance, the use of a pair of scissors, coloured chalks, clay, plasticine, to build with bricks, to do puzzles and play with marbles, to tie knots and learn to use buttons; (4) to learn self discipline and self control: to sit still, to listen to stories, to react to music, etc.; (5) to develop considerate behaviour: to balance dependence and independence in the relationship between adults and children, to control fear, anger, guilt feelings, to develop happiness, amusement, humour and healthy optimism; (6) psycho-sexual development: the discovery of identity, the role of the sexes and the development of conscience; (7) linguistic development; (8) intellectual development: cognitive learning, the formation of concepts, the understanding of self and self-respect, creativity and subjects preparatory to school.

Developmental psychology indicates that these needs are not all equally felt at different ages, which means that the effect expectations must of necessity be seen in relation to the stage of development reached by a

At the same time a new line of thought in developmental psychology suggests a hierarchical establishment of a child's needs, which in short means that a need arising at an early stage of development must be more or less satisfied before the child can move to the next stage. At the same time there are moments in a child's development when the satisfaction of a need has the optimal effect, while it will be difficult if not impossible at a later stage to achieve full development of this aspect of a child's personality, if the right moment is missed.

An example of this sort of theory on the development of needs is that of Maslow (1943 and 1954). After all the physiological needs for nourishment, sleep, movement etc. are satisfied, these being, of course, of fundamental importance, there comes a hierarchy of psychological needs, here listed with the most fundamental first: (1) the need for confidence and security; (2) the need for love and a sense of belonging; (3) the need for self-evaluation, self-confidence, self-assertion, respect and self-respect; (4) the need for self-realisation, for being able to do one's best and to achieve something; (5) the need for knowledge and understanding (curiosity); (6) aesthetic needs.

Maslow mentions other needs which arise later, but those listed here arise in normal children before school age. Maslow's thesis is that if one of the more fundamental needs predominates in a child, and is thus unfulfilled, the others will not show themselves, and the child's development in these other spheres will be harmed. For instance, if a child aged five or six, when the need for self-realisation, achievement, self-assertion and knowl-

32

edge will normally be predominent, suffers from an unsatisfied need for confidence and security, this need will take precedence. It will overshadow the other needs which at the given stage of development (5-6 years) ought to predominate. These theories also contribute to consideration of which effects of periods spent in daycare institutions for which age groups it is most important to examine.

Erikson (1950 a, 1950 b) has produced a similar theory on the emergence of a series of fundamental needs which must be satisfied at definite stages of development in order to ensure a healthy psychological development.

The fundamental need in the first year of life is the establishment of a basic confidence in the world around the child, which presupposes warm and constant contact with an adult. If the child does not achieve warm and stable contact, this side of the development of its personality is affected, and a fundamental lack of confidence in other people is established.

In the second stage, 2-3 years, the foundations are laid for the development of an individual personality. The child seeks to develop its independence, and the important factor in this period is the way in which these efforts are handled. If the child is thwarted in its attempts to achieve independence, it will develop doubts as to its own ability, and its personality may well become characterised by insecurity.

The main feature of the third stage, 4-6 years, concerns the development of initiative and self-realisation. The basis is created here for the child to become active and creative, to develop its initiative and become a person able to make the most of his or her abilities. At the same time the child's conscience is undergoing a rapid process of development. If the child's development at this stage is hindered, it will, according to Erikson, develop too strong a sense of guilt which will impair its initiative and creative achievement.

The problem which is always of supreme importance when a child is to be placed in an institution, the separation of mother and child, must thus be seen in the light of this development of needs in the child. The mother-child relationship varies in character and has differing significances at different stages of development. The institution will have correspondingly different tasks at different stages of separation from the mother. It may well be asked how the child's needs are fulfilled by the mother and the institution respectively at the different stages of its development: on the one hand the *security phase* with its need for love, security, confidence and a close relationship with a grown up; the *independence phase* with its self-assertion, wilfulness and the creation of self-confidence; the *initiative phase* with its urge to explore the surrounding world, the need for self-realisation and self-development through freedom to explore and create.

The essential question here is from what age a daycare institution can enrich a child's existence, from what age it can reasonably replace the home, and whether there is an early age at which the institution cannot fulfil the child's demands, but rather deprive it of its needs.

In the consideration of studies of the nursery school's effect on a child's development these aspects of psychological theories on development will be taken into account, and at the same time the extent to which the nursery school's own objectives are achieved will be examined.

The appearance of positive or the absence of negative effects

The next question in connection with the problem of effect is whether one should expect to find a positive effect from the child's time in nursery school in comparison with what a home upbringing would have achieved, or whether the mere absence of negative effects is sufficient. An examination of all the reports listed shows that almost all studies of day nurseries look for possible harmful effects of time spent in day nurseries. On the other hand most studies of nursery schools assume that nursery school will produce some positive effect.

There are, however, certain exceptions, studies carried out in West Germany, Holland and Switzerland often assume that nursery school might have some harmful effect on the child, whereas on the other hand Scandinavian, Anglo-Saxon and eastern European studies aim at deciding what are the positive effects of nursery school. The same is true of most French studies. Seen together, however, these two points of departure complement each other, since studies with positive expectations especially underline the advantages of nursery school, while studies with negative expectations point especially to their weaknesses.

Expectations of effect of this type can also vary according to the sort and quality of the nursery school in question. In American studies a positive effect is expected from time spent in nursery school, while studies of what are known there as daycare institutions usually expect neither a positive nor a negative effect, or possibly actually expect to demonstrate a negative effect.

At this point it is reasonable to relate the expectations of effect to the object of placing a child in nursery school. If the object in placing a child in a nursery school is to attain some educational aim, the expectation is presumably some positive effect which the institution can give, but which the home cannot; otherwise there would be no point in sending a child to nursery school for educational reasons. If, on the other hand, the object of sending the child to nursery school is what is usually referred to as social, i.e. to have the child looked after while, for instance, the mother is out at work, it must be sufficient simply to expect the absence of negative effects, that is to say that the child will develop in nursery school in the same way as it would at home.

Meanwhile, it is not established that the appearance of positive effects or the absence of a negative one should be related to how the child develops at home. In cases where the child cannot be at home it is reasonable to relate the effect of nursery school not to the child's development at home, but to the alternatives available to nursery school, i.e. private daytime care or some way of having the child cared for by someone other than the mother.

As has already been pointed out, nursery school is widely used in Denmark by parents who believe it will have a good effect on the child's development, that is to say for educational reasons. Danish nursery schools have indeed combined social and educational points of view in formulating their policy. While many other countries have two sorts of nursery school, the educational and the social, as is the case in England, USA and Sweden, both objects have been fused into one institution in Denmark. It therefore seems reasonable to expect that Danish nursery schools should have a positive effect on the child's development. On the other hand, when talking of day nurseries, which are mainly used by mothers who are prevented from looking after their children during the daytime, it is perhaps sufficient to be content with the absence of negative effects.

The occurrence of effects

When it comes to ascertaining the occurrence of effects, a number of questions immediately arise. It might well be that nursery school has a positive effect on all children, but it is also possible that it will only have a beneficial effect in the case of certain groups and will have a negative effect on others. Here we can distinguish between the *universal* effect of nursery school, an effect which it will have on all children, and its *partial* effect, an effect which will only be found in certain categories of children.

Then comes the question of whether nursery school has an effect on the whole of a child's development or only on certain aspects of it, whether that effect be positive or negative. Influence on the whole of a child's development can be termed the *general* effect of nursery school, while influence on certain aspects of development can be termed the *specific* effect.

In addition there is the question of how and for how long the effect will be discernible. Here, in contrast to the usual distinction between short term and long term effects, it is possible to distinguish between the following four forms of effect: (1) *the actual effect*: is the child's behaviour in nursery school different from its behaviour elsewhere?; (2) *transfer effect*: is the effect brought about in the child while under the influence of nursery school transferred to spheres outside the nursery school and will some mode of behaviour learned in nursery school occur at some time when the child is not at nursery school, for instance when it is at home?; (3) *temporary effect*: will the effect of nursery school on a child's behaviour show itself elsewere at a later time, for instance in the child's social behaviour when he or she starts school?; (4) *permanent effect*: will the effect of nursery school also be seen in the child's behaviour elsewhere and at all times and are there areas where nursery school will have a permanent effect on the development of a child's personality?

Among the studies listed there are examples of all these types of effect. The permanent effect of nursery school attendance is, for instance, dealt with by Skeels (1965) on the basis of an evaluation of the children's success in subsequent marriages and careers. The temporary effect was studied, for instance by Jersild and Fite (1939). The actual effect has been noted in the majority of studies.

This division implies the possibility of a distinction between the effect here and now and the effect elsewhere and later. Various studies of teachers' views on nursery school children do indicate that the freedom of self expression experienced in nursery school makes it, according to these teachers, more difficult for the children to adapt to school. And on the other hand, a positive effect later in life can be the result of a negative situation here and now. This matter is relevant to the question of the extent to which nursery school should prepare a child for school, possibly by means of activities which, at the moment of influence, do not have a positive effect, for instance learning to sit still in nursery school as a preparation for starting school proper. This problem can be called the nursery school's *preparation effect* as distinct from its actual effect. This leads to a fundamental educational problem: if a positive preparation effect presupposes a negative actual effect, e.g. training and exercises instead of play and personal development, is it really worth it? Here the value of the desired preparation effect must be weighed against possible disadvantages and undesirable long term effects in other areas resulting from a negative actual effect.

Views on psychological benefits and costs

This problem, however, concerns not only the nursery school as a preparation for school, but also all areas where there can be a conflict between present and future effect. In point of fact, in every single examination of effect it is necessary to ask whether any immediate positive effect will subsequently have to be paid for in the form of a negative effect. For instance, does the greater freedom afforded by nursery school mean that the child will later have difficulty in settling in at school? Or, on the other hand, does an immediate cost lead to a subsequent gain? Do the disadvantages coupled with the greater freedom to come through conflicts in nursery school lead to a positive gain in the form of greater maturity in the child when faced with conflict? The relationship between immediate and subsequent effect and between positive and negative effect can be combined in the following gain/cost possibilities:

+ + positive effect now and later.
+ o positive effect now but not in long term.
+ − positive effect now, but negative effect later.
o + no effect now, but positive in long term.
o o no effect either now or later.
o − no effect now, and negative effect later.
− + negative effect now, positive effect later.
− o negative effect now, no effect later.
− − negative effect now and later.

Furthermore the appearance of these effects can be correlated with the child's point of departure resulting from the psychological and social conditions of the home: especially well placed (+), average (o) and especially poorly placed (−). The home conditions can be taken into consideration in evaluating the immediate significance of the nursery school, which is thus seen in relationship to a child's subsequent development against a background of its situation before starting nursery school.

Since these combinations can vary further from one area of effect to another, each of these possible effects should in theory be studied for each of the areas.

In addition it can be of significance to combine the present and future gain/cost possibilities with the division 'here' and 'elsewhere'. A 'gain' in nursery school in the form of increased activity or increased independence can lead to a 'cost' at home in the form of more conflict with parents.

4 The Problem of Measuring Effects

The validity of effect measurements

The relevance of the material

The value of studies of the positive or negative effects of nursery school depends on whether the work has been carried out in relevant areas of development, at relevant points of time, after a relevant amount of influence and with the use of relevant methods.

One study consists merely of a projective test comparing one group of former nursery school pupils of which some had attended for a month, others for several years, with a corresponding group which had not attended nursery school. The tests were carried out 10 years after the children had left nursery school, and no differences were found between the groups. On this basis it is scarcely possible to conclude, as the study does, that nursery school has no effect.

Nor can a valid sign of the effect of nursery school be expected by studying children a month after they have started attending, and certainly not if they have only attended for two hours daily.

Conversely it is naturally impossible to take a positive effect demonstrated in one particular sphere of training with which the children have been particularly preoccupied as an expression of the general beneficial effect of nursery school.

Many of the studies registered were quite uncritical about the extent of the influence to which the children have been subjected, and the effects of which it is intented to study. Some have included all the children having attended nursery school, whether they had only spent a month there or whether they had spent all their pre-school life there, and these studies find it difficult to be specific about effects. The length of time spent in the institution each day can also be important. Attention should presumably be paid to what proportion of its day a child spends in nursery school. It could be that the influences a child is subjected to outside might counteract the effect of nursery school. If the child only spends a short time in nursery school, the influence it derives from it might be completely overshadowed by those from other sources. Presumably some minimum period of time spent in nursery school must be presupposed before any effect can be determined. This is probably of special importance when wider aspects of the development of a child's personality are to be studied, but perhaps less important if it is a question of some specific form of training.

A closer examination of the studies which conclude that nursery school has no effect can contribute to the solution of these methodological problems, especially when they are compared with studies concerned with positive and negative effects respectively.

The representative nature of the material and the general validity of the result.

A precondition for generalising on the basis of the results of one experimental group and transferring its findings to other nursery school groups or from one nursery school to another is that the experimental group or the nursery school studied is representative of the population or category for which the results of the study are claimed to have general validity. This means that the experimental groups should be taken either systematically from the larger group they are to represent or that a check is subsequently made to ensure experimental groups which are taken without such precautions are representative of the population as a whole. This problem has been overlooked in most studies, which is unfortunate, as much evidence points to the fact that nursery school children so far have not been entirely representative of the age groups from which they come. They are either, as in the American kindergarten, financially better off than other children (McCay et al., 1940) or as in the English nursery school financially worse off than other children (Gardner, 1967 a and b), so that it is not possible to generalise and say that so and so many effects are to be seen in children attending nursery school.

Even greater problems concerning representativeness can be supposed to be present in most studies when it comes to deciding which nursery schools to include. In many cases the initiative for a study of the effect comes from the nursery school itself. This in itself means that it cannot be representative of other nursery schools, and this distinction can be presumed to cover other qualitative differences, so that the results an individual nursery school of this type can arrive at cannot without further ado be applied to other nursery schools.

Other studies have been made in special experimental nursery schools concerned with teaching or research, and the results of effect studies from these can scarcely be applied to nursery schools in general (although it is obviously quite possible to carry out controlled methodological experiments in such special nursery schools).

A general effect study of nursery school must include a representative selection of nursery schools, which can presumably best be done by some independent research institute. But it will probably be of more practical interest to discover what effect specific categories of nursery school (e.g. 'good' and 'bad') have on children from specific backgrounds (e.g. 'better off' and 'worse off').

The basis for comparison (the problem of control groups)

Measuring the course of development

The earliest studies of the effect of nursery school often used the method of comparing the condition of children on entry with their later condition, and they often demonstrated a positive effect resulting from the time spent in nursery school. After a certain period of attendance a noticeable development could be traced in most of the areas studied. It was forgotten, however, that nursery school age is a time of rapid development, whether a child attends nursery school or not. Only when a group from nursery school is compared with a control group, i.e. with children not attending nursery school, is it possible to see whether nursery school children develop better or worse than do children at home. Later studies using this technique have been unable to demonstrate positive effects to the same extent as the earlier studies apparently could.

A very comprehensive study carried out in the Iowa Child Welfare Clinic of the intellectual development of children was able to show that the mental age rose 6 points during the winter six months, during which the children attended nursery school, but only 1 point during the summer six months, when the children did not attend. This was taken as a sign of the positive effect of attendance at nursery school. Meanwhile Jones (1951) studied the intellectual development of a corresponding group of children who did not attend nursery school and covering the same two periods; he demonstrated the same course of development in them. This has led to the conclusion that the changes were due to seasonal variation and not the effect of nursery school.

It is of crucial importance for the comparison that a control group should be chosen which corresponds as closely as possible to the nursery school group in all respects apart from nursery school attendence. Several of the studies registered suffer from the defect that the control group is a more or less a random group. Therefore it is not clear to what extent differences noted between the nursery school children and those in the control group should be ascribed to attendance at nursery school or to other differences.

The significance of this emerges from a study made by Trusal (1955). Trusal studied children starting school to see how far they were in fact ready for it. A division of the children into those who had attended nursery school and those who had not showed without any doubt that nursery school children led in all fields. Trusal then compared two groups of children, some of whom had attended nursery school and some of whom had not, composing the groups in such a way that their backgrounds were identical in many respects; there was then no difference in the two groups' readiness for school.

The important question is in which areas the experimental and control groups should be identical. It is obvious that the groups must from the start be identical with respect to the development areas in the child which are being studied. In addition, however, the groups should as far as possible be identical with respect to all the factors determining a child's development, i.e. the child's entire background. The first factor to attract attention was the child's milieu, including the parents' social status, education and financial situation. Then came the structure of the family, i.e. whether it was stable or broken, the child's sex, whether it was an only child or one of a group of brothers and sisters etc. More recently attention has been paid to selective factors implicit in the parents' decision whether to send the child to nursery school or not. This decision can cloak considerable differences with regard to the pattern of upbringing and the parents' attitude towards their children, so much so that these factors can themselves have different effects on children's development. Thus it is by on means certain that differences in the development of nursery school children and children staying at home should be ascribed to nursery school attendance as such; they may well result from the effect of different home attitudes.

Some of the most recent studies have solved this problem by choosing the control groups from children on waiting lists or from parents wishing to send their children to nursery school, but failing to find a place.

Another form of selection is to be found in the fact that some children attend nursery school because they are badly looked after at home.

Even in cases where poor care at home is not serious, it is doubtless one factor influencing the parents' decision to send the child to nursery school. Nursery school children might thus be rather more poorly placed than some children brought up at home, although this will not always be to such an extent that it can be measured by simple means.

Similarly the fact that some mothers send their children to nursery school because they want to spend their own time on something else can result in such children developing less successfully than children brought up at home by mothers who enjoy looking after the children themselves.

Not only can a positive attitude on the part of the parents towards nursery school be expected to have an effect on the child, but so can a negative attitude. There are mothers who do not wish to send their children to nursery school but are forced to for social reasons. Their dislike of nursery school can affect the child's attitude to it and thus militate against a positive effect.

A third selective factor which is difficult to control is the fact that children who settle down well at nursery school probably stay on longer than children who do not settle in. Thus, children who have attended nursery school for a long time and therefore must be considered as specially suited to effect studies, could for that very reason be an atypical positive group. A study of children taken out of nursery school after a short period of attendance would probably produce much useful information to complement our knowledge of the effect of nursery school. As yet, no such studies have been registered.

The greater the number of identical factors between an experiment group and the control group, the greater the number of children there must be to choose from. Stukat (1966), whose study is one of the few to fulfil all the criteria for homogeneity mentioned here, had some 1,200 children on the waiting list from whom to choose his control group, and of these he succeeded in finding 139 who could be paired with corresponding nursery school pupils.

The difficulty in attaining the ideal of finding sufficient identical pairs has resulted in most studies being satisfied with identical groups in the sense that the researchers have been content if the relevant factors have been more or less equally spread through the two groups, but not between individual children; this, however, must be likely to veil important factors.

These problems of comparison have, in some of the most recent studies, led researchers to adopt a new technique. Instead of the impossible task of composing two completely identical groups they have taken the experimental group and the control group as they are and sought to define the differences there must be between the two groups of material, and to take account of these differences in working out the results of their studies. This was done, for instance, in a Polish study of day nurseries for WHO (Gornicki, 1964). By using this approach it is possible to work with a larger amount of material.

Matching the groups can thus be done in two ways, either by making up two more or less similar groups before commencing the study, which for practical reasons means that the material will be fairly limited, or else by starting with a larger amount of material and subsequently correcting on a statistical basis the differences between the experimental group and the control group.

Prospective and retrospective studies

There are in principle two different ways of studying a course of development: it can be traced forwards from a given point in time, e.g. from starting in nursery school to starting school proper:

$$\text{from a} \longrightarrow \text{b}$$

Or it is possible to go from some given final point of time to the beginning of a given influence:

$$\text{to a} \longleftarrow \text{b}$$

For instance at some level in school the children can be divided into good and bad pupils, from which it can be seen where there are most nursery school children, or the pupils can be divided into those coming from nursery school and those who have been brought up without attending nursery school, and then it can be seen which group is the better.

The term used for following a development forward from its starting point is a prospective study. Following it back from a given point is called a retrospective study. By means of prospective studies it is possible to see the actual effect i.e. how the child is faring at nursery school, together with the duration of the effect throughout the period studied. In retrospective studies the later effects of nursery school attendance can be seen, but not its actual effect.

Prospective and retrospective studies make use of different points in time for comparing the experimental and control groups. In the first case they concentrate on the start of nursery school influence. In the second on its end. So in prospective studies the groups are identical at the beginning of the period of influence as far as background factors are concerned, though they are not necessarily so later. In retrospective studies the groups are identical in background factors at the end of the period of influence, but this was not necessarily the case at its commencement.

One important criterion for comparison which can only be met in prospective studies has already been mentioned: if the experimental group is a group which has applied to the nursery school from choice, the control group must also be one which is applying from choice, but which has not been accepted; they could for instance be on a waiting list. In retrospective studies it is impossible to know if there is a common attitude which both causes the child to attend nursery school and to do well at school. This could well be the reason why children from American university nursery schools tend to do better at school. The opposite might be the case in Danish nursery schools; *if* nursery school children did worse at school than children brought up at home, this would not necessarily be because of the influence of the nursery school, but because of a factor leading both to the child's being sent to nursery school and to its doing badly in school, i.e. the common factor to be expected is that more children with unfortunate backgrounds attend nursery school because of the demand for places to be awarded primarily on social grounds.

Retrospective studies fail completely if no use at all is made of control groups, but if it is thought to be sufficient to divide school children into, for instance, good and bad pupils and to see into which group most children having attended nursery school fall. A technique of this sort was used in a Danish school study in which it was stated that over 50 percent of the children who had difficulty in settling down in the town concerned had mothers who went out to work (which meant that many of them had attended nursery school); a control group, however, was forgotten, which would have indicated that in the town in question there was an equally large percentage of mothers at work whose children did not have difficulty in settling down.

Comparing groups who have spent varying periods of time in nursery school.

In certain early studies the technique used was a comparison of two groups of children who had attended nursery school for shorter and longer periods of time respectively, e.g. a maximum of a month and a minimum of a year, but who were of the same age. Comparisons were made of, for instance, the degree of social maturity, emotional stability, the ability to cooperate with others etc. (Caille, 1933; Jersild and Fite, 1939; Vitz,

1961). This technique implies that the parents in both the groups studied have wished to send their children to nursery school. On the other hand the problem arises here that children do not begin nursery school at the same age, though they had to be the same age at the time of the study. This might well affect the measurement of effect; there are various other studies indicating that the age at which nursery school attendance begins is of particular importance. There are also other difficulties in connection with this technique. Various studies have demonstrated that the effect of nursery school is noticeable at a relatively early stage, after which it does not increase to any significant extent. Thus there will not necessarily be any great difference between nursery school groups who have attended for long or short periods, while both will show differences from a control group of children brought up at home. It is also possible that the children who have only been in nursery school for a short time will show signs of beginners' difficulties which will no longer be present in those with more experience.

The reliability of effect measurement

Even though means have now been discovered to measure a relevant effect of attendance at nursery school, the question still remains whether the measurement is accurate enough to be relied on, i.e. whether it would be produced under similar conditions at other times and in other places.

Where should the effect be studied?

It is, for instance, of significance whether the studies are carried out in working nursery schools, i.e. as field studies, or whether they are laboratory studies carried out in special nursery schools attached to research or educational establishments. In the latter cases parents have often been invited to send their children to the nursery school. The advantage of laboratory studies is that it is possible to study and control many factors; on the other hand the number of persons available for research is usually small. The advantage of field studies is that they throw light on the effects of nursery school attendance as they normally function in the prevailing conditions at the given time. But on the other hand it is more difficult to check other factors which have played a part.

A special problem is the question of whether to study the nursery school group and the control group in the same locality or in different localities. Normally the nursery school children are studied in one place and the control group elsewhere; then they either go to some centre for the study to be carried out, or else visits are paid to the homes for the studies to be made. When the initial study is carried out the nursery school children might well be in the midst of beginner difficulties, while the children at home, at least if they are studied at home, are in a milieu where they feel secure and to which they are accustomed. When the next check is made, the nursery school children might well appear to have made great progress, while the children at home might well be relatively unchanged. The opposite problem might arise later, when the nursery school children have accustomed themselves to the experimental situation and to the person carrying out the study, while the children at home are less accustomed to either.

So it is not clear that the experimental group and the control group are being given the same conditions either by testing them in the same place or by carrying out the tests in different localities. One possibility would be to study the effect of nursery school on the nursery school group when the children concerned were at home, and similarly test the control goup at home. In this way it would be possible to study the transfer effect of nursery school attendance, but obviously not the actual effect.

These problems are particularly relevant to prospective studies, whereas retrospective studies avoid them.

Who describes the effect?

Should the effect be described by the person who has had the child in the nursery school, or the person who is later in charge of the child, for instance its teacher? Should the mother or the parents estimate the effect, or its playmates at school (e.g. by means of a sociometric test)? Or should the child itself say what it thought of attending nursery school?

The importance of this question is obvious from the fact that the results of many studies depend on who it is describing the effect. In particular the views of school teachers and nursery school teachers on the effect of nursery school appear to diverge considerably, in particular on the subject of social and personal development. The description given by a teacher of the personality of a nursery school child as opposed to a child brought up at home is very much dependent on whether he or she prefers 'the quiet, good, compliant' children brought up at home or the 'lively, active and independent' nursery school children, so that the report is really an expression of the teacher's attitude. A study carried out by the

Danish Institute of Education of unrestricted reports by teachers on 100 nursery school children indicated that preferences of this kind influenced their reports to a very considerable extent.

A Swedish report (*Daghem och förskolor*, 1951) describes a study of infant school teachers' views on beginners who had attended nursery school as distinct from those brought up at home.

Of those teachers seeing a difference between nursery school children and those brought up at home, half asserted that nursery school children were more restless and more of a disturbance than those brought up at home, while the other half said that nursery school children were able to adapt more easily, were more independent, more mature and had more manual ability.

It is possible that a teacher's judgement on more specific matters such as readiness for school etc. has some validity, provided that it is made without the teacher's knowing that it is to be used as the basis of a comparison between nursery school children and children brought up at home; this condition must, of course, be valid for all stages and not merely applied to the teachers' judgements.

The only study (Brown and Hunt, 1961) concluding that nursery school children have more difficulty in social adjustment than others, is based on a teachers' report on the subject. In another study (Angell, 1954) in which teachers maintained that there was no difference in social adjustment, a sociometric study carried out at the same time indicated that nursery school children did better socially than those who had not been to nursery school.

Lamson (1940), in a study in which teachers had been most positive in their judgement of the personalities of children brought up at home, could find no difference by other methods.

Kitano (1964) finds that children who have attended a nursery school attached to an ordinary school were by the teachers considered to be less well adjusted than children who had not attended. Kitano is of the opinion that the more spontaneous and self-assertive behaviour created by the tolerant atmosphere of the nursery school is not considered appropriate to the stricter school discipline.

Stendler (1949), who studied the views of teachers and clinic staff on children's adjustment, came to the conclusion that the points of view from which they judge behaviour problems are different but equally relevant, as the teachers look at adjustment with a view to class discipline, while the clinic staff look at the problem from the point of view of the individual.

Something similar emerges from a new Swedish study (Tjellström,

1967) of differences and similarities in elementary and nursery school teachers' assessments of children's behaviour. Various criteria for judgement are used, depending on differences in milieu and the assessors' own standards.

Hammond and Skipper (1962), using a detailed and specific questionnaire for the teachers' replies, seem to achieve more relevant replies which are less dependent on *a priori* attitudes than is the case when the teachers are allowed free range.

In the Swedish study by Tjellström referred to above it is demonstrated that while there is a conflict of teachers' views concerning the ability or the lack of ability to adjust, there was more agreement when it came to a more concrete description of the differences between nursery school children and those brought up at home.

A study based on mothers' comments on the effect of attendance at nursery school on the child's development would presumably throw light on their personal attitudes towards nursery school, but would scarcely say much about its effect. Partly because nursery school is of great practical help to the mothers, and partly because a certain sense of guilt at allowing their children to be looked after by others gives rise to a need to believe that nursery school is better, many mothers will report a more positive effect than can be measured by other methods.

Another source of unreliable information can arise if the mother feels that the relationship between her and her child undergoes a negative change, e.g. if the child becomes more independent of its mother.

A study of the effect of nursery school based on reports by nursery school teachers on the effect of nursery school on the children included in the study must be regarded as unscientific; the teacher is too closely implicated in the matter under consideration. However, no effect studies based on this method have been registered. On the other hand nursery school teachers can speak with great authority on the value of nursery school and thereby contribute to the discussion of objectives. Studies often make the mistake of allowing nursery school teachers both to describe the behaviour of the child (especially in connection with difficulties of adjusting) and at the same time to describe the reason for this. In doing this the reports ignore the elementary principle that two such sets of information must come from different sources in order to avoid false conclusions being reached.

Effect studies based on the comments of mothers and nursery school teachers have in common the mistaken assumption that the development occuring in all children during these years must be the result of nursery school and not of the child's natural development. In general there is insufficient knowledge about children who do not attend nursery school for this basis of comparison to be acceptable.

The instruments for measuring effect

It seems that the measurement of effect depends to a considerable extent on the instrument used in the study. For instance it appears that measuring aggression in a child by means of a projective technique based on games with dolls leads to a different result from that gained from watching for aggressive actions on the part of the child at play. Finally various intelligence tests do not always show the same development results as nursery school tests.

However, an evaluation of the validity and reliability of the individual instruments lies outside the scope of this study, and this problem is here only dealt with insofar as conflicting effect results necessitate comment.

Meanwhile three general problems concerned with the use of test instruments, which appear in many general nursery school studies, must be discussed.

The first is that many instruments used for study resemble toys and other materials used in the nursery school's everyday activities. This is true, for instance, of many intelligence tests using apparatus. If nursery school children are faced with these things more than the children brought up at home constituting the control group, it may well be that the test results will show differences which do not correspond to real differences in intellectual development (McHugh, 1945). Tests made in certain nursery schools specialising in teaching the children to use these things will be even more unreliable (Black, 1939).

Another problem is that a particular test routine can arise as the result of repeated tests with the same or related instruments; this can be due either to repeated practice in answering questions of this type, or to familiarity with a test situation. In some studies this difficulty has been removed by having both the experimental group and the control group tested at the same time and under identical circumstances. (Jones, 1954).

The third problem associated with a statistical phenomenon, regression effect, is found in connection with the repetition of tests measuring on the basis of some norm or other. At the first test of a given group, most of those on whom the experiment is being carried out will normally be fairly close to the average, with some rather more or less, and fewer rather further away and fewer still far from the average. The same will occur at the next testing, though it will not always be the same persons who come above, about or below average. In a suitable test the placings will by and large express the real differences between those being tested, but to a certain extent they can result from the uncertainty implied in all testing because of the impossibility of excluding all irrelevant factors. For instance, fatigue on the part of the person being tested can result in a lower placing. At the next test such subjects will very probably be placed differently, although no real change will have occurred in them in the sphere being tested (Goodenough and Maurer, 1940 a).

In nursery school testing the problem of regression effect arises when two groups are to be matched, if there are differences in intelligence levels in the two sections of population from which the experimental group and the control group are drawn. In American studies the average intelligence of kindergarten children has often been found to be higher than that of the section of population from which the control group was drawn. In order to find two groups who were identical at the beginning of the testing it was necessary to take more nursery school children who were below average and more control group children who were above average. Therefore the regression effect meant that when the next test took place it was possible because of the movement towards the average to point to a certain movement upwards in the case of the nursery school children and a movement downwards in the control group in the direction of the average for the population groups from which they came. Because of this the nursery school children appeared to be making intellectual progress in relation to the control group, which was incorrectly ascribed to the influence of nursery school attendance.

The surest way of avoiding this problem is to compose two similar groups drawn from the same sections of population, for instance by matching them in pairs from the list of applicants and letting one attend nursery school and putting the other into the control group. This, however, can only be done if there are twice as many applicants as places.

When to study the effect

A study of the effect of attendance at a daycare institution must take into consideration the time at which the presumed effect can be expected to appear. A study can presumably begin too soon as well as too late in respect of the effect being investigated. It might be that nursery school will create the preconditions for something which can only be measured later, and conversely it could be that nursery school will have a temporary effect which might be of significance at that particular time, but which

51

cannot be traced if the study comes too late. These problems of measurement assume particular importance in the light of theories on the hierarchical structure of need and development.

Next comes the problem of the length of the period during which the influence takes place. Some effect studies have given the nursery school too little time to achieve the effect to be studied. In some cases the authors have been in such a hurry that they have not even been able to give the nursery schools a month in which to influence the children before starting to study effect. Conversely it can be imagined that too much time has been allowed to elapse before commencing the study. This will be of significance in connection with the question of 'being tired of nursery school', a phenomenon which can either be due to a certain optimal duration of attendance at nursery school or to the nursery school's programme not being able to keep pace with the child's development.

A special problem is how long afterwards and how often the effects of nursery school attendance should be studied. In instances where researchers are seeking to study not only an actual effect but also a preparation effect, e.g. the nursery school as a means of easing the acceptance of school at a later date, it is necessary to compare a nursery school group and a control group not only at nursery school age but also after school attendance has begun, and not merely at the start of school attendance, but later again. Jersild and Fite (1939) demonstrated that nursery school children found social adjustment easier both while at nursery school and at the start of school, but one year later they could see no difference between them and other children. Durkin (1964) found among nursery school attenders who had had some training in reading a greater ability to read in the first form, but by the third form the children who had had nursery school training in reading were less competent than children who had not been trained early but only stimulated to the extent to which they appeared to be ready. One study (Skeels, 1965) found the greatest effect of nursery school when the pupils were well up into their twenties, demonstrating that nursery school children had managed better than the control group brought up at home both in their careers and their marriages. It appears that the start made by nursery school at a critical time can have a cumulative effect. As the control group children had come to a standstill, the difference between the groups had become bigger and bigger.

In psychological experiments it is not unusual for an effect ascribed to the experimental influence later to be seen to come from a completely different source.

In one experiment in which rats were taught certain tricks, it was later discovered that only one of the experimenters had achieved the desired result. A closer investigation showed that he had consciously stroked the rats' backs when they had behaved in a given manner. This 'reward' thus helped to strengthen the behaviour pattern. In another experiment the students taking part were told that half the rats were particularly intelligent and that the other half were particularly unintelligent. The predetermined attitudes thus created had their effect on the results of the study carried out.

A special effect, the 'placebo effect' (referred to in Rasborg and Florander, 1966) is a sort of suggestion resulting from the actual experimental situation, e.g. from the use of various unknown remedies, the director of the experiment wearing a white overall and so on, which can produce an expected effect in the person on whom the experiment is being carried out.

Another special effect has been called the 'Hawthorne effect' after the institute in which the experiment was carried out when its implication was realised for the first time (see Sjølund, 1965). The introduction of a number of improvements in the physical milieu during the course of the experiment had produced better work results in the experimental group, but when, as part of the experiment, the improvements were removed to see whether the effects in the form of increased production also disappeared, it was found that they did not. Production continued to increase every time an experiment was carried out on the group, irrespective of whether various features were introduced into or removed from the physical milieu. It turned out that it was not these factors, but the simple fact that interest was being shown in the group which had produced the results.

In school experiments it often happens that the mere experimental introduction of some new feature changes a number of other factors, sometimes the entire psychological climate of the class. Consequently experimental schools usually have a more favourable teaching climate than others. The result of this is that when attempts are made to transfer successful methods to other schools, the positive effect is suddenly found to be lacking for the simple reason that the school does not work under experimental conditions.

It is worth taking note that similar effects might make themselves felt in nursery schools which are made the objects of special studies, and in particular there is a risk of false conclusions being drawn from nursery schools established specially for experimental purposes.

Statistical reliability

It is obvious that there must be a difference in the measured effect between the experimental group and the control group which is sufficiently large to be statistically significant. The more limited the material on which the study is based, the more difficult it is to find statistically significant differences. On the other hand the result of an experiment need by no means be convincing even though there is a statistically significant difference between the experimental group and the control group. For instance in New York City material on no fewer than 12,000 former nursery school children was compiled for comparison with children who had not attended nursery school. The study showed a large statistically significant difference between the two groups to the advantage of the nursery school children. Since, in America, nursery school children often come from better milieus than children who do not attend nursery school however, the effect discovered in the study is unlikely to be the result of nursery school attendance.

A difference indicated with great statistical certainty need not, at the same time, be a difference of great significance. It may well be that differences discovered by means of a series of different studies all pointing in the same direction is more convincing, even if the statistical significance cannot be determined. At all events it is clear that studies leading to one result on one occasion and a completely different one on the next must create doubt as to the conclusions reached, even if the differences in each case are statistically significant.

This question will be relevant to the discussion of the results of studies available, as the studies of certain areas of effect seldom show statistically significant differences, but almost always differences pointing in the same direction.

5 Research Models

Expansion of the cause-effect analysis

Most of the studies registered are only concerned with one effect in one nursery school, and take little heed of other factors. This model can be illustrated thus:

$$\text{Nursery school} \longrightarrow \text{Effect}$$

However this model is an over-simplification. Some studies carried out according to it show positive effects of nursery school attendance, while others show negative effects, but cannot provide an answer to the question of why these differences occur. For instance, it is possible that nursery schools of a certain type have a positive effect while the effect of other types is negative, and it is particularly interesting to be able to demonstrate such relationships. Nor can one be content with a summary review which does not show the effect on a whole group of children attending nursery school. It is possible that some of the children have benefitted from attending, while the effect has been the opposite on others, so that the sum of effects on the group as a whole is nil.

Instead, the problem must be formulated as follows:

Which institution—
has which effect—
on which children?

This can be formulated in a two parameter model:

$$\text{Institution} \} \qquad \text{Effect} \qquad \{ \text{Person}$$

The institutional parameter

In order to discover which institutions have a precisely defined effect on a particular type of child, it is necessary to follow the children's development in varying institutional conditions.

The studies show that the institutional variables with which it is necessary to operate include, among other things, the following factors:

Type: day nursery, nursery school, nursery school classes, care in private families, etc;

Aim: social, educational, preparation for school, etc;

Quality of equipment: materials, layout, space available, etc.

Quality of teaching: teacher-pupil ratio, level of training, the quality of the principal, the philosophy of the institution, etc;

Length of daily attendance: all day, three quarters of the day, half day, two hours daily, etc (ranging from too little to too much);

Total duration of attendance: the number of months, etc (ranging from too short to too long, with child tired of nursery school).

The personality parameter

In order to discover which children derive a closely defined benefit from attending a certain type of institution, the children and their milieu must be described in some detail. When this is done, it will be possible to study the effects of similar institutional conditions on different sorts of children.

The studies show that it is necessary to operate with a number of person variables:

Stage of development: baby, toddler, 4-5 year-old, 6-7 year-old; personality and mental development;

Physical handicaps: deaf, blind, spastic etc;

Constitution and social status of the family;

The degree of stimulation of the child's environment, and the amount of conflict present in it.

The effect

Just as it is impossible to generalise about all nursery schools or all children when considering the benefit derived from attendance at nursery school, so, too, it is impossible to generalise on the effects of attendance at nursery school as a whole. In earlier studies there was a tendency to talk about negative or positive effects of nursery school attendance without any precise definition of what kind of effect was being discussed. Later studies, however, have been more concerned with specified kinds of effects from nursery school attendance.

When analysed in this light, available studies answer a number of questions concerning the kind of effect to be expected from precise types of institutions on precise types of children. The very large number of questions of this sort which it is possible to ask is far from being covered by available research, but this kind of analysis of results is presumably more valuable than an analysis seeking to draw general conclusions on the general effect experienced by all children in all types of institution.

On the basis of analyses taking account both of variations in institutions and variations among the children, it is possible to reach the general conclusion: (a) that the more highly qualified the institution, the more positive is its effect on different areas of a child's development; and (b) that the positive effect is more striking among children in need of what the institution has to offer.

This might sound like a truism, but it is the necessary point of departure for studies of what is needed for a nursery school to be a 'good' institution, and also for discovering which types of children derive particular benefit from attendance at a given type of institution, and which children will not benefit from it.

Model for studying the institutional parameter

In studies of the effects of educational institutions it is possible, according to Hagen and Thorndike (1960) to distinguish between structure, process and product analyses.

Structure analyses examine the effect of the arrangement of the institution and other structural factors.
Process analyses examine the effect of educational methods and other dynamic factors.
Product analyses seek in particular to evaluate the extent to which the institution fulfils the aims it sets itself.

Most studies of the effect of nursery school are product analyses in which a group of nursery school children is compared with a control group of children not attending nursery school. Product analyses of this sort show an effect, plus, nil, or minus, but they say nothing about the process or structural conditions leading to it.

A model for an analysis of the institution parameter must operate with three variables:

The framework of the institution (structure, i.e. layout, materials, space etc.) The teaching offered by the institution (process, i.e. the personality of the teacher, the behaviour of the teacher, the educational climate, the principal, etc.) The results of the institution (product , i.e. the extent to which the aims of the institution are achieved).

Unsuitable processes can explain why institutions with a suitable structure may not be able to achieve a positive effect, and conversely suitable educational processes can result in an institution achieving a positive effect despite an unsatisfactory structure. While satisfactory processes can compensate for unsatisfactory structure, it appears that the converse is not the case. But naturally satisfactory processes are strengthened when accompanied by an equally satisfactory structure.

The relationship can be illustrated by the following model:

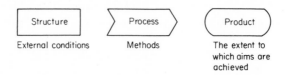

No studies have been registered which operate with this model and have at the same time a control group of children not attending nursery school. On the other hand a number of studies has been made of children in nursery schools, in which the three sets of variables have been employed with the object of studying which process and which structure lead to a given result. In other words attempts have been made to discover what a nursery school should be like or what it should do in order to achieve a given effect. In such studies the control group consists of another group of nursery school children with the same point of departure as an experimental group, but not subjected to the same experimental influence.

Model for the investigation of the child's personality parameter

While effect studies of the nursery school's preconditions for achieving a positive effect are few in number, some effort has been made to distinguish between the various pre-conditions necessary for the child to benefit from attendance at nursery school. It fairly soon became obvious that such differences existed, and it was quickly discovered that the factors responsible were largely those of milieu. Children from a less fortunate milieu had greater chances of deriving positive benefit from nursery school attendance, since the nursery school could hardly be worse than the milieu in which the children would otherwise have been placed. On the other hand it was by no means certain that children coming from a good milieu derived anything at all from nursery school attendance. However, there are no effect studies making a systematic examination of this.

In principle three sets of variables are also necessary here: structure, process and product.

The family background (structure, i.e. social and economic background, composition, the role of the child and its possibility of developing its personality etc.) The pattern of life and upbringing (process, i.e. the emotional climate, the personality and attitude of those bringing up the child, social and cultural activities, the ideology behind the way in which the child is brought up etc.) Relationship between the demands made by the child's role and their fulfilment (product, i.e. identification with and adaptation to the family group etc.)

These three sets of variables each exert an influence on the child and thereby on the basis of its personality when entering a daycare institution. Presumably the family processes are of greater significance for what the child is like than the family structure. Satisfactory processes can presumably make up for an unsatisfactory structure, while it is more difficult to assume the converse. On the other hand a satisfactory structure can make the presence of satisfactory processes easier, just as an unsatisfactory structure can make satisfactory processes difficult.

The relationship between these three variables can be illustrated by the following model:

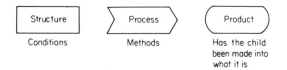

There are many studies seeking to explain the differences found in children when they start attending nursery school by means of different factors in the processes or structure of the home. These studies will be discussed in a later section on the influence of parental attitudes on and the significance of the child's milieu for its ability to adjust to nursery school. In addition a number of studies exist which divide the children according to certain rough milieu factors.

On the other hand there are no studies of the effect of nursery school seen in relation to the pattern of upbringing or parental attitudes.

Model for the relationship between the personality parameter and the institutional parameter

From the moment a child arrives in the nursery school and is subjected to its influence, there arises an interaction between factors in the home and factors in the institution which can be illustrated by the following model:

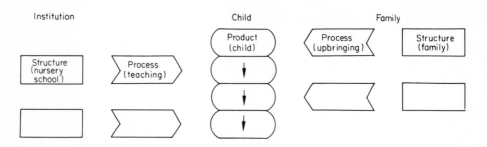

Read downwards, this arrangement shows the passage of time, and read horizontally the influences met by the child at a given moment.

The influence of the institution changes the child, so that it becomes a different child receiving impulses from the home, and this situation gradually results in its being a different child on which the institution exerts an influence.

This model is necessary for the understanding of a process such as the following: a child from a very authoritarian family milieu is placed in a situation requiring a good deal of independence and offering rich opportunities for personal development. This influences the child. It is changed from being a particularly obedient and compliant child into one who is more active and free, but at the same time less compliant. Through a transfer effect this change brings about new reactions in the parents. The child is placed between the demands of the home and those of the nursery school and is marked in the nursery school by conflict. In this way it has turned into a child needing a completely different sort of influence in the nursery school from what was originally the case.

PART III

Analysis of Effect Studies

6 Physical, Health and Motor Development

Physical and health development

Physical condition and health

When nursery schools were first started, great stress was laid on their ability to improve children's health. Indeed, some of the earliest effect studies are concerned with the question of how far this object was attained, Baldwin (1924), who studied 105 nursery school children aged from two to six years for a total of three years, discovered by means of systematic measurements that nursery school children benefitted physically from attending nursery school.

The Health Report of the London County Council stated in 1927 that of beginners in elementary school seven per cent of nursery school children were suffering from some illness as opposed to 30-40 per cent of children who had not attended nursery school. 80-90 per cent of two-year-olds starting nursery school had rickets which, however, were cured during the first year in nursery school. Infectious diseases and skin diseases were far less frequent amongst nursery school children than amongst others.

Sherman (1929), who carried out a study of normal children aged from two to four in nursery departments, discovered that they were better nourished and physically developed than children from the same milieu who did not attend nursery school.

Waddell and Greenwood (1931) summarised all studies made between 1924 and 1930 concerning physical development, stance and nourishment, and found nursery school to have a positive effect. One common factor in all these studies, however, was the fact that the development of these children was not compared with that of a corresponding control group.

Kawin et al. (1931) did compare 22 nursery school children with a corresponding control group of 22 children not attending nursery school, and came to the conclusion that the general health of nursery school children after one year's attendance was rather better than that of the other group, whereas the two groups had been identical at the beginning of the study. On the other hand there was no difference in height or other physical measurements.

A subsequent study of 25 nursery school children (Lamson, 1940), which also included a control group of 44 non-attenders, also concluded that there was no significant difference in physical measurement between the two groups.

Walsh (1931), who compared a group of 22 nursery school children between the ages of two and five with a corresponding group of children at home, demonstrated that the nursery school children had healthier habits. However, only a small number of children was included in the group. Meanwhile Hattwick (1936 a) made a similar discovery in a broader study. 106 nursery school children aged between three and four, who had attended nursery school for at least a year, were compared with a corresponding number who were just starting nursery school, but who were selected in such a way that they were of the same age and sex and came from the same milieu etc. The children who had attended nursery school had healthier habits.

Douglas & Blomfield (1958), in a study of more than 5,000 children born in the same year and for a number of years made the subject of extensive studies, sought to discover whether there was any difference between nursery school children and non-nursery school children as regards height. They discovered that nursery school children on average were a little taller, but not so much that any statistical significance could be attached to it. To this it must be added that the criterion for nursery school children was that they should have attended for at least two months, which is scarcely sufficient to bring about any noticeable physical changes.

Stukat (1966), in a Swedish study of children attending *lekskola*, which will be discussed at greater length in chapter 7, found that there was no difference between the *lekskola* group and the control group as far as physical development—i.e. height and weight—was concerned. He concluded that this was only to be expected, as *lekskola* scarcely has any effect on children's eating habits.

Eating habits

While the beneficial influence of nursery school on children's health might at first have been a direct one, ensuring that children from poorer homes were given better food and care than they otherwise would have had, the

64

significance of the nursery school in this field has perhaps now become more indirect, in that it accustoms the children to healthier eating habits.

Douglas and Blomfield (1958) thus found that nursery school children on the whole were given better and healthier food than children who did not attend nursery school.

Campbell (1933) carried out studies at a summer camp of 18 former nursery school children and a control group of 15 who had never attended nursery school. Their eating habits were studied for six weeks. The comparisons were made on the basis of a scale of values for eating habits, the time spent in eating, the type and quantity of the food eaten. The differences were not great, but nursery school children were more inclined to choose milk and vegetables than the other group. Children from the same home, where one had attended nursery school and the other had not, had identical habits, which indicates that the home influences eating habits more than the nursery school. The study also indicated that the sooner a child begins attending nursery school, the greater will be the influence of the nursery school on its eating habits.

Rhinehart (1942), whose study will be dealt with at greater length in chapter 7, examined the extent to which the nursery school could influence parents' understanding of their children's health. The study covered a group of parents, with children in nursery school, who took part in a special programme for training parents; the control group of parents of children not attending nursery school did not take part in this programme. In physical respects—height and weight—there was no difference in the children after a year, but in eating habits and other everyday behaviour, the group of children whose parents took part in the training programme showed progress. During the year the course lasted, more children from the latter group received treatment for physical defects. However, the study does not establish whether this difference was due to the training of parents or attendance at nursery school.

Infectious diseases

Thus, while studies do seem to indicate that the nursery school can have an effect on the children's state of nutrition, or that at least there is nothing indicating a negative effect, there is another health aspect where there have been fears that nursery school might have a negative effect, i.e. on the risk of contracting infectious diseases. Conrad & Jones (1932), who studied the frequency with which children contracted colds in a nursery school during a period of two years, noted that the number of cases rose from Monday to Friday and fell from Friday to Monday, when the children were not at nursery school. In the same way the frequency was diminished when the children had been away on holidays for longer periods.

Hesselvik (1949) studied literature concerning infectious diseases in nursery school and found a high frequency of infectious illness reported, especially among children under three years of age.

Between 1946 and 1949 a series of investigations of this problem was carried out in Sweden. The findings were contained in a report from 1951 concerning nursery school (Löfström, 1951). Löfström concluded that there appeared to be no greater risk for children of nursery school age, though there was a risk at day nursery age, and he suggested that this field should be further investigated.

Sandels (1952) discussed the increased risk of infection brought about by contact with a greater number of children; she concludes that, provided hygiene and health checks are not neglected, it is to be expected that the general standard of health among nursery school children will be better than among other children, as symptoms of illness are discovered during medical examinations and treated at an earlier stage.

This corresponds to the findings of Diehl (1949), who compared 25 nursery school children ranging in age from two to four and a half with a control group of 26 children taken from a corresponding milieu. This nursery school had a positive policy of keeping a watch on health, and sought, among other things, to reduce sources of infection to a minimum. The groups of children were checked for the incidence of colds for ten weeks from January to April; there was no difference in the incidence of colds in the two groups taken as a whole; likewise the incidence was the same in children of different ages. Nine children from the control group entered nursery school the following year; the incidence of colds among them did not increase. The study showed moreover that the nursery school children were given healthier food.

A study carried out by Drillien (1961) indicates that the milieu of the child might be significant in determining whether the risk of infection is greater in nursery school than at home. The study covered a group of two to five-year-olds attending nursery school and a corresponding control group. It concludes that children from good homes contract more infectious diseases when aged between two and three if they attend nursery school; after this age the risk is not so great. Children from poorer homes have at no age more infectious illnesses when attending nursery school than when they stay at home.

One study indicates that the incidence of infectious diseases is less in nursery schools than in residential establishments. Trautmann (1960)

66

compared the incidence in nursery schools and residential homes in the case of children aged from six weeks to six years. There was a greater tendency to illness among children in residential homes, and this was particularly noticeable between the ages of six weeks and three years. Children in residential institutions were also more prone to slight infections than children in nursery schools, and this was particularly the case with children under three years.

This situation is perhaps more closely connected with the extent of the separation of the child from its parents than with hygienic conditions in the two sorts of institution. Several studies dealing with the problems of the separation of mother and child touch on the extent to which babies separated from their mothers show a greater tendency to illness.

As far as infectious diseases are concerned, it is probable that the risk is greater in proportion to the greater number of children associating together, and on the whole it is true that these diseases occur more frequently among nursery school children than among other children below school age. Douglas and Blomfield (1958) found in their extensive study that the risk of infection among day nursery children was several times greater than it was among children who were kept at home even if the incidence had been the same in the two groups before the children started in day nurseries.

On the other hand an American study (Updegraff, 1933), covering 800 children between two and five years old, of whom rather more than half had attended nursery school, found that the incidence of infectious diseases was only half as great among nursery school children as among those kept at home. The author is of the opinion that this is due to regular health checks in the nursery schools, but the result is probably inconclusive, since the two groups were not socially identical. Moreover, it is pointed out that the nursery school children might well have had illnesses at an earlier age.

Stukat (1966) demonstrates that although the incidence of infectious diseases may well be greater among children attending nursery school than among those kept at home, the position is reversed when the children start school, as the incidence of infectious diseases in children who have not attended nursery school is correspondingly greater than in those who have. Stukat draws attention to the fact that it might well be possible to view this from an educational point of view and argue that, it is an advantage that the child should be absent as little as possible during the first important months at school. His study also shows that the incidence of colds etc., which is greater among nursery school pupils than among others when they are of school age, is of a more serious nature among children who have not attended nursery school than among those who have.

All in all it merely looks as though nursery school children contract these illnesses at an earlier stage than other children, so that the problem of contracting the 'things you are bound to get' is not serious, provided the children do not catch them too early. Thus the problem really becomes one concerning day nurseries rather than nursery schools.

In *Séminaire sur les crèches*, Paris 1960, there is an account of various pieces of research done on the problems of health in day nurseries. These will be discussed in more detail in the chapter on research into day nurseries.

As far as the general level of health is concerned, it must be taken that nursery school has a positive effect in that it has more thorough health checks than most homes. One can thus talk of a preventive effect, as the signs of approaching illness are detected earlier in nursery school, whereby the possibility of treating the condition is measurably increased. This is emphasised in various studies, i.e. Douglas and Blomfield (1958) and Sandels (1952).

Prevention of accidents

One important function which it is to be assumed the nursery school manages better than the home is the prevention of accidents. According to international statistics the commonest cause of death among children in technically developed countries is accidents. Of these road accidents are the most frequent. Accidents in the home such as burning, scalding and poisoning are also high on the list.

Sjölin (1964) points out that in Stockholm in 1959 there was not a single serious accident among the 1,400 nursery school children while they were actually at school.

Schorr (1963) discusses a study carried out in East Berlin. Of 1000 accidents which occurred between 1956 and 1958 among children of nursery school age, only 13 per cent occurred to nursery school children, even though only 37 per cent of all children attended nursery school. A third of all the accidents could, it was thought, have been avoided by better care, for instance in a nursery school.

Motor development

One of the aims of nursery school is to encourage the child's motor development (Gutteridge, 1939, Stukat, 1966). Enquiries made of 40 experienced Danish nursery school teachers led to the conclusion that motor development ranks fifth among the 12 most important aims of nursery school. In view of this it is remarkable how few studies have been made of the possible effects of nursery school in this field.

Skeels et al. (1938) compared a group of orphanage children attending nursery school with a control group of other orphanage children who did not attend nursery school, and discovered that the nursery school children showed better developed motor skills in the tests given to them. The tasks which the nursery school children managed best were typical motor activities such as are common in nursery schools, and which the orphanage children did not have access to. In other areas the differences were insignificant; this tends to indicate the result of specific training rather than general motor development.

Moustakas (1952) compared the results of several investigations into the relationship between nursery school attendance and motor achievement. The investigations indicated that the nursery school children on the whole showed a better motor development than the children in control groups, but the differences were rarely enough to be of significance. Moreover the comparability with the control groups was sometimes doubtful.

An Italian study (Barbiero and Galdo, 1960) covered 200 nursery school children aged from two and a half to four years and a control group of 40 children. Both groups came from financially and socially poor milieus; the mothers of both groups went out to work. The study demonstrated that a larger percentage of the nursery school children were retarded in psycho-motor development as compared to the children brought up at home, and the older the children and the longer they had been at nursery school, the greater was the percentage who were retarded. The authors were able to point out that the nursery schools had adequate buildings with a good standard of hygiene, but they had insufficient staff and too little equipment, so that the children attending nursery school had less opportunity for doing things than the children who stayed at home. The fact that retardation increased with age, however, could indicate that other factors than the nursery school were at work.

An East German study (Schmidt-Kolmer, 1963, 1964) indicated that nursery school children were inhibited in their motor development as compared to children brought up at home, especially if they had too little freedom of movement or too little opportunity to occupy themselves.

Rabin (1958 c), who compared 24 kibbutz children with a similar number of children from private homes, could find no difference either in gross or fine motor achievement.

Stukat (1966), studying motor development by means of gross and fine motor tests as well as a rhythm test, could find no statistically significant differences between the nursery school group and the children brought up at home. The material seemed, if anything, to indicate better motor achievements in boys brought up at home.

The number and extent of studies to hand are too small to come to any final conclusion, but there is nothing among them to indicate that nursery school has any obvious positive effect on a child's motor development, while there is the danger of a negative effect if the nursery school has not the necessary means of occupying the child. These results are really rather striking in view of nursery schools' insistence on the importance of a child's physical and motor development, but perhaps the truth is that children at home will find means of achieving the necessary motor activity.

On the other hand a couple of studies do seem to indicate that with a specific training programme (Painter, 1966) or where there is a more specific need on the part of the child (Argy, 1965) nursery school can further motor development. These studies will be discussed more fully in chapters 9 and 11 respectively.

The problem of the normal child's motor development in an ordinary nursery school is dealt with in an article by Sandels (1963) entitled *Neglected aspects of development in young children. 1. Children in nursery school: motor development, physical measurements, furniture.* Sandels points out that it is important that the nursery school should be able to complement the home milieu in the field of motor development as in other areas. With this object in view an investigation was started in 1958 aimed at studying the motor achievement of four to six-year-olds playing freely in nursery school. This study is now nearing completion. One important result of it is the discovery of small children's need for a variety of different movements. Accommodation and material, as well as the whole technique of nursery school education must be adapted so that this need can be catered for. With this object in view some new experiments have been started, and when the results of these are available it might be possible to understand why nursery schools have so far not been particularly successful in achieving their declared intention of furthering children's motor development.

7 Social and Emotional Development

Theories of developmental psychology

Developmental psychology has for a long time emphasised the fundamental importance of the pre-school age period for the development of personality, so that the first five or six years are thought to be decisive, while later years would only have a moderating influence or an influence in a specific direction. This point of view has been gradually supported by various pieces of experimental research.

More recent theories on development have thrown more light on which specific development problems are related to different ages, for instance Erikson's (1950 a), whose work has already been mentioned. He stresses the earlier years of childhood (from two to three years) as a period when a powerful urge for independence makes itself felt, while the urge for self-expression is particularly noticeable in later childhood years (from four to six).

The questionnaire sent to forty experienced Danish nursery school teachers, to which reference has already been made above, placed the child's social development and the development of its own personality as first and second respectively among the most important educational tasks of a nursery school. A similar Swedish questionnaire (Stukat, 1966) led to a similar result.

How are these aspects of a child's development attended to either in a nursery school or in the home atmosphere? The social situation in the nursery school is perhaps one of the areas in which the difference from the home is most pronounced. In a family group the child has relatively more to do with adults and relatively less with children of its own age, indeed sometimes it has scarcely any contact with children of its own age. In a nursery school group it is constantly surrounded by a fairly large number of children of a similar age and only one or two adults whom it must share with the other children. Thus the nursery school child is exposed to a greater social influence from children of its own age than are many children brought up at home.

Dependence on the nursery school group could, on the other hand, be

71

thought to have an inhibiting effect on a child's urge for independence, so that the independence attained in the family group is replaced by a new dependence on the group of playmates or on the nursery school teacher.

Children at home who have plenty of friends of their own age play on the one hand more independently and without adults being in charge of them, but on the other hand without educative guidance or any arrangement of their activities. The social situation is thus to a greater extent marked by 'the free play of forces' than is the group life in a nursery school. In nursery school there is the possibility of activity and self expression in fields in which the home offers more limited possibilities. On the other hand, there are the demands of group life. The child has to learn to adapt its own individual activities to the collective activities of the group. It has to learn to share both space and materials. It has to learn to find its place and to wait its turn. This creates many conflict situations leading to aggressive action, and is accompanied by various emotions which the child has to learn to control if it is to going to reach any degree of self expression. Personal development and adjustment to society must thus go hand in hand in nursery school.

The results of research

What do the various studies of this question reveal? Altogether 56 studies have been registered concerning the effect of the nursery school on the child's social and emotional development. In addition there is a number of studies of social development on the one hand of groups of children in special situations and on the other in particular educational environments, and these will be discussed in the relevant chapters. Of the studies to be discussed here, five are Israeli, four British, three Italian, three Swedish, one Indian and 40 American. 14 were carried out between 1920 and 1935, and of these five made use of control groups. 19 of the studies are from 1936-1949, and of these eight used control groups. From 1950-1965 23 research projects were carried out, 20 with control groups. All but the American studies have been carried out since 1949.

For the sake of comparability the American studies will be dealt with separately. Of the 40 studies, four were not available (Woolfolk, 1929; Carr, 1938; Little, 1940; Ryan, 1949). Of the 36 which were available 30 conclude that nursery school has a positive effect in one or more social and emotional fields; three conclude that the effect is negative, and three that nursery school has no effect.

In one of the studies showing a negative effect (Brown and Hunt, 1961) the researchers sought views of the subsequent schoolteachers of the children on their adjustment in school, their relations with their schoolmates and their teachers, and on their personal harmony. Thus the study is really one of the effect of nursery school on later social adjustment in school. The project concerned 42 children chosen from the school in such a way that half had attended nursery school and half had not. At the same time the children were very carefully matched in pairs according to intelligence, social and financial background and their placing among their brothers and sisters. There was an equal number of boys and girls in each group. Thus it was a retrospective study in which it was not possible to ensure comparability between the children at the time when nursery school influence began. The children who had attended nursery school were considered by their teacher to be less able to adjust to the various school activities and to their playmates, and to be personally less harmonious than the children who had not attended nursery school. The differences in these three fields were statistically significant, though when it came to the question of adjustment to the teacher's wishes, this was not the case.

Meanwhile it may well be that some of the negative results indicated in this study might be due to the difference already mentioned in both teachers' and nursery school teachers' ideas about how adaptable a child should be, so that the nursery school teacher might well not have seen the child's behaviour as negative.

The same is true of another study with a negative result, (Lamson, 1940): 25 nursery school children and 44 others, all of them beginners at school, were evaluated in various ways by their school teacher. A difference was only found in one area, that of personality development, where children brought up at home were judged more favourably. This difference could also have arisen because of differences in the children's milieus, as the groups were not matched.

The third study seeing a negative result of nursery school attendance (Jersild and Markey, 1935) measured the effect by counting the number of conflict situations arising. The group observed consisted of 54 two to four-year-olds from nursery school who were observed for 10-15 minute periods while at play. Their social conflicts, which varied from serious fights and quarrels to more subdued verbal or physical interchanges, were recorded. 36 of the children were studied in the same way a year later. The study showed a large increase in the number of conflicts arising among children who had attended nursery school for a year. However, there was no control group, and it can be assumed that this age is precisely one characterised by many conflicts, and it may well be a quite natural doubling of the number of conflicts which had taken place here. The study tells us nothing on this point.

There is also another way in which the method of measuring effect by means of counting conflicts is unreliable. It is obvious from the material produced in the studies that the appearance of conflicts in the various nursery school groups is closely tied to how much the adult, the teacher, is prepared to allow; for instance one of the groups had changed teacher between the first and the second study. The first teacher had a firm grip on the group's activities, while the second was more inclined to leave them to their own devices. The study showed that more conflicts arose in the group with too little control on the part of the teacher. It concludes that the emergence of conflicts is more closely associated with the social situation in the institution than with the personal qualities of the people observed.

One study reporting no effect from nursery school attendance, (Phillips, 1953), attempted to measure differences in personality resulting from nursery school attendance. The study covered two groups of children in the sixth school year, one group having attended nursery school, the other not. The groups were matched in pairs so that they were identical as far as sex, age, I.Q., home and parents' occupation were concerned. So at the time when the study was made, the groups were identical, but this can scarcely have been the case when the children started nursery school six to ten years previously. The two groups were assessed according to a personality scale covering 12 different areas. In none of these was it possible to establish any difference between the two groups of children. The weakness of the study, however, is that it contains no information on the length or type of nursery school influence. Finally, despite the matching, the two groups may well not have been compatible. In the classes containing the greatest proportion of former nursery school children there was a tendency for them to be judged more favourably than in classes where they were in a minority.

The other study concluding that nursery school has no effect (Nicholson, 1957) covered 402 schoolchildren ranging from their first to their sixth year; half had attended nursery school. The effect was measured partly by the children's sociometrical status among other children, measured by sociometrical tests, and partly by the teachers' assessment of the child's success in adjusting to society. In no area was it possible to discover differences between the children who had attended nursery school and those who had not. The author himself concludes that the reason for this is perhaps to be found in the fact that the nursery schools which the children had attended were by and large of a poor quality.

The one feature which most studies indicating a negative or neutral effect of nursery school have in common is that they are retrospective studies, that is to say, that the researcher starts from some point of time at school, divides the children into those who have attended nursery school and those who have not, and tries to discover what differences there may be between them. The studies thus tell us nothing of what effect nursery school had while the children were actually attending it.

However, this is not true of the third study which fails to find any effect from attendance at nursery school. On the other hand the assessment is based on the mothers' own judgements of their children's adaptability, which, as indicated in the chapter on measurement of effect, is an unreliable guide. Nye et al. (1963) studied the effect of nursery school attendance in connection with mothers going out to work, by interviewing two matched groups of 104 mothers (one of whom went out to work and had children at nursery school, while the other did not go out to work) on behaviour difficulties in their children. There was no significant difference in what the mothers had to tell of their children. However, the only conclusion one can reach here is that there is no difference in what mothers have to tell of their children's adaptability, whether they go out to work or not.

14 of the studies indicating a positive effect of attendance at nursery school were carried out without a control group. The method employed by most of the researchers, is study to the child at some preliminary stage, sometimes as it is starting to attend nursery school, followed by further study again after varing amounts of time have elapsed. However, without control material it is impossible to decide to what extent the changes noted are due to the child's own maturation processes and to what extent they can be ascribed to nursery school influence. The reason for including these studies in this book is that they do throw light on a child's development, and have intrinsic value for this reason. However, it remains uncertain whether the positive effect achieved is due to the influence of the nursery school or to other factors such as the child's maturation processes.

Baldwin and Stecher (1924) studied 105 nursery school children between the ages of two and six. The children were studied partly by means of observation, partly through tests. The authors conclude that the children had made such progress in social attitudes and willingness to cooperate between the first and second study that everything pointed to their having derived great benefit from their experiences in nursery school.

Ezekiel (1931), who studied four nursery school children throughout an 11 week period, found that children who at first were shy and reserved lost their reserve as their nursery school experiences progressed, and that they showed an increasing tendency to make themselves the focal point in activities. Children who had had plenty of confidence from the start retained that confidence.

Taylor and Frank (1931) studied the ease with which 38 children from four different nursery schools adjusted to school. They were able to demonstrate that many of the adjustment difficulties seen at nursery school age had disappeared after one to three years at school.

Mallay (1935) studied a nursery school group of 21 children first during their first three weeks in nursery school, and then again six months later. The study showed a rapid increase in social and mental activity after the six months in nursery school. The development covered the following areas: increase in time spent in social intercourse or in group contacts, increase in the use of such behaviour patterns as would produce successful contacts, increase in the number of children who were contacted, increase in the proportion of time spent using constructive materials, increase in the time spent making active use of materials and increase in the attention paid to the materials and to other children. The study showed that the average measurements for the two-year-olds after the study period were greater than the average for the three-year-olds before the period of study began. This could indicate a nursery school effect and not a mere maturation process. The author himself concludes that this development is due partly to the maturation process and partly to the experiences gained in nursery school.

Andrus and Horowitz (1938), who studied all the children in seven nursery schools with the aid of the teachers' accounts of uncertainty on the part of the children, came to the conclusion that the longer the children attended nursery school, the more confident they were emotionally. The children also showed signs of greater independence, were less inclined to accept authority and less receptive to criticism or suggestions. In addition, they were more active. The authors themselves are uncertain as to the validity of their results.

Horowitz and Smith (1939) studied social patterns in children in 13 nursery schools. They observed the children at play and while occupied indoors and out of doors and found that submissive and oppressive behaviour decreased with the length of time the child had spent at nursery school, while a willingness to cooperate with other children increased. Similarly a willingness to make constructive use of play material grew with the length of time spent in nursery school.

Horowitz (1940) concludes in his study of nursery school children that not all sorts of independence in the child are developed in nursery school.

It may well be that as a whole the child becomes more independent and self-reliant, the longer he or she attends nursery school, but by distinguishing between two different kinds of independence Horowitz is able to demonstrate that one of them, that concerned with outward activities and routine actions, decreases, while the other kind, concerned with contacts with adults, the urge for attracting the attention of adults, the need for love, support etc. increases, the longer the child attends nursery school.

Bender and Yarnell (1941) studied children with emotional problems who were attending nursery school as the result of some crisis in the family. The study concluded that, as a result of their attending nursery school, many of the children made progress, losing much of their shyness, and their neurotic symptoms decreased.

Koshuk (1947) carried out an extensive study of 500 nursery school children, all with working mothers; he collected his material between 1943 and 1946. The information was gathered from preliminary interviews with the mothers, from observations and reports on the part of the nursery school teachers, and a further interview with the mothers when the children were leaving nursery school. An analysis of the information gathered indicated that more than four fifths of the children were considered to have made good or excellent general progress, especially with regard to social and emotional development. Experience of nursery school had served to reduce emotional tensions and to develop a sense of how to adapt to other children in society. The mothers reported similar improvements in the children's behaviour at home, especially in social adjustment and independence in routine everyday actions such as eating, washing etc. The study showed that this effect was especially apparent in children who had started nursery school exhibiting behaviour problems in the home. The lack of a control group is particularly noticeable in a study of this nature, in which the effect is described partly by the teachers and partly by the mothers, as those concerned naturally notice the small improvements in behaviour without having anything to compare them with.

Vitz (1961) studied 40 nursery school children twice, with a seven week interval in between. The study included the observation of anti-social aggression defined as any expression of anger or destructive tendencies of a physical or verbal nature, e.g. hitting. fighting, scolding, using threats, critical remarks, spoiling equipment or other children's toys. 'Adult behaviour' was also studied in the sense that the children sought to act as adults in some way or another such as by playing mother and father, cowboys etc., giving advice or making announcements in the manner of an adult, helping each other or comforting other children. The study showed that anti-social aggression dropped by 40 per cent within the seven weeks.

Conversely 'adult behaviour' rose by a corresponding 40 per cent within the same period.

The factor common to all these studies is that they demonstrate a positive development in the children while they are at nursery school. As already pointed out, however, they do not tell to what extent this is due to the child's own maturation processes and to what extent it is the result of nursery school attendance. In some of the studies the authors themselves have sought, with the help of statistical methods, to decide how to apportion the development.

Williamson (1932), who studied 125 nursery school children, came to the conclusion that independence and a sense of responsibility were influenced by the child's age rather than by its attendance at nursery school.

Parten (1932), whose studies show a rapid growth in the child's willingness to take part in social activities, finds a greater correlation between this age group and I.Q. than between social activity and experiences in nursery school.

Caille (1933), who studied 36 nursery school children aged between two and four in order to discover how often they showed conscious opposition—i.e. the number of times the child either in words or actions refused to obey others, to make room for others etc.—found a close relationship between the amount of time the child had spent in nursery school and the incidence of opposition. The correlation was greater than could be accounted for by age. This study does not, of course, indicate that the children were obliged to renounce their independence as a result of their going to nursery school, as such expressions of independence increased according to length of attendance rather than according to age.

Mallay (1935) comes to the conclusion that this development is due partly to age and partly to nursery school attendance.

Andrus and Horowitz (1938) found that the longer a child had attended nursery school, the greater was its sense of confidence, but that the older the child was, the greater its lack of confidence.

Joel (1939) made a study of 425 nursery school children by getting their teachers to describe a large number of characteristics in them. He showed that the longer children of the same age had attended nursery school, the more mature was their behaviour. They acted in a more adult fashion, were more independent, showed greater self control and displayed more socially acceptable attitudes.

However, the studies including a control group are better able to distinguish between the nursery school's effect and the result of natural maturation processes, provided they do not suffer from other methodological weaknesses. Sherman (1929) found in his study that children who

had attended nursery school revealed a more favourable character development that children who had not attended. But the study is weakened
because the two groups compared are not identical. This weakness is the
greater as the study was carried out among ten year olds at school, the
two groups being first studied and then compared. If there was a difference in milieu between parents sending and parents not sending their children to nursery school the result need not necessarily reflect the effect of
nursery school, but may well rather be due to differences in the home
background.

Walsh (1931) compared two matched groups of 22 and 21 children
aged from two to five years, one group having attended nursery school,
and the other not. The children were studied by means of observations
and descriptions of their personalities when they began nursery school,
and then again after two, four and six months of attendance. After the six
months it was possible to discover in the children who had attended
nursery school, greater social and emotional development than could be
traced in children not attending. The nursery school children were less
inhibited, more spontaneous, more socially aware; they had more initiative and were more independent, showed greater self reliance and confidence, greater curiosity about the world around them, and had a better
sense of order and healthier habits. The author demonstrates that those
characteristics which were generally acceptable grew in the nursery school
children, while less acceptable habits developed in the control group. He
ascribes it to the influence of social forces at work in a group of children
who must constantly adjust to one another.

Green (1931) compared two groups of children starting school, partly
by means of observation and partly with the help of teachers' comments.
One group had been to nursery school, while the other had not. However,
the groups were not matched, and so differences in home background can
have been of significance. The nursery school children showed greater
independence and social awareness, gained through their contact with
other children; but they did also show a lack of adjustment when they
were bored at school. The teachers' views on the nursery school children
did not agree, as one considered them in general to be more able to adjust
than other children, while the other found them less so .

Kawin and Hoefer (1931) compared a nursery school group of 22 with
a control group of the same number, matched with regard to sex, age,
I.Q., physical development and the financial background of the homes.
This study is particularly interesting in that it was not carried out in the
nursery school, but seeks to discover the effect on the children at home.
The descriptions of the children are based partly on observations, partly

on discussions with the mothers at the beginning and end of the study. The whole project took a year. It concluded that as a whole the nursery school children had made greater social progress than the children who were kept at home. The nursery school children lost certain undesirable habits, for instance habits which indicated too great a degree of dependence; on the other hand they also acquired a large number of undesirable habits and habits indicating a greater degree of independence from adults. Both groups developed in the same way, but the change was more noticeable in the nursery school children.

Jersild and Fite (1937, 1939) carried out a very detailed study of 18 children, of whom half had attended nursery school by the time the study commenced. The children were studied individually for a number of short periods, partly at the start of the year, partly at the end. Moreover daily reports on their social behaviour were made. The analysis showed a striking measure of agreement between the various people assessing the children. On the whole the study concludes that nursery school improves a child's social development, but not so much as might be thought at first sight. The appearance of greater social contact in the children with experience at nursery school than in the control group was due less to a more social attitude than to the fact that the children knew each other beforehand. By the end of the year the children in the control group had just as frequent social contacts as the nursery school children. The study was also concerned with the question of what happens to a child's individuality in a nursery school group, and concludes that experience of nursery school does not seem to lead to a loss of individuality; on the contrary, the child continues to defend its own interests, property and activities against others, and will even do so with increased intensity. It also appears that the attitudes of the nursery school teachers are of great significance for the children's social development, both directly and indirectly: directly through personal contact and the technique used with the children; indirectly through the way in which the nursery school is equipped and activities organised. The social behaviour accepted by the teacher usually becomes that accepted by the children in the group.

Cushing (1934) compared the way in which 27 nursery school children adjusted to school with the behaviour of 25 who had not attended. The children were described with the help of teachers' comments on various behaviour characteristics under four main headings: habits concerned with health, social adjustment, use of surroundings and personal characteristics. The result indicates some differences between the two groups. The nursery school children were shown to be rather better in their total adjustment and in their attitudes, and they were far better than the control group in their use of materials and in their total number of activities. There seem, however, to be some problems connected with the social background of the two groups. On the whole the nursery school group was slightly younger, but presumably rather more intelligent. The study thus leaves open the question of whether the greater adaptability of the nursery school children was due to their superior intelligence or their experience of nursery school.

A study by Hattwick (1936 a) includes on the one hand a larger number of children and on the other two better controlled groups than the earlier studies. From 600 children in 17 nursery schools, two groups of 106 children were selected. The groups were similar with regard to age, sex and social and financial background. The difference between them was that one had been in nursery school for between six months and a year, on average for nine months, while the other had attended nursery school for a maximum of nine weeks and a minimum of three, averaging out at six. The children were described according to a personality scale covering three different spheres of behaviour. Each child was described by three teachers independently of each other, and the average of these three reports was used as a yardstick. Hattwick concludes that children's social behaviour develops more when they attend nursery school than could be expected otherwise. As a whole the group having attended nursery school longest showed signs of the greater social adjustment, was less inhibited and had better developed habits with regard to routine actions. In the emotional sphere it was also ahead, though not so pronouncedly. The children were less nervous and shy, less inclined to hang on to adults and avoid playing with other children. In certain expressions of emotion, however, there was no difference between the groups, for instance where tears were concerned, or fear of animals, sulking, pulling faces, tantrums and so on. The study also seems to indicate that the effects of nursery school are different at different ages. Especially the four-year-olds appeared to benefit from nursery school in their social habits, while the three year olds appeared to profit more when it came to independence in more elementary routine actions.

Skeels et al. (1938) carried out a research project which was of longer duration than any of the others, i.e. three years. The studies comprised two similar groups of orphans, one of 59 children attending nursery school, and a control group of 53 children who did not. The methods used were partly observation and partly a series of tests. The nursery school group obviously developed better in the field of social adjustment and social behaviour. Their emotional adjustment seemed to be better, and they had more contact with other children; their activities were more constructive, and the more extreme forms of social behaviour diminished. The nursery school group engaged in more spontaneous activities with other children and carried on for longer with individual activities. Their behaviour showed fewer signs of nervousness, and they were less inclined to refuse to join in. However, one important factor emerges in this protracted study: the progress observed in the nursery school group as opposed to the others began to diminish after a year, and after between eighteen months and two years the other group began to catch up in social behaviour. The author concludes that this was because nursery school was not in the long run able to satisfy the needs of the children or to keep pace with their development.

Peterson (1938) compared 20 five-year-old nursery school children with a control group of 15 of the same age. The two groups were similar in age, intelligence and social and financial background. Both were studied by means of observations and tests when they started school. The differences between them were statistically significant in various respects. The nursery school children wanted more attention paid to them. They cooperated more with each other, were more willing to take part in work and play, were easier to get on with, contributed more to the group's social development, were more inclined to mix and talk to others, more inclined to defend their rights; they competed more, tried to equal or exceed others, were more inclined to try to copy others, to tease, to defend themselves and to have a sense of responsibility towards others. The children kept at home were superior on two counts: they were more polite, saying thank you, excuse me and so on, and they showed a greater respect for the right of others to behave as they wished. The study also showed other differences which were not statistically significant. The nursery school children were less inclined to rely on adults for help, more affectionate, more likely to express their feelings, more inclined to do what was right and to influence other children and the group as a whole; they were better at inspiring others, more egoistic and had a greater sense of humour. Observation of the children's behaviour showed that the nursery school children were more imaginative in their play, more spontaneous and less in need of guidance from the teacher.

Van Alstyne and Hattwick (1939) studied the adjustment of a group of nursery school children two years after they had started school. The children were described on the one hand while in nursery school and on the other two years later when at school. Use was made both of observation of their behaviour and questionnaires concerning their physical and social development, which were answered by teachers and parents. The study covered 165 nursery school children who were compared with other children in the school who had not been to nursery school, altogether about 1,100 children. It appears that the nursery school children were of a slightly higher intelligence and came from more favourable milieus. Thus the two groups were not exactly matched. The study postulates that nursery school benefits social development, independence, self-expression, self-confidence and an interest in the child's surroundings, and that it improves emotional adjustment. Moreover, it looked as though nursery school developed qualities of leadership. The children who succeeded in becoming the leaders of nursery school groups appeared to the authors to be more likely than others to become leaders in their school. However, if a higher I.Q. and a more favourable milieu are beneficial in these areas, it is not possible to draw any conclusions from the comparison between the two groups. The study showed a certain stability in the children's ability to adjust in nursery school and elementary school. In school the nursery school children were divided into two groups, one comprised of the half who were best at adjusting, the other of the remainder. A comparison with their adjustment in nursery school showed that the same children were probably in the same half in each case, that is to say that children who adjust well to nursery school will probably go on to adjust to school, while those who do not adjust to nursery school also tend to have difficulty in adjusting to school. The author concludes that some action on the part of the teachers will be required if easier adjustment in school is to be achieved by previous attendance at nursery school.

Griffiths (1939) compared 24 former nursery school children with a corresponding control group. The children were studied by means of a series of personality tests which revealed no difference between the two groups. 48 of the 51 behaviour problems found in the nursery school children at the beginning of their nursery school career showed signs of improvement in subsequent tests, while 18 out of 19 desirable behaviour patterns were still to be seen. As there is a lack of corresponding information on the control group, it is not possible to see whether the change was due to normal development.

Rhinehart (1942) compared two groups of children from poor backgrounds, 21 nursery school children and 21 who did not attend nursery school. At the same time the parents of the nursery school children took part in a training programme, while the other parents did not. The study took a year. In nine of the 12 areas of emotional and social development on which assessments were based, there was statistically significant progress on the part of the nursery school children. It is, however, not possible to see whether the positive effect was due to nursery school attendance or the course in which the parents took part.

Angell (1954) compared 39 nursery school children with a control group of 39 non-attenders. The groups were similar with regard to sex, age, the fathers' profession and the size of the families. They were studied at school. The nursery school group had an obviously better social status than the other children in the school. Sociometrical tests showed that the former nursery school children were chosen as playmates more often than the others. An assessment by teachers indicated a greater social awareness on the part of the nursery school children.

Allen and Masling (1957) compared 34 nursery school children with 82 who had not attended nursery school. The two groups were similar in development, age and sex as well as the educational standards of their parents. In 14 of the 15 areas studied the nursery school children were judged better than the others. Only when it came to having respect for their teacher were the children brought up at home rated higher. On the whole the nursery school children were found by their comrades to be more spontaneous, more intelligent and to enjoy more prestige.

Axtell and Edmunds (1960) studied 506 children who had been members of nursery school classes, and compared them with children who had not. The experimental group was found to be superior in all respects, especially when it came to working independently, listening, paying attention, showing creative ability and respecting group rules and limitations. The study appears, however, to suffer from the fact that the two groups were not matched.

Saksena (1961) compared two groups of school children in India; each group consisted of 48 carefully matched children, and one group had attended nursery school. The study demonstrated that the nursery school children had far better developed personalities.

Stith and Connor (1962) found in their study that dependence on others diminished and helpfulness increased as a result of attending nursery school.

A Swedish study (Hansson et al., 1967) was particularly concerned with the development of independence and self-confidence in nursery school children. They compared the development of a group of children spending the whole day in nursery school with that in a corresponding group of children who had been kept at home, but who had just started going to *lekskola*, and had attended for a month at most. The study concludes that the children attending for a whole day are more self confident, less dependent on others and more thoroughly adjusted to reality than children who have been kept at home until they are about six years old. The differences between the two groups are statistically significant, but it may well be asked what the differences actually signify. The personal characteristics were measured with the help of special apparatus, and it might well be asked whether the differences discovered really were differences in personal characteristics, or whether there was simply a difference in the technical ability of the more experienced whole day attenders and the beginners at *lekskola*, who had scarcely had time, in one month, to accustom themselves to their new situation. Apart from the significance of the differences, it might also be asked what the differences are due to, for even though the groups were matched in many ways, there was one important aspect in which they were not similar: the mothers of the children attending nursery school for the whole day were all out at work, while the mothers of the others were all at home. Other studies (Sjølund 1963, Moore 1964) have in fact been able to indicate different attitudes towards education in mothers going out to work and those at home, which is relevant for the personal characteristics which Hansson and his colleagues are studying. Thus it is not possible to say with certainty whether the differences are due to the time spent in the daycare institutions or whether they stem from different attitudes towards education on the part of the mothers.

The study also points to some other special problems which are of interest. Boys at home were more inclined to consider their fathers as representing authority than were those spending all day at nursery school. Girls in an institution all day had greater difficulty with their feminine identification than was the case with those who were kept at home, a state of affairs which is also indicated by other studies: boys' masculine identification is more difficult when they are alone with their mothers too much, while girls' identification process is made more difficult when they spend too little time with their mothers. Finally, this study demonstrates that the good results of whole day institutions are only achieved when children are not sent there too soon. If they start at between two and three years, the development of their individualities is slower than the development of children kept at home.

Contributory factors

The attitude of the parents

One thing that most of the studies with the control groups have in common is that however well matched they may have been in a variety of important ways, there has always been one factor which has not been constant: the parents' attitude to the question of whether the child should attend nursery school or not. As has already been said, it can be taken that the parents who send their children to nursery school have an attitude different from that of parents who prefer to keep their child at home, and this can itself result in a difference in social adjustment between children who have attended nursery school and those who have not. A Swedish study (Stukat 1966) succeded, however, in overcoming this problem of matching. Stukat made a study of *lekskola's* effect on a child's development. The group studied was compared with a corresponding group of children who had been entered on the waiting list for *lekskola*, but who had not yet been given places, so that the two groups were similar in that all the parents wanted to have their children in *lekskola*. The two groups of children were matched in pairs, so that there were 139 pairs in all, matched in all relative respects. A large number of aspects in these children was studied after they started school. The study showed that there was little difference between the groups. As regards social adjustment there were no differences of statistical significance; the *lekskola* children, however, were more outward going, more self-confident and spontaneous as well as more importunate. The longer the children had attended *lekskola*, the more highly-developed was the tendency. The *lekskola* children's greater ability to look after themselves was the only significant difference. Stukat emphasises that this is not necessarily the result of systematic teaching, but might be due to the fact that the child finds itself in situations in which it is forced to manage on its own. He also stresses that the lack of difference might be due to the fact that both groups were taken from families in relatively good circumstances; children from less fortunate milieus might possibly derive more benefit from attending *lekskola*. The material used in the study does indicate that the differences are greater in cases where the children come from social group III (the poorest). A subsequent study was made two years later, based on teachers' assessments, and this, too, only showed slight differences. The children from *lekskola* were considered better adjusted as a whole, and they were more extrovert than the children who had not attended. Rather more children with an exclusively home upbringing were sent for treatment for adjustment difficulties, but the difference was not significant.

Unfortunately, Stukat's study is the only one to have overcome the problem of parental attitudes in both groups, a question which makes the positive conclusions of the earlier studies unreliable. On the other hand there are some aspects of Stukat's study which make difficult to say how far one can generalise and transfer his conclusions to nursery schools as a whole.

The apparently small influence which *lekskola* apparently had on the children's development could be the result of the relatively short time spent there each day, while children were placed in the nursery school for the entire day. This problem will be discussed in the section dealing with the significance of the total length of attendance. Studies carried out in Israeli kibbutzes, where the children find themselves in a totally institutional milieu, do point to a greater effect. Here, however, it might well be that the attitude of the parents towards upbringing is of even greater importance than in a study of nursery school.

Irvine (1952), basing himself on a series of clinical discussions, finds that children from kibbutzes have greater self-confidence and show fewer signs of emotional disturbance than other children. This study does not, however, base itself on controlled data.

Kaffman (1961), who compared 219 kibbutz children of pre-school age with a group of American children of the same age from similar backgrounds, was particularly interested in disturbed behaviour, but found no significant difference. Three times as many of the children from the kibbutz resorted to sucking their fingers, but three times as many of the American children refused their food. This difference is ascribed to the greater freedom found in the teaching methods in the kibbutz.

Rabin (1958 b) compares a group of ten-year-old kibbutz children with a corresponding group of non-kibbutz children. The children from the kibbutz were more open and friendly, more generous and more willing to share with others; the other children were less trusting and more reserved than those from the kibbutz. The children from the kibbutz were intellectually better developed and showed greater emotional maturity; in addition their attitudes towards their families were more positive than those of the control group.

In another study (Rabin 1957) the author finds that children from the kibbutz nursery school show greater emotional stability and maturity than those brought up at home.

In a third study, Rabin (1958 a) compared 24 kibbutz babies with a similar group from outside the kibbutz. There was no difference between the groups in physical development, but certain differences in social and personal development could be observed, and the kibbutz children did not react to others as quickly as the control group. On the whole the development of the kibbutz babies was behind that of the babies in the control group; this was in contrast to the situation found regarding older children in Rabin's other studies.

The need for caution in assuming anything from a comparison with a single group of institution children emerges indirecty from a study carried out by Faigin (1958). He carried out a very detailed study of three groups of children aged from one and a half to three years. The children were observed for six months. They came from two different institutions with widely differing educational principles, one working according to liberal educational theories, the other being more restrictive. This again had its effect on the children's development. A comparison of one of the groups with children brought up at home indicated a positive effect from the kibbutz institution, but a comparison with the other group made the kibbutz institution appear to have a negative effect.

Cultural background

It also appears that differences in cultural backgrounds play their part in producing a negative or positive effect from nursery school attendance. In an Italian study (Barbiero and Galdo, 1960) a comparison was made between 200 nursery school children aged from two and a half to four years, and a control group of 40 children who had been brought up entirely at home. Both groups came from financially and socially poor milieus, and the mothers of both groups went out to work. The nursery schools were described as having good accommodation and a good standard of hygiene, but too small a staff and insufficient material to occupy the children. The study concluded that the children attending nursery school showed signs of emotional difficulties and disturbances in their psycho-motor development. The start at nursery school was accompanied by difficulties in adapting to the new milieu. After a few days most of the children had overcome their adjustment crisis; often, however, it was only a formal adjustment, accompanied by a lack of a more fundamental emotional adjustment, which showed itself in emotional resignation and a feeling of loneliness. The most common symptoms were enuresis, difficulty in sleeping, long or short attacks of crying, a tendency to isolation and a refusal to take part in general games, and an urge to boss others about. The emotional disturbances were accompanied by a complete or partial retarding of psycho-motor development. It was suggested that the retardation of psycho-motor development and the adjustment difficulties found in the children attending nursery school were ultimately due to the lack of stimulus in their milieu and to their limited personal relations with adults.

The Italian authors ascribed this to the psychologically-speaking poor nursery school milieus. However, as the mothers of both groups went out to work, it might also be that the control group had a better family background, as the child *could* have been looked after at home, while the mothers who were obliged to put their children in nursery school were, by Italian standards, less fortunately placed.

Another Italian study (Barbiero and Villone Betocchi, 1962) looked at the behaviour of the same children in nursery school and at home respectively, and dealt in particular with the children's social adjustment. 385 children aged between three and four years from five nursery schools in Naples were studied. They were described according to the same scale by the nursery school teachers on the one hand and the mothers on the other, and in addition by a psychologist. 44 per cent of the children were considered in all three instances to be socially well adjusted, 22 per cent to be disturbed in various ways; 12 per cent were considered by the nursery school teachers and psychologists to be disturbed in nursery school, but not by the mothers at home; nine per cent were considered by the mothers to be disturbed at home, but not in nursery school by the teacher and psychologist. These last differences are explained by differences in family conditions. The children who were well adjusted at home but not at nursery school appeared to come from more harmonious family backgrounds, and vice versa. The study concludes that it did not appear that an early start in the collective milieu of a nursery school influenced the development of psychological structure either in the case of those with normal psycho-motor development and normal family background, or in the case of those showing mental disturbance and irregular family backgrounds.

Another Italian study (Asprea, 1962) is particularly concerned with the question of how much of the behaviour developed by the child in nursery school is transferred to the home. A group of 77 nursery school children was studied, all aged between three and four years, and all having spent between six months and two years at nursery school. The children were assessed in respect of mental development and social maturity. The assessment was made by the nursery school teachers and the parents. The object was to collect the relative data for mental and social behaviour at home and at nursery school respectively.

As a whole the assessment was more positive in the nursery school. There were, however, some specific differences: whereas they were judged better able to look after themselves in nursery school, their manners were considered better at home. The biggest differences were found in the field of social development. The very considerable number of areas of behaviour which were given a positive assessment in the nursery school could be caused by the social stimulus, typical of numbers of children together, to join in at play, to attract the attention of the others and so on. Although the assessment of social development as a whole was higher at home than in nursery school, there was only one field, the ability to look after themselves, i.e. to carry out specific functions, which appeared to be the result more of the collective situation than of normal social maturity. A positive nursery school assessment of this sort does not necessarily mean that the child has developed any real degree of independence, as it is found that when at home the same child does not receive a positive assessment in these fields. The reduced independence at home might, according to the authors, be due to the fact that the mother's protective attitude produces an opposite effect.

The study then points out that the children's linguistic development was also unsatisfactory in various respects. This is ascribed partly to too little aural contact with the nursery school staff and partly to the fact that the language used in exchanges between the children themselves was not yet sufficiently structured to act as a positive stimulus to the improvement of their language or to establish real verbal relations. The study concludes that the collective life in the nursery school, while apparently stimulating a capacity for independence and self-sufficiency, does not appear to lead to more fundamental social maturity at this age.

Age on entry

A number of English studies are also concerned with the negative effects of nursery school attendance, and are particularly concerned to discover at what age negative effects can be discerned. One of the first of these (Freud, 1949) was made in nursery schools during the war. It concludes that the nursery school children showed insufficient emotional development, as the nursery school gave rise to a further sense of anxiety in children who were already under pressure. It might be, of course, that the wartime situation played a greater part here than the attendance at nursery school. Freud does admittedly argue that even under normal circumstances nursery school cannot replace parental care, but this can certainly not be deduced from her study, which was made during the war.

Glass (1949) compared 48 nursery school children aged between 20 and 62 months in an industrial town near London with a corresponding group of children kept at home. The study aimed in particular at discovering whether attendance at nursery school did have any negative effects. The eating and sleeping habits and the cleanliness of the children were observed,

90

and attention was paid to the appearance of personality and behaviour disturbances. The study concluded that there was no difference and therefore no reason to believe that the children who attended nursery school were exposed to a greater risk of development problems than those brought up at home, despite the fact that more than half the group had begun nursery school before reaching the age of three.

The most recent English studies are particularly concerned with the effect of nursery school at various ages, and come to the conclusion that there is a greater probability of a negative effect if the child begins at a very early age, particularly if it starts before reaching the age of three years.

Moore (1954, 1959, 1963) has carried out a very carefully controlled protracted study of 167 children whose mothers go out to work, and of whom some proportion or other has attended nursery school for some amount of time. Of the various ways in which the children were looked after, care at home, private care and various sorts of care outside the home, nursery school was that which had the best effect. By comparing the nursery school children who had gone to nursery school before reaching the age of two with those who had started at three or more, however, she discovers that the first group had developed a greater degree of independence than the others, and then she goes on to conclude that a start before the age of three is unfortunate. In addition she compares the children who had a stable milieu with those who experienced changing milieus, either residential institutions or daycare institutions; the latter group showed more nervous symptoms; the children showed signs of fear, they had difficulty in sleeping and were more inclined to bite their nails; in addition they were more dependent and had a more pronounced tendency towards self pity.

Another comparison was made between children who had been subjected to changing milieus outside the home and children under four who had experienced total separation from their mothers for up to 35 days. This latter group, one which is inclined to be thought of as being particularly threatened, was not so maladjusted as those whose milieus had constantly changed. Moore's study concludes that, provided the circumstances are favourable, children from three years and upwards can manage in nursery school for a portion of each day without suffering unfortunate psychological effects; on the contrary such children are less nervous and more independent. On the other hand they are more self-assertive and possibly less willing to seek the approval of adults before trying to achieve what they want to do.

These differences perhaps point to an area in which there is a fundamental difference between the effects of home upbringing and nursery school attendance: the child's attitude to authority. Moore (1946) studied this problem on the basis of the material mentioned above. She compares the development of the ego and the formation of a super-ego in the nursery school children and those brought up at home respectively, and concludes that the children used to institutions develop a less rigorous super-ego, while the constant presence of a mother appears to teach self-control at an earlier age, but can often be inhibiting.

Freud and Dann (1954), in a study of children placed in institutions during the war, say that as a result of the absence of their parents the children identify with each other, replace the relationship with their parents with a group relationship and attach their libido to the group or to some members of the group.

Similarly Rabin (1958 b), in a kibbutz study, finds that the kibbutz group showed fewer oedipal problems, a more diffuse positive identification and a less intense jealousy of brothers and sisters than children brought up at home.

Moore (1964) concludes in her study that the experience of greater freedom in nursery school seems to produce children who are less nervous and more self-confident and perhaps less inclined to social conformity. How fundamental and how permanent these effects are, however, it is not possible to say. It is obvious that more research is necessary to confirm what can only be seen as interim results.

While the positive significance of nursery school in the realms of social adjustment and the development of independence seems to be reasonably well documented, the question of its emotional impact remains unanswered. The anxiety conditions of nursery school children, seen in numerous instances, need further study. These problems appear to emerge particularly between the ages of two and three and might thus be simply a phenomenon related to that age, i.e. the result of too early a start in nursery school, or they may be merely the sign of a transitional problem, i.e. beginner difficulties in nursery school. A questionnaire sent to 40 experienced Danish nursery school teachers showed that in Denmark, too, these anxiety problems are found at this age in nursery school. However, no study of this problem has been undertaken in which a control group has been included for purposes of comparison, and as long as it is uncertain whether similar cases of anxiety occur at this age in children at home, it is impossible to ascribe the responsibility for these cases of anxiety to the nursery schools.

Tizard (1967) says that in his experience there is a greater sense of anxiety and greater behaviour difficulties in nursery school children than in children brought up at home. The differences disappear when the child is aged four, and from the age of five nursery school children are more independent than those brought up at home.

8 Research into Day Nurseries

The effect of time spent in day nurseries

On the basis of the tendency found in studies of nursery school for an early start to create greater adjustment difficulties, it might well be feared that an even more obviously negative effect would be found in studying day nurseries. Expectations of this nature are indeed often expressed in the general discussions of research into day nurseries. While nursery school studies usually aim at demonstrating the extent to which nursery school achieves some positive effect, day nursery research tends to look for possible negative effects of attendance. Such studies of day nurseries as are available, however, tend not to confirm these fears. The anxiety conditions which have been seen in the youngest nursery school children, i.e. those of two and three years of age, might on the one hand be due to transitional difficulties and on the other to the fact that the start at nursery school occurs at some particularly critical phase, when the child is especially sensitive. One obvious object of research is to study to what extent similar anxiety states are found in two to three-year-olds who are kept at home, just as it might also be of interest to discover whether three-year-olds being transferred from day nurseries to nursery schools, and who thus have been used to institutionalised care, experience similar anxiety states when aged between two and three.

There are only a few empirical studies comparing the day nursery and its effect with that of the nursery school. On the other hand the discussion of the effects of day nurseries is carried on with such vehemence that it results, in the case of England and parts of Germany, in a policy aimed at preventing the establishment of day nurseries in order to persuade mothers to stay at home instead of going out to work. There is, however, plenty of evidence to indicate that such measures merely lead mothers to find other, often inferior, ways of having their children looked after.

Most studies of day nurseries are mentioned and thoroughly discussed in Public Health Paper no. 24: *Care of Children in Day-Centres*, published by the World Health Organisation, 1964. Other studies, especially those concerning the effect of day nurseries on health and their contribution to the prevention of accidents, as well as a lengthy discussion of the sort of equipment desirable in a day nursery, are dealt with in *Séminaire sur les Crèches*, Paris, 1961, published by Centre Internationale de l'Enfance.

While the very large number of studies of the nursery school are normally concerned with the child's outward behaviour in the intellectual and social fields, studies of day nurseries often deal with more fundamental emotional problems and with the development of personality, all of which are probably inspired by the debate carried on throughout the past fifteen years concerning the significance of taking the child away from its mother at a very early age.

Day nursery studies are usually more comprehensive and better controlled than nursery school studies. Whether this is because the problem mentioned above demands it, or whether it is due to a different research tradition, it is impossible to say. Day nursery studies are predominantly European (French and east European), while nursery school studies are mainly American. The better quality of day nursery studies may also be due to the fact that they are more recent; all have appeared within the past ten years. The fact that day nursery studies are mainly east European while nursery school studies are predominantly American is perhaps connected with the expected positive effect of day nurseries and negative expectations of nursery school, as the American nursery schools are set up with an educational objective, while the European day nurseries are created as a social necessity. In the first case a positive effect is expected. In the second a negative effect is feared.

In a Polish study (Gornicki, 1964) a comparison was made between 500 children at home and 400 in day nurseries, all aged between nine months and three years, from Warsaw and Krakow. The groups were not composed from the start to be identical in character. On the other hand a thorough study was made of the differences which were to be expected between the two groups. Of these differences it is worth mentioning that five times as many of the day nursery children had mothers unsupported by husbands as did those who were kept at home. Some of the parents had a very poor education. Alcoholism was more common among the parents of day nursery children, especially among those with the poorest education. Many of the parents of day nursery children lived in single room flats, while far more of the parents of children brought up at home lived in three or four room flats. The standard of the flats and the sanitary arrangements were of a lower quality in the case of parents placing their children in day nurseries.

The two groups of children were studied by a fairly large research team consisting of sociologists, anthropologists, psychologists, paediatricians, social workers and statisticians. The children were subjected to extensive psychological, physiological and medical examinations, and all the families were interviewed.

The study showed that physically speaking the day nursery children had had a poorer start in life; but as time went on they caught up with and overtook the children brought up at home. The poor start was ascribed to the fact that they came from a poorer milieu, so that it was possible to conclude that the improved physical development was a result of their attendance at day nursery. As for psychological development the study showed that both groups as a whole were normal; but more of the children brought up at home were above average than were those in the day nurseries, which was seen to be a result of the better educational standards of the parents. In the psycho-motor field both groups developed in the same way, and they were both quite normal.

In two areas the day nursery children were obviously inferior to those brought up at home. Coordination between eye and hand was less well developed in the day nursery children than in the others; this difference was more pronounced towards the end of the first and the beginning of the second year. This was ascribed to the fact that the children brought up at home had more opportunities to occupy themselves with a variety of things, e.g. toys, than the children in day nurseries. The other area was linguistic development. The day nursery children were clearly behind those brought up at home, and this was ascribed to the fact that, on the one hand, the day nursery children had too little stimulus, due to shortage of staff and perhaps also because the staff available were unable to stimulate the child sufficiently, and on the other, that the children brought up at home came from a milieu where the parents were better educated. As for social adjustment, in the first year the day nursery children were clearly ahead of those staying at home, but in the second and third years no significant difference was discernible. The initially faster development of the day, nursery children was thought to be due to the fact that the day nursery milieu gave the child the possibility of making contact with others earlier than was normally the case at home. Both groups, when aged between two and three, were in fact well above average in social development, which could be explained by the fact that the children kept at home were favoured by a better home background, while the day nursery children were favoured by the social contacts which they made in the day nurseries. As for health, there appeared to be both advantages and disadvantages in going to day nurseries. Infectious diseases common in childhood occured with much greater frequency among day nursery children, which was naturally due to the increased risk of infection; but this evened out at a later stage. The difference was merely that the day nursery children had their illnesses at an earlier age. On the other hand such illnesses as bronchitis were more common among day nursery children, which again was obviously due to the greater risk of infection. However, there were fewer stomach infections among the day nursery children, which was ascribed to the more nourishing food they received.

As a whole the study does not suggest that children placed in day nurseries are given a poorer start than others. There were both advantages and disadvantages in day nurseries compared with home upbringing; but the disadvantages could be due to the control group's coming from a better milieu than the day nursery children, or possibly due to weaknesses in the day nursery milieu itself-especially a lack of toys and other materials to occupy the children, and also of staff to guide them, both weaknesses which can be remedied. On the basis of information available it is not unreasonable to assume that the day nursery children would have had a relatively less favourable development than the others if they had been kept at home.

It would have been interesting if the Polish study had related the effect of day nurseries to good and bad examples of nurseries. More attention was paid to this question in an East German study (Schmidt-Kolmer, 1964). She compared a sizable group of children from varying milieus, who were brought up at home with children brought up either in daycare institutions or residential institutions. She found no differences caused by milieu, but on the other hand she found that the institution children showed poorer motor development and physical coordination, less active play and poorer social contacts if they had too little freedom of movement, spent most of their time in bed, were without any degree of contact with adults or were not stimulated through play. The retardation was particularly noticeable between the ages of six and twelve months.

Adjustment difficulties, disturbed behaviour and an inhibited development are particularly noticeable in day nursery children in their second year. This was ascribed in particular to certain factors in the institution itself: a lack of educational activities, so that the opportunities given to the children for doing things were limited and monotonous; routine treatment of them which did not encourage their urge for independent development, and thus inhibited motor development and physical achievement; the long periods of waiting, during which the child was unoccupied despite the fact that at that age it was awake for longer periods at a time; and finally the fact that the children were moved from the baby group to the toddler group soon after their first birthday, which produced difficulties of adjustment in some.

The study demonstated that the younger the child, the more difficult it is for it to adjust to new circumstances. This was particularly true of children aged between six and eighteen months. The study also shows that in the cases when institution children have less well developed speech than children brought up at home, it is because adults do not talk to them enough, and the children do not have sufficient contacts with adults. Their development was retarded both with regard to knowing what things were called, to imitating the speech of others and to formulating ideas; all these can only be developed by means of contact with adults. The study concludes that provided the day nursery is of a sufficiently high standard the development of the children is not strikingly different from that of children brought up at home, whereas children placed in residential homes appeared to be retarded in relationship to those brought up at home.

Davidson (1964) discusses the results of a French study from 1961 covering 12 day nurseries in the Paris region, in which the quality of the institutions was again related to various aspects of the child's development. The children were divided into three age groups, the first consisting of children until they learned to stand, the next of children until they could walk, the third of the remainder until they attained the age of three years. In the first group no apparent difference was found in children from different institutions; and it appeared that the children of this age were treated in more or less the same way in all the institutions. The next group, children who had learned to stand but could not yet walk, were assessed for motor development and their ability to occupy themselves with the materials they were provided with. This aspect of their development was closely related to the amount of stimulus they received from the institution. The children in the four institutions judged best in this respect were given a development quotient of 100, while children from the three poorest had a development quotient in these two fields of between 92 and 95. The third group, consisting of children from the age when they learned to walk until they attained the age of three, was studied from the point of view of general intellectual development. Here, too, there was a close relationship between the children's development and the educational standards of the institution. The study showed at the same time that it was not always the same institutions which were best and worst at providing stimuli in various fields. Some of those which had been judged poor at furthering motor development and occupying the children, were found to be superior at providing intellectual stimuli. The differences between the institutions are dealt with at length in the study.

The conclusion is that institutions as such do not cause retardation— and indeed, they may well act as a stimulus for children from poor milieus.

It appears that the architecture and of the institutions are not without significance; however these features are not nearly as important as the organisation of daily life and the institution's equipment, especially toys and material for occupying the children's minds. The most important factor is the staff, in particular the personality of the person in charge, the standard of training of the staff together with their backgrounds, and finally the question of whether there is sufficient trained staff. In some of the institutions there were qualified nursery school teachers for the third group—those who could walk but were not three years old—and the study concludes that this type of training appears to be the best suited to this age group. It is also demonstrated that staff with this training could completely transform the atmosphere of an institution from one of restlessness and agressiveness on the part of the children to one of peace and good humour.

The study shows that the day nursery is an unnatural milieu for the first age group: from birth until the child can stand; for these children the natural milieu is proximity to the mother. However, a child's ability to adjust is quite considerable, as it is capable of growing and developing in a satisfactory manner even without its mother, provided it receives a minimal amount of maternal love and care each day, and provided that certain other conditions, which are now recognised, are fulfilled. The study concludes that the creation of such conditions is the essential problem of the day nursery.

Davidson (1964) also discusses a study of the health of children in day nurseries. The study concludes that their physical development is equal to that of the most fortunate children brought up at home, despite the fact that day nursery children as a whole come from poorer milieus.

Schorr (1963), in an East German study of 300 babies, found that while infectious diseases and respiratory diseases were some fifty per cent more common in children in day nurseries than in children kept at home, the opposite was the case when it came to ailments caused through insufficient nourishment.

One constant theme in the studies of day nursery children's general health, which is discussed in *The Care of Children in Day-Centres* and in *Séminaire sur les Crèches*, is that the general health of these children is better than that of children brought up at home, and the differences are more pronounced in children coming from particularly poor milieus. Only one study has come to the opposite conclusion (Menzies, 1946), but it was carried out in England during the war. The study, dealing with children aged between one and two years in wartime day nurseries, showed that despite the children receiving double the rations they would have

100

received at home, their weight charts were not satisfactory. This was put down to emotional disturbances resulting from the children's being taken from their mothers at such an early age.

Another aspect of the importance of day nurseries for children's development is the prevention of accidents, a subject which was dealt with at the *Séminaire sur les Crèches*, in Paris in 1961. Mention was made there of a comparative study carried out in Stockholm in 1959 in which it was demonstrated that the number of accidents which occurred in institutions was particularly small; and it was concluded that measures for the prevention of accidents in institutions can reduce the number of accidents to far below that of children at home. This, of course, is an important aspect of pre-school institutions, when it is considered that in technically developed countries accidents are the most common cause of death in children below school age.

Douglas and Blomfield (1958) demonstrated in their study that children meeting with accidents such as burns and scalds in the first year of their lives often came from homes where their mother devoted insufficient care to them, homes which were overcrowded, and poor milieus–i.e. from circumstances where attendance at day nursery would have a preventative effect.

As for the state of mental health in day nursery children, Lebovici (1964) demonstrates on the basis of a study carried out in the Paris region that psychiatric treatment is given to comparatively speaking as many children brought up at home as to institution children. He is of the opinion that many mothers at home are such perfectionists in their upbringing that they produce adjustment difficulties as a reaction, while mothers who go out to work but know their children are being well looked after can come home in the evening in a relatively relaxed frame of mind and provide emotionally more suitable care for their children than might be the case if they felt themselves to be prisoners of the children and exaggerated the difficulties of looking after them.

Another French study (Lézine and Spionek, 1958) studied the educational methods employed in the home and day nursery respectively in the case of children aged from seven to 15 months. It was demonstrated that the home upbringing is far from satisfactory. The most common faults were exaggerated demands on the child, too high expectations and too much stimulus. On the other hand there was a greater probability in the day nursery that there would be a lack of suitable stimulus.

In a number of studies, Spitz has demonstrated that the development of intelligence can also be influenced by the conditions under which a child grows up, and that the factor which he calls 'mothering' is also of significance for a child's intellectual development in its first year. Spitz (1945; 1946 a) used the Bühler-Hetzer test to compare the development of babies in two institutions. In one of them (a foundling home) the children were given very little attention or variation in stimulus once their mothers had ceased looking after them at the age of three months. The other (a nursery) was a day nursery connected to a women's prison, where the mothers were permitted to look after their children every day during its early years. The mothers of the children in the foundling home were socially well adjusted. Their sole handicap was the fact that they were financially unable to stand on their own feet. The mothers of the children in the nursery, on the other hand, were a group with social adjustment difficulties, unintelligent, sometimes with psychological disorders, psychopaths and criminals. The study showed that the development quotient for the 61 children in the foundling home gradually dropped in the course of the first year of the children's lives from a starting point of 131 to a final 72. On the other hand the development quotient for the children in the nursery school started at 97 and had reached 100 within a year. Spitz explained the fall in the development quotient in the children from the foundling home as the result of a lack of mothering. The babies in the nursery were looked after by their mothers. Spitz called the drop in the development quotient hospitalism. He also found another syndrome which he called anaclinic depression. It consists of continuous crying, a refusal to make contact, loss of weight and reduced resistance to infection (Spitz, 1946 b).

Pinnau (1955), however, stresses that these conclusions cannot be derived directly from the facts. The reported lack of variety in stimuli, the lack of toys and even excessively dark surroundings can be factors just as important as the lack of a strong emotional contact with the mother when trying to explain the emergence of a falling development quotient in the children in the foundling home as opposed to those in the nursery. These problems will be further dealt with in the section on deprived children.

Plowman (1948), on the other hand, finds in a study of 11 day nursery children aged between two and two and a half that it looks as though the children with the most stable and affectionate backgrounds were those who derived the greatest benefit from day nurseries.

Sjölin (1964), after discussing various studies, concludes that it looks as though being brought up in a daycare institution is just as good for a child's mental development as being brought up by its mother.

The alternative to placing a child in a day nursery is, however, by no means always for the mother to bring it up. If the mother is forced to go out to work the alternative will either be to have the child cared for away from the home or else in the home by a stranger. In these cases the effect of placing a child in a day nursery must be compared with the effect of these forms of upbringing. Placing a child outside the home can in most countries take the form of controlled child minding or of more casual minding; and care in the home can be either carried out by someone specially employed for this purpose, or by other members of the family. Apart from English and Swedish comparative studies of institutional and private care, which are referred to in connection with nursery school studies, no other comparative studies have been made. The educational differences found in these studies tend to favour institutional care, but they are scarcely as relevant to the early stage of development represented by day nurseries.

On the other hand Lebovici (1964) is of the opinion that a home upbringing in France can have an unfortunate effect on the child's development. As one of the most important arguments he points out that childminders are not usually particularly young; they have often lost all genuine maternal feelings and see themselves at best as 'aunts' or 'grandmothers'. They take in the children for financial reasons, often have too many, and provide them only with playthings; they can give them no educational stimulus.

The effect of a completely different alternative, that the mother should be at home with the child for the first year and provided with a suitable financial compensation for not going out to work—e.g. the approximate cost to the state of placing them in a day nursery—has not been examined. Partial attemps at compensation have been tried in France, but their effect has not been studied.

Stimulating and unstimulating milieus

Differences in effect

As a whole the available studies show that day nurseries offer both advantages and disadvantages for the development of a child as compared with a home upbringing. The advantages are found particularly in the children's health, and then again especially in the case of children coming from poorer milieus, while the disadvantages appear in particular to be psychological in nature, occasioned by the fact that many day nurseries do not offer a sufficiently stimulating milieu. Several of the studies have demonstrated that children from day nurseries as a whole are subject to too little linguistic stimulus because of insufficient contact with the adult staff.

Lézine (1962) made a special comparative study of linguistic development in day nursery children growing up in institutions offering different ranges of stimulus. One milieu was without positive stimulus and had a rigid, restrictive educational atmosphere, while the other had a kindly atmosphere with a reasonable amount of linguistic stimulation. In the first of these the children sat for ten minutes waiting for their food; they took no part in its preparation, but were just told to sit still, with the result that they became restless, pulled faces at each other, pushed at each other and wet themselves, which again led to more restrictions on the part of the grown-ups. They were rushed through their food in ten minutes, and apart from a few outbursts here and there there was hardly any talking. A count showed that within the ten minutes the children were told 27 times to hurry up, were scolded ten times and told five times to keep quiet; only twice were they encouraged or comforted. The meal was a veritable trial of strength which ended in tears on the part of the children. This day nursery produced the most difficult and disobedient children; both boys and girls were far behind in linguistic development, with an average quotient of 85 for the girls and 80 for the boys.

In the other nursery the children were encouraged to help with preparations for the meal; the adults talked to them a lot in a friendly tone; the meal lasted twice as long, and only once was there a remark that they should hurry, only once a reprimand with the remark: 'That's not nice.' On the other hand they were encouraged fifteen times, were not reproved, and had kindly remarks directed at them on 11 occasions. The development quotient was 105 for the girls and 99 for the boys. The study concludes that backwardness in linguistic development in toddlers growing up in day nurseries is mainly due to a lack of social stimulation through contact with adults and insufficient preparation of activities from an educational point of view; in particular it is due to the very common idea that linguistic development takes care of itself.

Another French study (David and Appel, 1961, 1962) first looked at the stimuli provided for a group of 20 day nursery children in their earliest years. To begin with a survey was made of the number of people concerned with looking after the child, then the degree of social contact and isolation were considered, and thirdly the interrelationship between the nurse and the baby. It emerged that during the whole of their time in the day nursery the children were on average looked after by no fewer than 25 different people, varying between 16 for some children and 33 for others. It also emerged that the nurse particularly concerned with a certain child only actually looked after it for a period varying between 26 and 46 per cent of the time. Whilst awake the children were isolated for between 68 and 81 per cent of the time, and only in contact with others for the remainder of the day. Social contact while being given physical care of one kind or another was between 18 and 29 per cent of the time awake. The interrelationship between the nurse and the child was limited. The conclusion was that two effects of day nursery care could be seen: firstly, the feeling of isolation resulting from the lack of external stimulation or the lack of contact resulting from tears, smiles etc.; secondly, there was the lack of communication and interrelationship between the child and an adult. The researchers designated this kind of care as routine care. It is characterised by the large number of people looking after the child, by the small extent of social contact and a great deal of isolation, and thirdly by the lack of emotional contact between the nurse and the child—when there is any contact at all.

A new educational programme was then devised for the institution, designated intensive individualised care. The aim was to give as few people as possible responsibility for the care of the child, and to have as few changes as possible. In addition an attempt was made to establish maximal contact with the child and to isolate it as little as possible, besides which there should be as close a relationship as possible between the nurse and the child. The result then was that the children were each looked after by between ten and 13 people as against 25 in the previous programme, and that two nurses accounted for 88 per cent of the care of each child. The periods spent in isolation were reduced by half, and the amount of social contact while being tended was more than doubled. Interplay between the child and the nurse was more than doubled.

The significance of the quality of the institution

Another area in which the studies show day nurseries to provide too little stimulation is that of motor development and play activities. Lézine (1964) reports the conclusion arrived at by a specialist committee in 1960 with regard to materials for occupying children of day nursery age. Suitable toys must be chosen, and activities must be arranged; a positive relationship must be created amongst the children, and special attention must be paid to those who are easily tired or upset.

Schmidt-Kolmer (1963) carried out a three-year experiment to test the effect on the children's development of an ideally equipped day nursery. She included 77 children aged between one and three years who were divided into groups of varying ages with four adults to each group, two trained teachers and two assistants. For purposes of comparison 76 children were selected from ordinary day nurseries.

The following educational principles were adhered to:

(1) Each individual child was in the same group and was looked after by the same adults;
(2) It was not be allowed to lie and look after itself. It was be in active contact with its surroundings as long as awake;
(3) Twice daily the children were grouped together according to the stage of their development for activities which could develop and establish new forms of behaviour corresponding to the child's stage of development:

The two groups were compared every three months with regard to behaviour, which was divided into linguistic reactions and physical reactions (including activities and play). The result was that in relation to ordinary development norms the experimental group was some 20 per cent ahead of the control group.

Lebovici (1964), basing himself on his own French studies, emphasises his experience that the most critical stage in the care of a child is when it begins in the institution, especially if the child is more than six months old but less than between eighteen months and two years. Once the separation is accepted it will no longer give pain. Therefore the start is particularly important.

Schmidt-Kolmer (1964) argues that the babies must gradually be introduced to the institution, for instance by being left for one or two hours at a time for the first few days, and then gradually for longer periods. Moreover, she says, children should be moved as little as possible from one group to another. In her East German study she found that a change at the beginning of the second year often produced adjustment difficulties.

The unfortunate effects of staff changes become obvious from a French study (Bertoye, P. and Dumorand, C., 1957). In a day nursery connected with a training college deep psychological adjustment difficulties were experienced every month during the regular change of nurses.

A Norwegian paper (Östlyngen, 1956) emphasises that a child can derive benefit from a daycare institution when aged from eighteen months to two years, but that this will depend on a period of slow adjustment, with a maximum time spent in the day nursery of six hours in small groups.

Schmidt-Kolmer (1963) enumerates the most important educational aims of day nurseries as follows:

(1) To develop and further cultural and hygienic habits and independence;

(2) To further motor development and physical control;
(3) To develop senses, abilities and skills;
(4) To develop language and thought;
(5) To develop knowledge of nature and the society in which the child lives;
(6) To develop feelings, the ability to establish contact and to get on with others.

A West German discussion of the question (Mehringer, 1966) stresses the following important points: the number of children per nurse should be small, six at the most; changes of surroundings should be avoided; attention must be paid to both educational and psychological development, not merely the child's health. This last point necessitates the staff's being trained in teaching techniques as well as child care.

The last point—the transfer of the main emphasis from health to teaching and psychological care is also underlined by Mallet (1964) as well as many others among the studies referred to already. Problems related to this are discussed at length in *Séminaire sur les Crèches*, Paris 1961 and in *Care of Children in Day-Centres*, 1964.

The tendency in several countries to move the emphasis from hygienic aspects to educational and psychological aspects has had as one of its results the fact that the Soviet Union (Usova, 1961 a) has moved pre-school institutions from the Ministry of Health to the Ministry of Education and has established a special research institute for research into the pre-school age group under the Academy of Educational Studies.

There is also interest in the USA in carrying out research into the educational functions of day nurseries. Pease and Gardner (1958) note a positive effect on children placed in good institutions. Caldwell et al. (1965) describes a complex new research programme which is being launched in order to study what an 'enriched milieu' could mean for children of day nursery age who come from poorer milieus.

The deprivation problem

Partial and complete separation of mother and child

The expectation of a negative effect with which many day nursery studies begin has obviously been caused by the discussion started by a report which the English psychiatrist J. Bowlby prepared for the World Health Organisation: *Maternal care and mental health*, Geneva 1951. He summarised in his report a large number of studies demonstrating that children growing up in full-time institutions showed clear signs of a development inferior to that of children being brought up at home.

Although the report was strongly criticised by social psychologists and anthropologists (O'Connor, 1956; Mead, 1954), the effects of placing children in institutions noted in it were immediately ascribed to other forms of institutional care of children. This was despite the fact that Bowlby himself draws a clear distinction in his report between the effect on children completely separated from their home and those who are only away from home for part of the day. He even goes so far as to quote studies showing that the development of children placed in a daycare institution because their mothers were going out to work was completely normal, in contrast to that of children completely removed from their mothers' care. On the other hand, there is a risk that the child will feel rejected by its mother if she is prevented from going out to work and in consequence finds the child a burden. This matter will be more fully treated in Chapter 13, the subject of which is children whose mothers go out to work.

The uncritical use of Bowlby's results in the discussion concerning day nurseries is presumably due to the emotional and ideological overtones of the entire discussion of the justification of mothers' going out to work. On this superficial basis some countries, such as Great Britain and West Germany, have even prevented the creation of day nurseries in an effort to persuade the mothers of small children not to go out to work. According to figures for Great Britain (Yudkin, 1963), however, these measures have not had the desired effect, but have merely led to less desirable arrangements being made for the children.

The day nursery studies summarised above agree that the placing of children in daycare institutions produces an effect closer to that of a home upbringing than placing them in full time institutions. Lebovici (1964) says that the danger implicit in removing children from their mothers and placing them in day nurseries is infinitely less than that in putting them in residential institutions. Sjölin (1964) argues that care in a day nursery probably harms the child less than care in a full-time institution. Schmidt-Kolmer (1964) comes to the same conclusion.

A few studies have been made comparing children growing up in day nurseries and children's homes respectively. A Danish study (Simonsen, 1947), which occupies a place of importance in Bowlby's report, compares 140 children in full time institutions with 165 attending day nurseries and nursery schools. The two groups were from the same working class milieu, and they were compared by means of the Bühler-Hetzer development test. The average development quotient for the two to four-year-olds in day nurseries and nursery school was quite up to normal, while the children of the same age in full time institutions had a development quotient of 93 points.

Simonsen operates with a special term, 'the passage age', by which he means the age at which a child can manage the individual tests. For 43 of the 77 tests there was no difference between the groups, but in the others the children in daycare institutions were ahead in 29 tests, while those in residential institutions were ahead in five. The children in full time institutions showed a more sustained interest in the toys given to them, which was explained as a result of the training methods used in their case. These children showed a greater respect for authority, and they were less accustomed to toys; they were also less spontaneous. Emotionally they were less well developed. They were more nervous and inhibited, and their language was less well developed except in the case of memory tests. Their general experience was less than that of children in daycare institutions.

The differences are partly ascribed to the fact that there were fewer possibilities of contact with adults, and that there was too little stimulation from the other children, who had themselves not achieved a higher degree of development. The milieu in the children's home was too enclosed and provided too little stimulation and there was too small a staff, who had too little time to look after the children.

An English study (Heinicke, 1956; Heinicke and Westheimer, 1965) compared a group from a day nursery with a group from a children's home. The groups were small, but carefully controlled and studied, both by observation of their daily lives and by testing in individual play situations. Both groups showed signs of disturbance at first, especially on the first two days, but after this the day nursery children became less concerned with their separation from their mothers, while those in the children's home continued to show evidence of considerably greater difficulties in a number of areas. At first, both groups tried to go home with their parents; but those in the day nursery soon stopped worrying much about that problem and were quite obviously able to work it out in their imagination and with fewer signs of antipathy. Their needs were satisfied by the mere physical presence of adults, and they spent a greater proportion of their time engaged in activities with the other children or playing with dolls than they did in turning their attention to the adults. Their reactions when their parents came to fetch them were reasonable and showed no signs of a disturbed relationship with them.

The children in residential care, however, showed massive reactions: uncleanliness, serious antipathy, an urge to eat sweets, a powerful desire for attention from grown-ups, resistance to the wishes of adults even while seeking their attention, increased auto-erotic behaviour, especially finger-sucking, and a greater number of illnesses and colds. When their parents came to visit them, there was a tendency to shun them, despite the fact that they had only been separated from them for three weeks.

It appears, then, that placing a child in a day nursery for part of its time does not have the detrimental effect which many researchers have found to result from putting a child in a children's home. Meanwhile the studies of the deprivation problem made after Bowlby's original report give reason to consider the educational situation in daycare institutions. The World Health Organisation, in a new report, *Deprivation of Maternal Care, a Reassessment of its Effects* (Ainsworth et al., 1962) has made a reassessment of the problem based on new research. Other attempts at reassessing the problem have been made by Casler (1961) and Yarrow (1961, 1963, 1964, 1965). The following section will attempt to synthesise the points of view expressed in this work and to consider their practical implications for the work of day nurseries.

The problem of deprivation in day nurseries

A summary of the results of research into the deprivation effects produces a series of problems which might well be relevant to the study of the effect of day nurseries.

(1) *How prolonged is the separation of mothers and child?* Bowlby (1951) was already aware that a distinction must be drawn between total and partial separation. This is confirmed by the other studies of day nurseries mentioned above. Yarrow (1965) and Ainsworth et al. (1962) went on to specify other varying categories of separation. It is useful to distinguish between complete and partial separation and in the latter case to specify the length of separation each day. Then comes the question of the total length of separation, whether it is only of short duration or whether it is permanent. Finally, the question is raised as to whether it is a continuous or an intermittent separation, or one occurring at irregular intervals.

(2) *At what stage in the child's development does the separation occur?* Ainsworth and Bowlby (1954) stress that it is necessary to distinguish between a separation of mother and child taking place before a stable and secure relationship between them has been formed and after such a relationship has emerged but before the child is old enough to be

110

independent. Most researchers agree that the close relationship between mother and child is only established around the age of six months. Casler (1961) maintains that there can really be no question of maternal deprivation in the first six months of a child's life, as the ties between them have simply not been established. Bowlby (1951) also distinguished between two sorts of separation: privation, i.e. separation before a close relationship has ever been established, and deprivation, where an established relationship is broken, usually after the child has reached the age of six months. Yarrow (1965) refers to various pieces of research indicating that the most violent reactions immediately after separation are to be found in children who before the separation had developed a strong emotional relationship with the mother, while children taken away at an earlier age were apparently unaffected by the experience.

(3)   *The fact that the critical point for the separation is not reached until the child is six months old does not necessarily mean that it would have been less harmful to place the child in care at an earlier age.* Yarrow (1965) emphasises that if the child is separated from its mother at too early an age, i.e. before it has begun to develop a strong emotional link with her, and if it is then placed in an institution where it has no possibility of making emotional contact with a mother figure, the child will not develop a normal capacity for making emotional contact with other people. The critical point for learning to have emotional contacts will in this case have passed.

(4)   *What is the quality of the relationships which are broken off and of the new relationships taking their place?* Yarrow (1965) points out that the mother-child relationship before the separation can have been of such a quality that a separation can only benefit the child. If it has not had the possibility of establishing a close contact with its mother either because of her unwillingness to do so, or because she is prevented from looking after it, the child might, by being removed to a good institution or a foster mother who really cares for it, actually find many of its emotional and social needs fulfilled, and thus perhaps avoid reaching the critical time without having had the opportunity of establishing emotional relationships. Lebovici (1964) argues that being placed in an institution can very well mean an improvement in the child's situation. On the other hand it is of crucial importance that the institution should be able to give the child the same as it would have received at home; in other words, the quality of the institution is decisive. In his work on kibbutz babies, Spiro (1957; 1958) demonstrates that they have as much daily contact (two hours)

with their mothers as children at home, and moreover he finds the contact to be of a better quality.

(5) *Individual differences in children with regard to the effect a separation from their mothers has on them.* It must be assumed that constitutional factors play their part in deciding how susceptible a child is to the effects of a separation from its mother. Some children are presumably more sensitive than others and will thus suffer more from a separation from their mothers. This aspect of the problem, however, is much more difficult to study than the others, and for that reason no work has been done which can give any indication of its importance.

The decisive question for day nurseries is what it is in the mother-child relationship which the child loses by being placed in an institution, and how and to what extent an institution can replace this.

How a day nursery can stimulate

Recent research has attempted to isolate the factors relevant to the separation of mother and child, and it has been seen that the general term of maternal deprivation must be broken down into a number of specific forms of deprivation.

Thus, as has been said above, there can be no question of maternal deprivation before a close relationship between the child and its mother has been established, normally around the age of six months. Casler (1961) has paid special attention to the question of what sort of deprivation is present when it is possible to find signs of retardation in children who have been placed in institutions before this age, and considers that a lack of sensory and perceptual stimulation in the institution, i.e. the opportunity of receiving different sense impressions, including tactile impressions, must be the explanation.

Yarrow (1963) has tried to discover what forms of stimulus are particularly important to children aged six months or more. He concludes that progress appears to be very largely dependent on stimulation on the part of the mother. Then he goes on to discuss certain forms of stimulation from the mother which are particularly closely related to specific aspects of the child's development; for instance emotional stimulation and contacts are important for the child's ability to deal with emotionally charged situations and for the development of its social interests. Physical stimulus resulting from care for the child is of even greater significance.

These kinds of stimulation are less closely connected with other aspects of the child's development, such as, for instance, intelligence, curiosity and an urge to be occupied with things. In these fields there are other forms of stimulus which seem to be of far greater significance, e.g. communication, stimulation to achieve things, and stimulating materials and experiences.

It is possible to summarise the ways in which a day nursery can be sufficiently stimulating for a child in the following manner:

(1) *Sensory stimulation.* The time and opportunity must be found for looking after the child, fondling it and showing affection.

(2) *Perceptual stimulation.* The child must be given as much opportunity as possible for sense impressions, not least by means of the materials given it to play with.

(3) *Motor stimulation.* The child must be given room and freedom to move around.

(4) *Social stimulation.* It must have a great deal of contact with others.

(5) *Cognitive stimulation.* It must be talked to, so that it has the opportunity of developing its ability to speak.

(6) *Emotional stimulation.* It must be given the opportunity to feel that someone is fond of it.

9 Intellectual Development

General intellectual development

Basic psychological research has not yet finally demonstrated to what extent individual intelligence is influenced by milieu. The older theory that intelligence was hereditary and will emerge irrespective of the external circumstances under which it must develop, has, however, been undermined recently. Numerous studies have shown that children growing up in a milieu incapable of providing them with sufficient stimulation (often in an institution of one sort or another) are retarded in their development in comparison with other children, and that this cannot be explained simply on the basis of their having come from a particularly unfortunate milieu in the first place.

Simonsen (1947) compared Danish children from residential homes and nursery school; they belonged to the same milieu, but whereas the second group showed normal intellectual development, those in the children's home were on average some ten points lower.

Crissey (1937) found a connection between the degree of retardation and the duration of stay in institutions providing insufficient stimulation.

On the other hand Skeels (Skeels and Fillmore, 1937; Skeels, 1940) found a relationship between retardation and an insufficiently stimulating home background as distinct from a stimulating institution milieu.

While most researchers agree that an insufficiently stimulating milieu can retard a child's intellectual development, there is less agreement as to whether a particularly stimulating milieu can accelerate it.

If milieus do play a role in the intellectual development, whether it is a question of a poor milieu retarding it or a particularly good milieu accelerating it, this must be a specially good area in which to measure the effect of nursery school. In a short questionnaire sent to 40 Danish nursery school teachers, asking what they considered to be the most important tasks of nursery school with regard to the children's development, intellectual development was given eighth place. Other areas, however, must be included when talking of intellectual development. Linguistic development was given third place, and the need to stimulate a child's imagination and curiosity came sixth, followed by the need to teach the children to create and be constructive. In this chapter consideration will be given to a number of studies of nursery school's significance for the child's intellectual development, including both the development of intelligence and the more specific aspects of intellectual development.

36 research reports concerning the effect of nursery school on a child's general intellectual development have been registered and analysed, and in addition a number of papers containing theoretical commentaries have been noted. Besides these are various studies of the development of children in special circumstances, either intellectually retarded or culturally deprived or subject to particular educational situations, which will be discussed in the relevant chapters. Finally, the question will also be dealt with in connection with the preparation of a child for school; 21 of the 36 studies conclude that nursery school has a positive effect on a child's intelligence, 15 studies report no effect. None reports negative effects in the form of reduced intelligence resulting from attendance at nursery school (in contrast with results of research into the effect of residential institutions). Of the 15 studies reporting no effect, several had small numerical differences which favoured nursery school, while none contained any differences detrimental to it. These figures, however, were not statistically significant.

Most of the studies are American, and most of these again were carried out in the second half of the 1930s. A few, including all the European studies, appeared after 1960; of these an English one and a Swedish one are complete, while others from Israel and Italy are still not finished. These more recent studies all point to a positive effect if the milieu factor is controlled.

Most of these studies have included control groups which were more or less well matched. Some of them, however, have based themselves on an intelligence test of the child at the beginning of its attendance at nursery school, and then again after varying periods of attendance, comparing the results.

Baldwin and Stecher (1924) studied the development during three years at nursery school of 105 children aged between two and six years. The children were both observed and tested periodically. When they showed progress in their test results, the authors concluded that it looked as though their intellectual development was accelerated by their experience of nursery school. As there was no control group undergoing similar tests, this study could not provide conclusive evidence of the extent to which the better results after attendance at nursery school were the result of attendance or of other factors such as familiarity with testing procedures.

Woolley (1925) included a control group in his study, however; it consisted of children on the waiting list for nursery school, but for whom no place was available. When the two groups were tested a second time it was found that 63 per cent of those attending nursery school showed a rise in their intelligence quotient, while only 33 per cent of the group on the waiting list showed an improvement. However, these results were not followed up, and it could be that the differences resulted from the materials with which the nursery school children were occupied giving them more experience, which was useful to them in the subsequent tests. The result can only be considered reliable if the difference is maintained over a prolonged period.

Hildreth (1928) also investigated this problem. She compared 41 children starting school, who had spent at least four months in nursery school, with another group of children who had not attended nursery school. The groups were matched so as to be similar in age, milieu, race and sex. The two groups were tested as they started school and again after an average of eighteen months. At the start of school the nursery school children were on average six points ahead of the control group. At the second test the difference had largely been eliminated, the control group having risen by 3-4 points on average. The author concludes that the study points to no essential difference between the groups, but that the advantage which the nursery school children had at the start had not really been lost at school. The situation was merely that the other group had caught up with them at a later stage.

Goodenough (1928) found no difference between nursery school attenders and a control group. There were 28 children in each group, and the groups were carefully composed so as to be as similar as possible. In doing this the author placed special emphasis on the educational standard and the intellectual capacity of the parents. During the year spent on the study a certain rise was discernible in both groups, slightly greater in the case of the nursery school group, but not sufficient to be significant, and so the author assumes that the rise must be due to a degree of unreliability in the testing. No connection was found between the level of intelligence and the length of attendance at nursery school. The study does not indicate that the rise in the nursery school children's test result is due to the nursery schools' use of materials similar to those used in the tests, as the nursery school children did not appear better than the control group in managing those parts of the tests most closely resembling activities in the nursery school, as Woolley (1925) had thought might be the case.

Sherman (1929), who compared nursery school children aged between two and three and a half years with a control group of the same age, concluded that a faster growth in intelligence was discernible in the nursery school children.

Barrett and Koch (1930) compared a group of children from a children's home, who spent a year at nursery school, with another group of children from the home who did not attend nursery school. There were 17 children in each group, and they were carefully matched in pairs. The average intelligence of the group attending nursery school rose from 92 point to 112, while the control group rose from 92 to 98 points. The study showed no correlation between the individual parts of the test and the extent to which the children had worked with similar material in the nursery school. On the other hand, it was demonstrated that the children making the greatest intellectual progress in the nursery school were the ones who showed the greatest development of personality. This can be interpreted as showing that intellectual development is helped more by an emotionally warm atmosphere than by direct training in intellectual activities.

Kawin et al. (1931) compared 22 nursery school children with a carefully matched control group. The children were observed for a year and studied from various points of view. While the nursery school had positive effects in other areas, no difference was found between the nursery school children and the control group with regard to mental development.

Kawin's group was drawn from the upper middle class. Ripin (1933) studied children from a poor social milieu and found that attendance at nursery school provided a clear stimulus to intellectual development.

Mallay (1935) observed 21 nursery school children at the beginning of the nursery school year and again at the end of it and found a clear development in mental activity. No measurement was made of intelligence, but the author described how far the children made use of materials with which they were provided, and whether their use of apparatus was constructive. In addition a study was made of the attention the children paid to the apparatus and to what was going on around them in the nursery school. However, as the study did not include a control group it is not possible to decide whether this development was due to normal maturation processes or the particular influence of the nursery school.

Skeels et al. (1938) compared a group of children attending nursery school for five to six hours daily with a corresponding group from a children's home who were not sent to nursery school and spent their day in the home. This home provided little stimulation for the children, while the nursery school was outstandingly good. There were 21 children in it, ranging from eighteen months to five and a half years. Each of these children was matched with one from the children's home for age, mental development and I.Q. Intelligence tests were carried out on each group every six months throughout a period of almost three years. The result was a rise in intelligence for the children in nursery school, but a drop for those from the children's home. Those who had been at nursery school for between 200 and 400 days rose on average by just under four points. Those who had attended for more than 400 days rose by an average of just over six points. The corresponding control groups showed a fall of just over one point and just under five points respectively. The differences were statistically significant.

It must be pointed out, however, that the nursery school group, too, was below average for this age. So instead of saying that nursery school has a positive effect, it is fairer to say that it appears that the children's home had a negative effect.

McNemar (1940) checked the statistical data and found them to be unreliable. The small difference remaining between the groups, which was not significant, he ascribed to a greater ability to make contact on the part of the children who had attended nursery school, which put them at an advantage when it came to testing them.

Skeels et al. (1940) replied to the suggestion that there was a regression effect by re-analysing the data for a group with an I.Q. of under 80 and another with and I.Q. of over 80. Eleven children who had attended nursery school for at least 400 days and had an I.Q. of over 80 at the start rose by half a point on average, but the control group feel by 16 points. The two corresponding groups with an original I.Q. of under 80 rose by an average of 7.7 points, while the control group rose by only three points. The differences were significant in each case. At the same time the authors demonstrated that the test-retest effects showed a fall for the brighter group (I.Q. more than 80) and a rise for the slower group (I.Q. less than 80). So an increased ability to make contact on the part of the nursery school children cannot be the explanation of the better test results, as this would be valid in both instances.

Wellmann and Pegram (1944) undertook a further re-analysis of the original material and concluded: (1) that the children's home produced a tangible diminution in intelligence when the child was kept there for a long period; (2) that attendance at nursery school, which supplemented the children's home milieu, counteracted such as diminution; (3) that the progress produced by the nursery school milieu depended on the length of the daily attendance and the total period of attendance.

In his reply to this McNemar (1945) accepts Wellman and Pegram's conclusion that the nursery school milieu promotes an acceleration, but argues that their conclusion that the fall in the level of intelligence on the part of the control group was produced by a prolonged stay in the home cannot be accepted; rather than being the result of their time spent in the children's home, this change should, he believes, be ascribed to various selective factors.

Page (1939, 1940) compared the intelligence of 72 beginners at school, all of whom had attended nursery school, with the intelligence of their elder brothers and sisters, averaging about ten years of age, who had not been to nursery school, and found no difference between them. Nor did a control group of other schoolchildren who had not attended nursery school but were comparable from the point of view of age and social and financial status, show any significant difference.

Rhinehart (1942) compared the development of intelligence in 21 three-year-old nursery school children from a milieu described as lower middle class, and whose parents at the same time took part in a training course for parents, with a corresponding control group of 21 children not attending nursery school, and whose parents did not take part in the course. The nursery school group, who at the start had been seven points below the control group, was two points above them at the end of a year, a relative improvement of nine points. As the experiment was arranged, however, it is not possible to determine how much of the rise in I.Q. was due to the direct influence of the nursery school and how much to the indirect influence of the increased educational awareness of the parents resulting from their participation in the course.

The Iowa Child Welfare Research Station, under the direction of B. Wellmann, carried out in the 1930s a series of studies of the development of intelligence in children of pre-school age, seeking to discover the significance of the milieu in this connection, (Wellmann, 1932 a; 1932 b; 1933, 1934, 1938), and in particular to pinpoint the importance of nursery school for a child's intellectual development.

In the report from 1933 Wellmann surveyed the results for the first 600 children who had attended the institution. Repeated tests indicated a rise in the children's achievements, which seemed to be connected with their attendance at nursery school. The rise was also connected with other factors such as the length of time they had attended, the duration of each day's attendance and the level of intelligence at the beginning. The study concludes that intelligence is influenced by milieu to some extent. However, it contains no control group, so the objections referred to before are also valid for this. In his work, however, Wellmann has considered the validity of the various intelligence tests in nursery school and finds them sufficiently reliable.

The following six studies were also carried out in the Iowa Institute under the directorship of Wellmann:

Coffey and Wellmann (1936) studied the cultural status of the children's milieu and its significance for the development of intelligence in 400 of the children who were included in the previous study. The study concludes that while there is a connection between the child's intelligence and the cultural status of their parents when the child starts in nursery school, these differences are evened out as a result of attendance at nursery school to such an extent that subsequent testing showed no statistical connection between the intelligence of the children and the parents' cultural standard.

McCandles (1938) studied two similar groups of four-year-olds with an average I.Q. of about 140. However, there were only six children in each group. One of the groups was sent to an ordinary, good nursery school, while the other was given a particularly inspiring programme of constructive activity. For instance the children visited a farm, after which they were given the task of constructing a miniature farm in the nursery school. Similarly, visits were made to stores, hotels etc., and when, after a year, the children were tested again, the experimental group were found to be ten points above the control group.

Peterson (1938) compared 20 nursery school children with a control group of 15, made up in a comparable manner, when the two groups started school. The children who had been to nursery school had a higher I.Q. on starting school. This difference, however, was eliminated after a year's schooling.

Griffiths (1939) compared 24 nursery school children with a corresponding control group and found that the nursery school children were of significantly higher intelligence than the control group.There was a significant rise in the I.Q. of the nursery school children from the time they started attending and until they left.

Kounin (1939) compared 26 nursery school children, who on average had attended nursery school for a year, with 31 children who did not attend nursery school. At the age of three, the groups had had identical I.Q.s and when the study commenced had an average of 118, but at the end of the year the nursery school group were significantly higher.

Messenger (1940) compared two identically composed groups: 20 nursery school children and a control group of 22. The groups were identical with respect to the social status of the parents, the children's age and intelligence when the study commenced. After two years the intelligence of the nursery school children had risen, while that of the control group had not. The difference was statistically significant.

Wellmann (1940 b) summarises the results of these studies as follows:

(1)   The I.Q. of nursery school children is increased while they attend nursery school, not before or after.
(2)   The rise is cumulative during the first two years in nursery school.
(3)   The I.Q. of children not attending nursery school does not rise.
(4)   There is no connection between the time spent in nursery school and the changes in I.Q.
(5)   The cultural status of the parents is not the explanation of changes in I.Q.
(6)   A suitable educational programme appears to raise the I.Q. of particularly intelligent children.
(7)   Progress resulting from attendance at nursery school appears to be reflected in achievement in school.
(8)   Children from residential homes not attending nursery school showed a drop in I.Q.
(9)   The effect of practice or training cannot be the explanation of the changes. The tests used at pre-school age are quite reliable and valid.

These results are in conflict with Goodenough's study, and Goodenough does indeed criticise the conclusions. (Goodenough, 1939; Goodenough and Maurer, (1940 a). She is of the opinion that statistical regression is the explanation of the apparent improvement in intelligence in nursery school children tested at intervals over a given period. If she treated her data from the University of Minnesota Nursery School in the same way as the data from Iowa was treated, she would reach similar conclusions. She is convinced that the statistical laboratory in Iowa has played a much greater part in the rise of intelligence in the children than did the Iowa nursery school.

Stoddard and Wellmann (1940) replied to this that the conclusion reached by Goodenough and Maurer was based on the use of the Minnesota Nursery School intelligence test, which had not been so carefully conceived as had the Binet test which they had used.

These problems were further discussed in connection with a conference on the significance of the milieu for the development of intelligence in the National Society for the Study of Education, the results of which were published in the Society's 39th yearbook (Stoddard, 1940). This included a further series of original studies of the significance of nursery school for the development of intelligence, and these will be the basis of the following summaries.

Anderson (1940) compared 17 nursery school children with a control group which at the beginning of the study was comparable in I.Q., social and financial background, sex and the parents' education. After six months the nursery school group had risen by an average of 2.41 points, while the control group showed a decline of 1.23 points. However, this difference is not statistically significant. Then Anderson examined the extent to which these differences were either increased or diminished by a prolonged attendance at nursery school, comparing groups of nursery school children of various ages who had spent varying lengths of time at nursery school with corresponding control groups. The results show no differences between the nursery school children and the control groups, and Anderson concludes that there is no support for the thesis that nursery school improves a child's I.Q., or that the increase is dependent on the amount of time spent at nursery school.

Bayley (1940) adopted a different method. She studied the mental development of 48 children throughout their first nine years. The development was compared with various milieu factors, including attendance at nursery school, but no relationship emerged.

Bird (1940) carried out observations on 54 nursery school children aged between three and a half and seven years at the beginning of their nursery school attendance and again at the end of it. The periods of attendance varied between one month and one year, and the time spent there each day was two and a half hours for five days a week. The nursery school was of unusually high educational quality. The average intelligence rose by just under two points; in the case of most children only slight variations were found, but a few of them made considerable advances. The differences between children from particularly affluent homes and those from notably poor ones were of the same dimensions.

Frandsen and Barlow (1940) compared a group of 30 nursery school children aged from two to five years with a corresponding control group of 28 children matched in sex, age, social and financial background and the level of training reached in the home. The groups were examined when the nursery school group was starting attendance and again six months later. The nursery school group had risen by 3.34 points, while the control group had only risen by 0.53 points. The difference was almost statistically significant, and the authors conclude that over a longer period it could well be that the differences would be big enough to be statistically significant.

Goodenough and Maurer (1940 b) compared the results of tests made over 13 years for 147 nursery school children divided into groups having spent from just over a month to just under two years at nursery school, with those of a control group of 260 children from comparable milieus.

The material was divided according to the children's ages and social and financial milieus, so that the experimental groups and the control groups were alike in this respect without being matched in pairs or with regard to intelligence at the start of nursery school attendance. The study concludes that the time spent at nursery school has no measurable effect on the child's mental development.

Jones and Jorgensen (1940) compared 54 nursery school children with a corresponding control group composed in such a way that the I.Q. s were equal at a given age, as were the parents' educational standards. No difference was found between the two groups, not even if the length of attendance at nursery school was taken into consideration, and the study concludes that under the given conditions nursery school has no measurable effect on mental growth.

Lamson (1940) compared 25 beginners at school, who had spent an average of two years at nursery school, with a corresponding group of children who had not attended nursery school. The control group was selected at random, though the school class and sex were kept constant. The study found no difference in I.Q. or school achievement. It concludes that nursery school attendance neither improves nor impairs mental development.

Olson and Hughes (1940) compared 28 nursery school children with 28 others. The mental development of the nursery school children was demonstrably better. However, the groups were not identical in composition, and when those children whose parents had particularly high levels of education were excluded, there was no difference in the groups. So the improvement was found in children coming from homes with a poor level of education. When the nursery school children were divided into a group consisting of those who had attended on average for 225 days and one who had spent an average of 117 days in nursery school, no significant differences were found. The study concludes that there is no particular advantage in nursery school for children coming from privileged milieus, and it might be that children coming from such a background have already been given optimal mental stimulation at home. If, however, the children come from a milieu deprived in one way or another it might well be that attendance at nursery school can help the child to realise its potential. To arrive at a definite conclusion tests would be necessary on children from other milieus.

Reyment and Hinton (1940) looked at this problem. They studied the intellectual development of 100 children throughout a four year period. The children's age at the start ranged from three to 14 years, and the I.Q.'s varied between 70 and 130. The milieu in nursery school and school was in general considerably better than the home background of most of the children concerned. Most of the parents were either skilled or unskilled workers. Taken as a whole there was no difference in the I.Q. s of the children at the start and end of four years attendance, but if they were divided into those who started before reaching the age of six and those starting later, it was clear that those who started at nursery school age both individually and as a group showed a significant rise in I.Q. after one year at nursery school. Smaller though still significant rises continued for the next four years for this group, while the older children showed no rise. The authors cannot say to what extent the increase in the younger children is due to nursery school training or to their becoming increasingly accustomed to the testing, which the older children had not had. However, if it were not due to this latter factor, it looks as though a start must be made on stimulating a child's milieu at nursery school age. A division of the children into those below average and those above showed that the changes taking place were distributed equally in both groups.

Starkweather and Roberts (1940) studied 209 children at the beginning of nursery school attendance and again after an interval of between six and 40 months, while the children were still at nursery school. The study showed a significant rise in intelligence in relation to the first test carried out. A further test carried out at school showed that the improvement was maintained. The rise in the level of intelligence bore no relationship to the length of attendance at nursery school. The I.Q. of the children who had only been there between 50 and 150 days rose just as much as in the children who had attended for longer. This certainly seems to indicate that the rise registered can be due to the effect of the testing, in that the children when being tested for the second time are in a situation which they have experienced before, irrespective of the length of time they have spent in nursery school. Unfortunately no control group was included in this study. Taken individually, the intelligence of six per cent of the children was identical in each test. 34 per cent fell ten points or more, and 60 per cent rose 14 points or more, and of these 12 per cent rose by 20 points. The average rise was thus due to a particularly noticeable improvement in a few of the children, while the remainder showed rises or falls close to the average.

Voas (1940) compared 114 schoolchildren who had attended school for between one and three years, and who had previously been to nursery school, with a larger group who had not been to nursery school, and found it impossible to discover any difference in intelligence between the two groups, despite the fact that the nursery school concerned had been modern and well equipped. On the other hand, the two groups were not matched with regard to personal and social factors.

Goodenough (1940) published a number of criticisms of these studies:

Woolley's study (1925) probably showed a temporary effect at least, but since the children were not tested again on leaving nursery school, its significance for their subsequent development remained unknown. Nor can it be decided with any certainty to what extent the effect observed was wholly or partly produced by the fact that the children were given toys to play with which were similar in nature to the material used in testing them, so that there could be a question of unintentional training.

In Barrett and Koch's study (1930) the children constituting the control group were taken from institutions other than the group given nursery school training, and even if the nursery school was similar to the control institutions in equipment and organisation, there might well have been a difference in their psychological climate. The difference in the development of intelligence might also be due to a faster development of the nursery school pupils' personality, as the three children who showed the greatest improvement in the test results were also thought to have developed most in personality. This was also the opinion of their teachers, who did not know the results of the tests.

Wellmann's study (1933) of a group of nursery school children about to start middle school suffers from the defect that these children were tested twice a year while they were at nursery school, and thereafter once a year, while the control group was only tested once in all, i.e. when it started school, so that the slight difference favouring the nursery school group might well be due to a greater routine in testing. Then the test results are presented separately for groups with different test levels at the start, with the result that the regression effect, resulting from a greater unreliability of tests at nursery school age, might well have resulted in the children who at first were at the top managing less well in later tests, while those who were lower on the scale showed clear progress. Since the various factors which can be grouped together as results of practice have almost without exception been seen to produce an improvement on a second test compared with the first, the advance made by the group which originally was at the bottom is usually greater than the decline in the group from the top.

The results in the report by Starkweather and Roberts can likewise be explained as regression effect. Moreover, no control group was included in this study.

Goodenough concludes that it is not certain whether attendance at any unspecified nursery school can bring about an acceleration of intellectual development in the average child. In most studies of this sort, no conclusive evidence has been produced of such an effect. It looks as though only certain nursery schools further intellectual progress. The differences between nursery schools achieving this effect and those which do not, have not yet been investigated. Thus it is not reasonable to ask the question whether nursery school as such develops a child's intelligence, but whether any nursery schools do, and if so, then in what way do they differ from others with regard to equipment and educational policy. Moreover there is the question whether, in an ideal situation, all children could benefit from the possibilities which such nursery schools have of accelerating their intellectual development, or whether only certain types of children can. And if so, then which types? Is the effect temporary or permanent, and if it is permanent, then does the improvement only take place while the child is at nursery school, or does it continue when it has left?

Wellmann (1940 a) answers Goodenough's criticisms. When there are changes in the same child being examined, there can be no question of mistakes in the choice of control groups. The changes in intelligence have been studied in the same children, on the one hand at a time when they were not attending nursery school, and on the other at a time when they were. This avoids all the problems associated with making up a control group suitable for comparison purposes. At the same time an extra control group of children not attending nursery school has been examined. The suggestion that the improvements were due to practice in testing also seems unlikely, as various comparisons were made in which the number of tests carried out was the same for both groups. Nor can regression effect be the complete explanation of the various changes, as two groups of children with the same level at the start ought to show the same changes. However, they do not do so when milieu factors are different. The changes are not, for instance, the same in winter, when the children are at nursery school, as in summer, when they are not.

Stoddard (1940), on the other hand, criticises the studies which have not been able to point to an intellectual improvement resulting from attendance at nursery school.

The study made by Goodenough and Maurer, which started with 147 nursery school children and 260 control group children, ended by studying only 13 nursery school children and 15 others. Furthermore these small groups are divided into three on the basis of the parents' occupations. The result is thereby based on numbers which are far too small to be significant.

In Lamson's study the control group was almost three months older than the nursery school group. This factor alone could be expected to account for a difference of four points in intelligence, and since Lamson himself indicates a difference of three points in favour of the nursery school group, there might well in practice be as much as seven points in their favour.

Hildreth's study comprised children who had been problem children long before starting nursery school, which was considered a last resort in helping them with their difficulties.

Goodenough and Maurer (1940 a), in another paper, point out that generally speaking only Iowa indicates a positive effect, while other institutions with equally high standards, such as the nursery schools at the University of California, the University of Minnesota, the University of Cincinnati and Winetca Public School System can demontrate no positive effect resulting from attendance at nursery school.

In a couple of later articles (1943, 1945) Wellmann has taken up this question. She has analysed 50 studies in all and divided them up according to whether they issue from Iowa or elswhere, and according to whether the intelligence tests were made on the basis of the Binet system or the Merrill-Palmer test. The tests based on the Binet method showed a rise in Iowa of an average of six points against the 0.7 of the control group, while studies done elsewhere showed an average increase of 4.6 points against 1.3 in the control groups. Studies based on the Merrill-Palmer test showed for the Iowa group an average increase of 8.2 points for the nursery school group and 3 points for the control group, while studies elsewhere showed an average increase for the nursery school groups of 18 points and for the control groups of nine points. In the material as a whole 22 nursery school groups and 14 other groups were tested with the Binét method. Half of the nursery school groups rose by an average of at least six points, while only 14 per cent of the others had an increase of this magnitude when tested by the Merrill-Palmer method. Of seven nursery school groups and four others, six of the nursery school groups rose by at least six points, while only one of the others rose by this amount.

In yet another study (Wellmann and McCandles, 1946) attention is drawn to a number of factors in nursery schools which are related to an accelerated intellectual development.

This discussion has been very fruitful indeed, as it has helped to point to problems of a methodological nature, which has been to the advantage of subsequent studies of other aspects. After this culmination of the 1930s' experiments with and discussion of the possible influence of nursery school on the intellectual development of the child, further research in this area seems to have come to a halt until recent years when studies have been carried out, in the main, in the USA.

Rabin (1958 c), on studying 30 ten-year-old children who had attended a kibbutz nursery school, and comparing them with a corresponding control group, found that there were signs of a superior level of intellectual development in the nursery school children. Specific details are not included, and even if the groups are described as being identical, the factor of attitudes might well have played its part.

A Swedish study (Erasmie, 1964 a and b) (discussed at length in the section dealing with linguistic development), which included a comparison of the development of intelligence in nursery school children and other children from a comparable milieu, found a significantly greater increase in nursery school children aged between four and six, after which the difference diminished.

Borum and Livson (1965) compared 152 children who had attended nursery school, with a matched control group who had not. The nursery school group showed a more rapid increase than the control group. In the case of girls the increase was significant, but not in the case of boys. In boys the tendency was for the increase to be greater, the younger they were on commencing. The duration of attendance at nursery school, however, bore no relationship to the increase in intelligence either in boys or girls.

Moore (1967), in a study of English nursery school children, found no difference between those who had attended and those who had not.

Gardner (1967 a and b) reports as his experience from English studies that there is no clear evidence to indicate whether academic achievement is better in children who have been to nursery school. But in view of the fact that most children attending nursery school in England come from very underprivileged homes, the fact that they are on a level with other children when they start school is in itself evidence of the positive effect of nursery school on the children's intellectual development, as it could otherwise be assumed they would lag behind.

Douglas and Ross (1964) also find an improved intellectual capacity in nursery school children in comparison with others from similar milieus. This can still demonstrated at the age of eight and to some extent at 11, but by 15 the difference has been eliminated. Both the nursery school children and the control group were from unfavourable milieus.

Smilansky (1958, 1967) carried out a series of experiments with nursery school children in Israel, the children coming from socially and culturally underdeveloped areas, and aimed to discover whether a specially devised nursery school training could put these children on a level with others by the time they started school. Previous experience had indicated

129

that they were not sufficiently well developed intellectually. The preliminary results of this study indicate a rise in I.Q. of 30 points.

The result indicates a change of culture rather than an increase in intelligence, but naturally that, too, is of importance if the most is to be made of school attendance.

In recent years a number of experiments have been carried out in the USA similar in style to the Israeli ones, and aimed at throwing light on the question of whether, through what is called an enriched milieu, it is possible to stimulate the intellectual development of underprivileged children who come from culturally deprived milieus and therefore have not attained their maximal intellectual development. These experiments will be discussed in the chapter dealing with the extent to which culturally deprived children are ready for school.

While studies concerning groups of children from a reasonably good milieu give no clear picture of a possible beneficial influence of nursery school on the child's intellectual development, the results concerning children from a poor milieu are more in agreement in indicating a positive effect.

All the studies specifically indicating that the children come from a poor milieu (Ripin, 1933; Olson and Hughes, 1940; Reyment and Hinton, 1940; Rhinehart, 1942; Smilansky, 1967; Douglas and Ross, 1964) indicate that nursery school has a positive effect on intellectual development. The same is true of children from children's homes who attend nursery school (Barret and Koch, 1930; Skeels et al., 1938).

All in all it appears that the poorer the milieu from which the child comes, the more a nursery school can do for its intellectual development. This point of view is supported by most of the studies discussed in the chapter on culturally deprived children and the section on mentally retarded children.

Half of the studies of children not coming from retarded milieus report a positive effect, and half report no effect at all from nursery school attendance. Of these latter, however, several show a slight bias in favour of nursery schools, though they are not statistically significant. No report indicates that nursery school has a negative effect on intellectual development, although many of the children in these studies come from above average milieus and are of above average intelligence.

At the same time it looks as though the better the educational standards of the nursery school, the better it will be able to stimulate the child's intellectual development. One single study specifically devoted to particularly intelligent children (McCandles, 1938) indicates that a nursery school of particularly high calibre can accelerate intellectual development even at this level.

Specific aspects of intellectual development

All the studies of intellectual development discussed above have in common the fact that they are concerned with testing general intelligence and usually include a comparison of I.Q. before and after attendance at nursery school.

While nursery school teachers seldom talk of increasing the intelligence of the children as one of their educational objectives, they do more often mention specific aspects of intellectual development such as, for instance, the development of their ability to express themselves, the encouragement of creativity in the sense of constructive self-expression, the formation of ideas and orientation in the world arround them. These three spheres came in third, seventh and eleventh place in the Danish questionnaire on the twelve most important objectives of nursery school. Swedish teachers (Stukat, 1966) place them in eighth, ninth and twelfth places of thirteen.

Linguistic development

Altogether 12 studies have been registered dealing with the effect on the general pattern of development of linguistic development. They come from various countries, but are predominently European, and while five are based on a comparison of nursery school children and children kept at home, the other seven compare nursery school children with children from residential institutions.

In addition there are other studies concerning the linguistic development either of children in special circumstances or children subject to special educational programmes in nursery school, and they will be dealt with in the relevant chapters.

The linguistic development of children appears to be an area which has been neglected in nursery school teaching theories. Most studies indicate that the speech of nursery school children is less well developed than that of children kept at home. Only two Swedish studies show signs of a slightly positive effect, but this is not statistically significant.

Bergamini and Swanson (1954) took a group of school beginners and compared those who had attended nursery school with those who had not. On the basis of tests to see whether they were ready for school they

131

noted the extent of their vocabularies and their understanding of language. The children brought up at home produced the best results.

An English contribution (Moore, 1966) was a protracted study of 76 children, some of whom attended daycare institutions and some of whom were at home. The observations, which were very thorough, were made when the children were six months, eighteen months, three years, five years and eight years of age, and the object was to discover the importance of language for mental development at an early age. The children who had attended daycare institutions from an early age tended to be linguistically retarded even when they had not been much affected in other directions. The difference was statistically significant; at the same time the study pointed to a slight difference between boys and girls, indicating that girls from the daycare institutions were linguistically less developed than boys.

Langmeier and Zdenek (1963), in a study of Czech institutions, note that one in eight of children in institutions showed normal linguistic development at the age of twelve months while nine out of ten children brought up at home did.

In a study carried out in Poland, Gornicki (1964) points out that children brought up at home were clearly superior to day nursery children in linguistic development, though the position was reversed in other areas.

Schmidt-Kolmer (1964) notes in her East German study that children from institutions, particularly those in which the children resided permanently or throughout the week, but also to some extent daycare institutions, were less well developed linguistically than children brought up at home, and concludes that the reason for this is that the adults in the institutions do not talk to the children sufficiently. The second year seems to be crucial in this respect. This study also demonstrates that linguistic development is furthered by having the children in mixed age groups both in day nurseries and in nursery school. However, it was demonstrated in an experimental institution that the children's linguistic development could be fostered to such an extent that it exceeded the normal development of children brought up at home. But this presupposed great and well planned efforts on the part of the teachers.

Several studies are concerned with the reason for unsatisfactory development of children in institutions. McCarthy (1943, 1954) emphasises that most children from better milieus will, on starting nursery school, have more contact with other children and less with adults than the case would be at home. The adult linguistic patterns will thus develop more slowly in children attending nursery school. She does not, however, think that this retardation should be interpreted as a negative effect of nursery school, but as a result of the child's total development in the sense that on starting nursery school the child becomes more concerned with things other than learning to talk to adults, and develops other abilities rather than the ability to speak well.

Lézine (1962) notes that the linguistic development of children is closely associated with the linguistic stimulation to which they are exposed. In another study (Lézine and Spionek, 1958) she finds that on the other hand children can be over-stimulated in the home, while there is a risk of inadequate stimulation in nursery schools. Her paper ends with a number of suggestions for ways of improving linguistic development.

A Russian paper (Radina, 1963) stresses the importance of the correct teaching methods for the desired linguistic development. On the basis of studies carried out in the institute for research in educational methods in nursery schools it is emphasised that linguistic development is most important as it is of significance for other aspects of mental development.

Yakubovskaya (1963) finds that the extent to which children aged between two and three understand words depends on their linguistic development in their first year, the social milieu during that time and the extent of communication with older children to whom they have access.

The two Swedish studies showing slight signs of a positive effect were made in *lekskola*, which is a form of pre-school institution which emphasises intellectual linguistic stimulus more than nursery schools usually do; this in itself confirms the points of view expressed above.

For Stukat's study (1966) use was made of vocabulary tests and a test of linguistic expression, while a note was made of speech errors. Relatively acceptable and partially significant differences are found, and they are such as would be expected, taking the aims of the nursery school into account. In the vocabulary test the nursery school children of both sexes, but especially the girls, did better than the children brought up at home. Notes on which this assessment was based show a greater ability to produce connected sentences, to remember details more correctly, to express themselves in a more lively fashion and with fewer stereotyped ideas. Speech difficulties were observed in more children brought up at home than in those attending nursery school. All in all, these results indicate that attendance at nursery school has a positive effect on the development of speech. In the subsequent study, carried out in school, there was still a tendency for the nursery school children to be in advance of the others. Stukat himself argues that the wider vocabulary and the greater ability to express themselves which he found in the nursery school children must be seen as the direct result of conscious training in these skills, and it is clear from his description of the Swedish half-day nursery school, the *lekskola*,

133

that it provides ample opportunity for such training.

Another Swedish study (Erasmie, 1963, 1964 a and 1964 b) is particularly concerned with language development in children of nursery school age. In this a group of children attending nursery school is compared with a group staying at home. A representative selection was made of 147 children aged between four and six and a half, living in Norrköping. They were given a series of tests aimed at assessing both intelligence and linguistic ability. The material collected was then divided up according to whether the child attended nursery school or not. Attention was also paid to certain social variables such as the parents' education, income and social status.

The conclusion reached was that attendance at nursery school seemed to have a positive effect, in that it accelerated the growth of vocabulary. The language tests were divided into two categories: definition tests and recognition tests. The definition tests showed the greatest difference, and Erasmie is of the opinion that the explanation is to be found in the speech training given in *lekskola*, as active speech is required more for definition tests than for the others. All ages taken together, nursery school children are significantly better in definition tests, but not in recognition tests. When they are divided into age groups, the difference is most marked in six-year-olds, which is the age at which optimal results are found in recognition tests. The difference in definition tests increases, in favour of nursery school, until the age of six. In the oldest group, however, there seems to be a negative connection, in that children at home between the ages of six and seven (school begins at seven in Sweden) appear to do better than those in nursery school. It seems that the oldest children in nursery school are those who risk being exposed to insufficient linguistic stimulation.

In an article (Erasmie, 1963), the author argues that a change is necessary in the nursery school programme if it is to attain its object of making a child intellectually more ready for school than it otherwise would be. A flexible nursery school with a greater variety of training methods for six-year-olds, so that the brighter ones were given greater opportunities for satisfying their intellectual needs, would have a beneficial effect on their readiness for school.

While the youngest children in nursery school are stimulated by other, slightly older children, the top class in nursery school has no possibility of stimulation from children older than itself, and if their teacher has too little opportunity for indulging in 'grown up talk' with these children, they will receive less stimulation than children at home who have both adults to talk to and possibly older children to play with.

An important factor in deciding whether a milieu is linguistically stimulating is that it should not be too homogeneous; for instance, the children should not be too close in age. A number of psychological experiments comparing the linguistic development of twins, triplets, quadruplets and quintuplets with that of children who had only older or younger brothers and sisters shows that the more brothers and sisters there are of a given age, the more linguistically retarded they are likely to be in relation to families where there is a greater age spread. This problem might well be relevant to day nurseries, where, for practical reasons, the children are divided into groups at the same stage of development. In this way there is not merely a question of triplets, quadruplets and quintuplets, but of groups of up to ten of the same age, and so it is easy to understand that linguistic retardation in children attending institutions is to be found more in day nurseries than elsewhere. The problem is, however, also present in nursery schools where the children are divided according to age.

In Russian nursery schools, which used to have a very strict division according to age, experiments have produced great linguistic progress in two-year-olds by putting them in with groups of three-year-olds. The experiment says nothing about what happened to the three-year-olds, or whether they might have benefitted from being put in with a group of four-year-olds.

Although nursery school might retard children's linguistic development in certain respects, there are two categories of children whose linguistic development appears to be accelerated by attendance at nursery school. These are children from milieus with low cultural standards on the one hand, and on the other, children from residential homes, who, as a result of deprivation, already show signs of retardment in their linguistic development. Studies of the effect of nursery school on children from culturally deprived milieus usually touch on readiness for school and are discussed in Chapter 11.

Psychologists studying children's linguistic development soon became aware of the difference between children growing up in a children's home and those growing up at home. However, the first comparative studies sought primarily to discover the factors determining linguistic development. Meanwhile they all pointed to the fact that children from residential institutions were far less well developed. It is impossible here to recapitulate the very large number of studies indicating linguistic retardation in children from residential institutions, but Pringle (1965) and McCarthy (1954) both provide summaries. The intention here is only to summarise studies concerned with the effect of nursery school on the linguistic development of children from residential homes.

A Danish study (Simonsen, 1947) pointed to a difference in development between children from residential institutions and nursery school children. Simonsen showed that, apart from memory tests, children from residential institutions were in all fields inferior to those merely attending nursery school. He explains the difference as originating from insufficient contact with adults and no stimulation from the other children who were equally unfortunately placed. The milieu was too enclosed and lacking in stimulation, and there was too small a staff for them to be able to devote sufficient time to the children. In order to improve conditions it was suggested that efforts should be made to bring the children into greater contact with life outside, to provide more staff, and to move the children from the nursery to groups of older children at an earlier stage.

Skeels et al. (1938), in their study comparing two groups of children from residential homes, one of which attended nursery school, found that while the nursery school children were clearly superior to the control group in many fields, nursery school only had a slight positive effect with regard to improving linguistic development, which was below normal in any case.

Dawe (1942) examined the linguistic development of two groups of children from residential homes, one of which was taking part in a special language training programme in a nursery school, the aim being to provide them with stimulation comparable with that given to children living in a good home. The two groups, consisting of 11 children each, were matched in pairs with regard to sex, age, education, intelligence and linguistic development at the start of the experiment. When the study was completed there were statistically significant differences between the groups. The experimental group rose from 80 to 95 per cent of normal, while the control group fell from 81 to 79 per cent.

Pringle and Tanner (1958) compared four-year-old nursery school children with children of the same age from a children's home, each group consisting of 18 children who were matched in such a way that the relevant background factors were as nearly identical as possible. The children were studied both through a series of verbal tests and by means of recordings of their manner of speaking while at play. Data was gathered on their vocabulary and their sentence structure both when they knew they were being tested and when they did not, on their ability to understand and to express themselves in simple sentences, and on their ability to express themselves when in the company of others. In all quantitative comparisons the nursery school children were seen to be ahead of those from the children's home. Among the qualitative differences found were the nursery school children's ability to establish social contacts with others of the same age by means of speech, and to retain the interest of adults.

Pringle and Bossio (1958 b) note in their study of the linguistic development of children from residential homes that retardation of linguistic development is notably greater than retardation in other areas, such as intelligence; this is in agreement with other studies maintaining that the deprivation effect is far more marked in a child's linguistic development than in any other area of the development of its personality.

Moore (1967) finds in the study already referred to that while other areas are not affected, the linguistic development of children with a daily substitute for a mother is poorer than that of the children in the control group. This is particularly noticeable in girls.

Roudinesco and Appell (1950) tried to make up for the effects of institutional life on small children by introducing another kind of educational practice which entailed more individual attention being paid to the children by the staff. A subsequent check carried out eighteen months later showed progress in various areas, but practically none in the field of language.

It looks, then, as though it is necessary to distinguish between two sets of reasons for linguistic retardation in residential institutions. On the one hand it is caused by the child's emotional suffering from maternal deprivation, and on the other by the lack of adequate linguistic stimulation in the institution. In the early years (at day nursery age), the first of these two reasons is probably the more potent, while the second plays a greater role at a later age (at nursery school age).

Linguistic retardation as a result of deprivation will be dealt with at greater length in the section on day nursery studies; as for nursery school, there are numerous studies which tell something of what factors are important for stimulating the children's linguistic development. As has already been pointed out, it is beneficial for small children's linguistic development to put them amongst older children who have a larger vocabulary. Smith (1935) found that children used longer sentences and a more highly developed pattern of language in talking to adults than in talking to other children. McCarthy (1943) discovered that when older children were talking to adults they used considerably longer sentences than in talking to other children. Hahn (1948) studied a group of six-and-a-half-year-olds and found, on the other hand, that a group discussion with other children was more likely to stimulate a mature language than a conversation with a single adult. From this it looks as though, while a child's language is stimulated by talking to an adult more than by conversation with another child, it is stimulated even more by a group discussion with other children.

More carefully controlled experiments are necessary, however, before anything can be said with certainty.

Other studies also indicate the importance of the group for the child's language. Williams and Mattson (1942) studied three to four-year-old nursery school children in groups consisting of an adult and one, two or three children respectively in addition to the person in charge of the experiment. Tape recordings of 17 different games, lasting ten minutes in all, were made. The length of sentences was more or less the same in the various groups, but there was more chatter and more social contact in the largest group. The use of adjectives diminished, and the use of adverbs increased with the size of the group. The larger the group, the more social and the less egocentric was the type of language used.

Hahn's study (1948) noted that the sentences used were longer in group conversations than in conversations with the adult. During conversations with adults incomplete sentences were used six times more frequently than in talk with other children. Moreover, it was observed that when a conversation on some subject or event was not based on visual terms, the sentences used by the children were longer.

Another study (Dawe, 1934 b) was concerned with the effect of the size of the group on a child's understanding of a story, and the extent to which the children took part in a subsequent discussion of it. It indicated a slight tendency for more children in larger groups to get less out of the story. It was quite plain that the bigger the group, the more children there were who were left out of discussion of the tale.

Various studies have shown that the physical situation in which the child finds itself produces varying linguistic reactions. McConnon (1935) studied 28 nursery school children in various situations: eating, playing out of doors, playing indoors, acting etc., and noted that they all produced quite different expressions in the language the children used.

Van Alstyne (1932) found that the playthings used were also of significance. Certain types of playthings had a greater 'conversational value' than others. Playing with dolls, building with bricks, crayoning and modelling encouraged the children to talk, while painting and cutting out shapes had the opposite effect.

Young (1941) looked at linguistic usage in four different nursery school situations. Each child was observed for a total of six hours in ten minute periods spread over a fortnight. The four situations studied were outdoor play, indoor play, mealtimes and periods during which the children were looking at books. It was shown that the situation in which the child found itself was of great importance for the language it used. Outdoor play and looking at pictures were the situations leading to most discussion.

138

The results of these studies, banal as they may seem, do, however, show that situations can be created which will stimulate more use of language on the part of the children. For instance, it is possible to devise types of games which encourage them to talk; materials can be used which have more 'conversational value', and group situations can be arranged which lead to discussion and conversation on a more mature level.

In short, it can be said of the effect of nursery school on a child's linguistic development, that it can be negative for children coming from good backgrounds, but that it has a good effect on those coming from poorer backgrounds. The situation is also that nursery school has a negative effect if it itself provides an unstimulating milieu, but a positive effect if special programmes are arranged, or if play situations are devised which will stimulate the use of language. This has been done in connection with experiments carried out to test a child's readiness for school, and will be discussed more fully in the section on laboratory experiments in nursery school (Chapter 17).

Creativity

The concept of creativity, in the sense of the ability to create something new or to construct something original as distinct from re-creation or reproduction, is now being placed by psychologists alongside intelligence, and research in this field is attracting a great deal of interest from psychologists and teachers, for in the final analysis it may well be that a person's creativity is of greater practical significance than his or her intelligence. Various studies, e.g. Getzels and Jackson (1962) indicate that intelligence and creativity do not necessarily go hand in hand. A person can be highly intelligent without being particularly creative, and vice versa.

As it appears that creativity is more directly influenced by the stimulation to which a child is subjected than is intelligence, and as it seems that the pre-school age is a time of special importance for this development, it must be assumed that nursery school has a special educational task in this area, which has indeed always been included amongst its aims. Getzels and Jackson, who compared a group of young people described as highly creative with another group described as highly intelligent but not creative, found a difference in the manner in which the two groups had been brought up. The general impression formed by the manner in which the creative group had been brought up was that they had been allowed plenty of scope for individual self-expression, and that it was accepted that they should be allowed to try doing things for themselves. The opposite was the case with the highly intelligent group. They had been allowed only a limited scope for self-expression, and the extent to which they had been allowed to try things for themselves had been minial.

Other studies have demonstrated that group psychological factors are decisive for the extent to which creativity is allowed to develop freely. Torrance (1960 and 1962), who studied 25 highly creative children, each of whom had been placed in a group with five other children, discovered that a certain amount of group pressure was exerted against the creative members of the groups. The ability of the creative children to express themselves and to develop as was natural to them, was controlled by the group through teasing, criticism, rejection or neglect, and by a general tendency to oppose their ideas. In another study (Torrance, 1962) a tendency was found for teachers to prefer highly intelligent children to highly creative ones. In a third study (Torrance, 1960), he tried to discover in which ways the creative children differed from the others, and it appeared that they did so in particular in three fields. Firstly, they had the reputation for producing mad and ridiculous ideas, a view shared both by their schoolmates and their teachers. Then the results of their efforts showed great productivity, but did not keep to well trodden paths. Thirdly their attitude to work was seen to be humorous and playful.

Someone with mad ideas who goes his own way and has a playful attitude to work is liable to be subjected to pressures both from his own group and from those in charge. As, however, such qualities appear to be closely connected with creativity, it is the teacher's task to produce a milieu which allows these qualities to thrive, and this means creating a tolerant atmosphere in the group and behaving in a permissive rather than an authoritarian manner. This has long been the practice in nursery school. The studies referred to above were all made at school and dealt with children aged between seven and 15 years. In the following a look will be taken at such studies of creativity in nursery school as have been carried out.

Creativity and intelligence have one thing in common: the difficulty of definition and delineation. This fact in itself creates certain difficulties in measuring the effect of nursery school attendance on the child's creative activity. Taylor (1959) examined more than 100 definitions of creativity, and tried to group them into different levels and stages. He found, however, that none of the definitions which he included in his study contradicted each other. It was merely that the individual studies were concerned with different aspects of creativity. Taylor talks of five levels, of which one is described as the expressive level and is characterised by spontaneity and freedom of expression. As an example of expressive creativity the author mentions small children's drawings. Expressive creativity is probably that form of creativity which comes closest to the nursery school concept of it. However, it must be assumed that creativity in nursery school is something different from creativity in adulthood. It is not yet known whether there is any connection between these two stages of development, which is naturally a limitation on any assessment of the significance of nursery school for creativity in the long run. This has not yet been studied.

It will be necessary completely to ignore the question of definition in the following, as the studies are evaluated exclusively with regard to what the authors themselves regard as creativity. Moreover the word creativity is relatively new. In nursery school such terms as free activities, constructive use of materials, free play, etc. are used, all of which are contained in Taylor's definition of expressive creativity.

Mallay (1935) found that the amount of time children spent with the active use of materials and the constructive use of equipment rose in the course of the time spent in nursery school. His study, which did not make use of a control group, ascribed this partly to greater maturity on the part of the children and partly to what they learned while attending, both through their own experiences and directly through the teaching.

Peterson (1938), in the study mentioned earlier, discovered that nursery school children were freer, more spontaneous and more imaginative on starting school than other children from the control group.

Horowitz and Smith (1939) found in their studies that there was a positive correlation between the constructive use of materials and the length of attendance at nursery school, and they were of the opinion that this was true irrespective of age. The longer the period of attendance at nursery school, the greater the interest in constructive activities together with other children.

Axtell and Edmunds (1960) found in their study that the children who had taken part in the nursery school programme were considered by their teachers to score better in creative activity than those who had not taken part.

Cushing (1934) discovered that nursery school children showed more signs of activity in more fields and chose a greater variety of materials than children in a control group.

All studies indicate that nursery school attendance has a positive effect on the child's creativity. However, the studies so far reviewed cannot be considered sufficiently controlled, as the control groups, where there are any at all, are not exactly matched with the nursery school groups. For instance, it is apparent in Cushing's study that the nursery school children were of a higher average intelligence than the control group, and similarly it can be taken that the nursery school children in all these studies come from milieus and homes with the greatest interest in their education.

Stukat's Swedish study (1966) is the only effect study of this subject to be reasonably well controlled. He discovered that children in *lekskola* needed more manual constructive work than children at home. When it came to drawing, which was judged on a sense of form, intensity of colour and originality in the choice of motif, the *lekskola* children were also ahead of the others. Although the differences were not significant, the author believes he can indicate a certain influence from the creative activities of *lekskola*.

The educational activities and the milieu of the nursery school must presumably be of special significance in the achievement of a positive effect.

Reichenberg-Hackett (1964) made a study of the effect of the nursery school milieu on children's creativity. The work covered 120 nursery school children from the same milieu with an average age of just over four. A quantitative and qualitative analysis was made of their drawings. The results were then seen in relationship to the psychological climate of the nursery school. The groups of children were divided into the three which enjoyed the freest and most encouraging climate, and the three who had the strictest and most authoritarian climate. The drawings produced by the children in the first three groups indicated greater creativity than those by the other children. The results of this study support the suggestion, which is based on primary psychological research, that the educational climate is of importance for children's creative self-expression.

This also emerges from Simonsen's Danish study (1947), in which she compared nursery school children and children brought up in children's homes, and discovered that the latter category managed less well in most fields. The study concludes that the main reason for the lower degree of spontaneous productivity in the children from the residential home was the more pronounced sense of authority, which in its turn was explained as resulting from a milieu which was cramped and unstimulating, with too little staff and too little possibility for the children to have contact with adults.

There is much evidence pointing to a correlation between the factors causing conformity of behaviour and those limiting creativity in a child. An upbringing emphasising what is the done thing, or pressure from a group to be like all the others, hampers creativity in itself. In this respect the strongest factors are the family group on the one hand, and the group of playmates on the other. In this area nursery school has an important function in creating a milieu which allows the child to develop its creative instincts. Such studies as are available indicate that nursery school can achieve this.

The formation of basic concepts

Developmental psychology has shown that the pre-school years are the most important period for the formation of basic concepts, and that development takes place in a particular order, so that the acquisition of certain basic concepts at the right time is necessary for the development of concepts at a later age. Unsatisfactory development of concepts in the areas relative to a particular age can thus have fateful consequences for subsequent-developments. This problem will be dealt with at greater length in the section on the effect of cultural deprivation.

The unsatisfactory development of concepts is especially caused by unsatisfactory and inadequate stimulation. It is one of the effects most often mentioned in studies of children from residential homes.

Schmidt-Kolmer (1963 and 1964), in a very thorough study carried out in East Germany, has proved that while the formation of concepts in daycare institutions is on a par with normal development, it falls below this level in residential homes and homes for weekly boarders. At the same time her experiments indicate that such a state of affairs is not necessary provided the residential institution is of a sufficiently high quality.

In nursery school children an unsatisfactory formation of concepts is most noticeable among the older children. Sandels (1956) demonstrates that many six-year-old children, especially when gifted, tire of nursery school, as they no longer find materials presenting them with new problems with which to occupy their minds, and which could lead to the development of new concepts.

Wann (1962), however, maintains that because of its educational methods nursery school can produce above average intellectual development by furthering the children's understanding and helping them to develop new concepts. He argues that the years from three to six are of particular importance for this development and must receive more attention than has so far been the case.

He asserts, as does Piaget, that this age is of prime importance for the establishment of certain elementary concepts which are significant for subsequent intellectual development, concepts which may never be properly formed if the right occasion is missed. It has been shown that this problem is of particular importance for culturally deprived children and an important reason for their having a poorer intellectual development than children from other milieus.

Church (1963) stresses how important it is for a child at nursery school to be systematically guided so as to be able to explore the world around him, to understand the essential qualities of the things he sees, to learn what can be done with them, and to appreciate such concepts of measurement as bigger, smaller, heavier, lighter and so on.

McCandles (1938) carried out a special training programme aimed at developing the children's understanding of concepts and giving them a knowledge of the world around them. The groups consisted of four-year-old nursery school children, matched, and both highly intelligent. One of the groups took part in an ordinary, good nursery school programme, while the experimental group was specially stimulated by, for instance, visits to a farm, a store etc. Then, on returning to the nursery school, these children were expected to construct a miniature farm, store, hotel etc. for themselves, and to talk about their experiences during their visits. After a year's experiments of this nature this group was ten points above the other in intelligence, while they had been identical at the beginning of the experiment.

Thus the question of the effect of nursery school on the development of concepts must also be divided into two: (1) Are there circumstances limiting development in comparison with circumstances considered normal?; (2) Can certain circumstances produce a development beyond what is considered normal? Very few studies have been made of this.

Peterson (1938) did not find that nursery school children were better informed than those in the control group. Stukat (1966), on the other hand, found a significant difference between children in *lekskola* and children brought up at home. Those attending *lekskola* were distinctly better informed. A subsequent study two years later, and based on teachers' reports, showed them still to be ahead.

None of the children in these studies came from a particularly poor milieu. Studies of this nature will be discussed in Chapter 11 on the significance of nursery school in preparing culturally deprived children for school, as the experiments undertaken were mainly aimed at preparing children for school.

10 Preparation for School

Readiness for school

The question of the effect of nursery school on a child's readiness to attend school proper differs in several respects from the problems already dealt with. To prepare a child for attending school implies a more conscious effort to attain a specified goal than has been the case in other fields of nursery school effect. At the same time it means that we are not concerned with the present effect but with a future effect, i.e. the effect at some point of school education, perhaps throughout a child's entire school career. The main point is, then, not the actual effect, but some subsequent effect.

In some countries parts of nursery school have been a sort of pre-school, closely connected with school proper like, for instance, the American kindergarten, the Swedish *lekskola* and now Danish nursery school classes. In Russian nursery schools, too, emphasis has been laid on direct preparation for school (Zaluzhskaka, 1960; Leont'eva, 1960; Usova, 1961 a). (For a large number of indications that nursery school is seen as a part of the school system, see Unesco, 1955, 1960, 1961 a, 1961 b). These nursery schools at least formerly aimed more at giving a direct preparation for school than was the case in nursery schools elsewhere, e.g. those in Denmark, which considered the child's development and growth to be the prime aim (and thereby only entailed an indirect preparation for school).

This leads to some difficult and so far unsolved problems as to whether the best form of preparation is direct training aimed at making a child ready for school when it reaches the right age, or whether a nursery school seeking to enrich the child's experience and to develop its personality is preferable.

Moreover, the question of loss and gain must be considered. Are the gains for the child at school attained at the expense of other aspects of its development, either now or later?

These questions are doubtless relevant to the present development of nursery school classes in Denmark. However, it is difficult to apply the results of foreign studies to Danish conditions, as attempts such as these, which are aimed at a specific object, are far more closely allied to the particular national situation than the studies so far considered, in which the effect has had more general significance.

Apart from the theoretical questions, there are also many problems of a methodological nature involved in the study of the effect of nursery school on a child's readiness for school. Most studies have been carried out at some point in a child's school career, the children concerned being divided into groups consisting of those who have attended nursery school and those who have not. These are, then, retrospective studies in which conclusions concerning previous conditions are reached on the basis of the present state of affairs. This method makes it difficult to match the two groups exactly in relevant respects, as the point of departure is precisely the difference between them now, while the question of differences between them when of nursery school age cannot be answered. A more reliable method is to start the study in nursery school and then see how the children concerned fare at school, but this method has seldom been used.

Another problem is caused by the fact that the basis for evaluation of both categories of children is often a teacher's report, which is often coloured by the teacher's personal attitude to nursery school. A short Danish study (Sjølund, 1963) comprising 100 teachers' assessments of former nursery school pupils showed plainly that the teachers themselves could be divided into two roughly equal groups, those who preferred nursery school pupils and those who preferred children brought up at home.

A Swedish report on all-day nursery school and pre-schools (1951) summarises a study made of infant school teachers' opinions of children who had attended pre-school institutions of one sort or another as opposed to children brought up at home. 60 per cent of the teachers saw no difference between children who had attended all-day nursery school and those brought up at home. Of the remainder, however, half said that the pre-school institution children were more restless and constituted more of a disturbance than children who had been brought up at home, while the other half found certain features in the nursery school children which were better developed than in the others, e.g. a greater ability to adjust, greater independence and manual dexterity and a more obvious readiness for school. A roughly equal proportion of these teachers, then, found negative and positive effects from attendance at all-day nursery school.

While there were differences of opinion as to whether these children were more or less adaptable, there was greater agreement on the way in which the children differed from others. Far more of the teachers found greater independence in nursery school children than in those brought up

146

at home, and far more found the children with a home upbringing gentler than nursery school pupils.

In answer to the question of what nursery school ought to be like, roughly equal proportions wrote that more emphasis should be placed on writing and arithmetic, or the opposite: that nursery school should not be run on the lines of school proper. Roughly as many argued that the children ought to be taught better discipline as maintained that they ought to be given a greater opportunity for individual self-expression.

American studies indicate that teachers on the whole are critical of daycare children, but positive in their assessments of kindergarten children (see Hammond, 1957; Brown and Hunt, 1961; Kitano, 1964). As the second of these categories is mainly drawn from the same middle class background as the teachers themselves, while the daycare children come to a greater extent from working class milieus, this may well explain the difference. The explanation could, however, also be the fact that kindergarten aims more directly at preparing children for school. Even if the teacher assessments are replaced by more objective measurements, such as moving the child up to the next class, it is impossible to be certain that prejudice does not play its part. Only measurements such as achievement or intelligence tests are uninfluenced by such factors, but even here an indirect effect might well be present.

In the next section of this chapter, consideration will first be given to studies of readiness for school and adjustment to school in general, these being based on such things as detentions and the degree of adjustment aimed at. Then there will be a review of studies of more specific aspects of the readiness for school, such as reading, writing, musical ability and language, where the effect in many studies results from direct training.

In all, 47 studies of effects have been registered, all concerned with different aspects of the significance of nursery school for the child's readiness for school. Of these it has been impossible to trace three (Hofmann, 1957; Shaw, 1957; Girolami-Boulinier, 1963).

Five studies are of the effect of nursery school measured by the child's progress at school. Of these four report a positive effect, and one no effect. 11 studies are interested in adjustment in school. Eight report a positive effect; one no effect; two a negative effect. 18 studies are concerned with reading. Of these 13 report a positive effect; four no effect; one a negative effect. Nine studies are concerned with arithmetic. Five report a positive effect and four no effect. Five studies are concerned with singing and music. The three dealing with singing all report a positive effect, while the two on music find no effect. Five studies are concerned with the development of speech and language. All deal with children who are handicapped in some way, and all report a positive effect from attendance at nursery school.

Altogether, then, the 44 studies contain 53 effect studies. 38 of these report positive effect, 12 no effect and three negative effects.

Studies of the effect on readiness for school and adjustment to school

Progress and detention

Morrison (1938), studying the reports on 13,730 children in first forms in New York schools, found that six per cent of former kindergarten pupils were given detentions as against 20 per cent of others. More than 80 per cent of kindergarten children made normal or accelerated progress as against 58 per cent of the others. It appeared, moreover, that these tendencies continued and even increased throughout the following classes.

These studies, however, tell us nothing of the effect of nursery school if the children attending nursery school came from the better off section of society, as much suggests is the case. The same objection can be made to a study by McLatchy (1924), which concludes that a greater percentage of kindergarten children are put up at the end of their first year at school, and to a study by Hammond (1957) covering several thousand children and reporting that almost all the teachers (98 per cent) found a relationship between kindergarten training and adjustment and progress in the first form of school.

In his more carefully matched study, which was followed up by a study of the same children two years later, Stukat (1966) found that there was no noticeable difference in the number of detentions given to *lekskola* children and children brought up at home.

There are thus no studies documenting with certainty that nursery school children do better in school than children from an ordinary good milieu.

On the other hand there is evidence to suggest that nursery school children do better than children from residential institutions. Schmidt-Kolmer (1963) included in her work a comparative study of school beginners, 129 of whom had attended nursery school, while 85 came from residential institutions. Despite the fact that the children from the children's home were on average six months older than those from nursery school, they made poorer progress in school. No less than 50 per cent of them did badly, as against only 8.6 per cent of the nursery school children. 36.5 per cent of the children from the home were retarded as against

6.2 per cent of the nursery school children. 3.5 per cent of the children from the home were placed in remedial school in their first year as against only 0.8 per cent of the nursery school children. In the second year no fewer than 10 per cent of the children from the home were put in a remedial class as against 1.6 per cent of the nursery school children. Psychiatric studies showed that the differences could not be due to either organic causes or abnormally low intelligence, but must be the result of an educationally poorer milieu.

Schütter-Janikulla and Krohne (1966), in a West German study, carried out an experiment in which retarded beginners at school were placed in a sort of remedial nursery school, where they were given special teaching to make them ready for school.

Twenty-eight children took part in the experiment, most of them coming after an unsuccessful start at school. After a test to see to what extent they were ready for school, in which the average quotient was found to be 88, they were divided into two groups which were matched for sex, age, social and economic background and readiness for school.

One of the groups was given a training programme lasting four weeks. With the help of a specially designed book the children were taught such concepts as form and space, they were trained to coordinate hand and eye, to orientate themselves, to form general concepts and basic linguistic expressions, and to reflect and to think logically.

At a second test of readiness for school, carried out at the end of the training period, the experimental group was significantly better than the control group. They were now at the normal level. On the other hand intelligence tests still showed no difference between the groups.

However, no studies have been made to discover how long the effect lasted, but even if it was only a short term effect, it could be of value at the particularly important stage of a child's life which the start at school represents.

In an American study (Painter, 1966) an attempt was made by means of a special training programme to improve the readiness for school in the lower half of a nursery class. For this the group was divided into an experimental group of ten children and a corresponding control group matched with regard to sex, age and intelligence.

The object was to develop the children's basic perceptual and motor abilities, which are taken to be of fundamental importance for the development of more complex activities such as reading, writing and arithmetic. It is generally taken that perception and motor development are indeed the two areas in which culturally deprived and mentally retarded children show poor development. Therefore the training programme, which lasted seven weeks and consisted of three sessions weekly, aimed at systematic rhythmic, sensory and motor activity.

Before the experiment the groups were given a test of language and a test of their ability to appreciate form, plus a draw a man test. At this time they achieved similar results. After the training programme the experimental group were significantly better than the control group.

It is still an open question, however, whether progress of this nature is of any significance for progress at school. As there was no re-testing, it may well merely have been a temporary effect resulting from the special training.

General adjustment

Numerous studies have sought to judge the effect of nursery school on the child's settling in at school, and on the basis of an earlier chapter in which it was seen that nursery school has a positive effect on the child's social and personal development, it would also be expected to play its part in this field.

Cushing (1934) did indeed find that nursery school children were assessed higher both for their ability to adapt to certain situations and for their general attitude to the school, despite the fact that the average age of the nursery school children was lower while their average intelligence was possibly a little higher. The matching of the two groups is thus insufficient for anything decisive to be said on the basis of this study.

Matching problems with the opposite effect might be present in a study by Kitano (1964) in which teachers were of the opinion that nursery school children had settled in less well than children brought up at home. The nursery school children came from a poorer milieu than the children in the control group. Kitano remarks that the result might also be due to the fact that the more confident and spontaneous behaviour which nursery school produces might not be considered desirable in a school with a stricter discipline.

The same might be said of a study by Brown and Hunt (1961), who found that 42 former nursery school children who were compared with a corresponding control group were considered by their teachers to have settled in less satisfactorily. The two groups were assessed as equally 'bright'.

The problems of matching are also apparent in a study by Hammond and Skipper (1962). The material on which they base themselves consisted of rather over 1,000 children from the first forms of eight different schools

150

in Florida. On the basis of teachers' reports the 25 per cent who had adapted best and the 25 per cent who had settled down with the greatest difficulty were selected, after which a statistical analysis was made with the aim of discovering what differences there were between the two groups in various respects. Of those who had settled best, 53 per cent had attended nursery school. Of the others, only 25 per cent had done so. This difference is statistically significant. The result, however, does not tell us much about the effect of nursery school, as it is very possible that the children who had attended nursery school came from backgrounds which would themselves have given them better preparation for school. This emerges indirectly from the study, as the social status of the family is also a factor acting in a positive manner on a child's willingness to adapt to school. In other words, social status and nursery school attendance follow the same pattern. Nor does the study take into account how long the children had attended kindergarten, which might also have produced some differences.

Trusal (1955), in a doctoral thesis, analysing the results of a large number of tests to determine whether children were ready for school, found that nursery school children appeared to be ahead of other children in school in all fields, both in the general sense of being ready for school and in the more particular aspects such as achievement in reading and arithmetic. However, when he compared two carefully matched groups all differences in all fields disappeared.

Most reports, however, suggest that nursery school does have some positive influence on preparing a child for school, especially with regard to independence and getting on with other children.

Peterson (1938) found that the nursery school children as opposed to the matched control group had improved their I.Q. on starting school. Moreover, according to various tests, the school beginners who had attended nursery school were more self-assured, independent and sociable, and they were more mature in 'social competence', by which the author appears to mean that they could make a more positive contribution to the activities of a group. On the other hand they were no further advanced in their readiness to read, in their vocabulary or in their understanding of concepts than the others.

Axtell and Edmunds (1960), comparing 506 children who had taken part in a pre-school programme with a corresponding control group from the same milieu, found that the nursery school children were better adjusted in all fields, especially with regard to independent work, attentiveness and obedience to rules and restrictions.

Saguisag (1960), studying children in the Philipines, found the influence of nursery school very obvious, even in individual subjects, in the first two classes, but then it was less evident in the following two classes and finally disappeared.

Johansson (1965) examined the influence of nursery school on readiness for school as part of an extensive study of the question of readiness for school. 211 children were included in the study, being divided into two comparable groups, nursery school children and others, and it was shown that the nursery school children were obviously better at social adjustment to the school milieu than the control group. They were also more mature in other areas, but here the difference was not statistically significant. Only in their attitude to other adults was there no difference.

Stukat (1966), who supplemented his study with teachers' reports, discovered that children from *lekskola* found it easier to adapt generally than children who had been brought up at home, but their achievements at school were as a whole insignificantly better. Relatively more children brought up at home were sent for counselling or for remedial teaching, but this difference was not statistically significant. A test of readiness for school carried out at the beginning of their school career showed no difference between them, but at the end of the first year the children from *lekskola* were judged by their teachers to be better than the other children, and this same difference was still apparent two years later.

Douglas and Ross (1964), as part of the comprehensive British *National Survey of Health and Development*, compared 224 boys and girls who had attended nursery school at the age of four with the remainder of the school population. The nursery school children as a whole lived in inferior and more overcrowded homes. They were generally considered to be worse looked after at home than the other children; 39 per cent of the mothers of nursery school children went out to work as against 18 per cent of other mothers. Nevertheless, the nursery school children were thought to be better adjusted than the others at the age of eight years, as well adjusted at 11, but less well adjusted at 15.

So it appears that the compensatory effect of nursery school lasts until the age of 11, and only then does the children's poor milieu make itself felt.

Effects in specific fields

Readiness to read and ability to read

Studies concerned with the effect of teaching directly aimed at preparing a child for school, for instance teaching it to read or add up, normally report a positive effect of these efforts, but apart from other weaknesses, these studies all suffer from the great weakness of not having been followed up by subsequent tests.

Meanwhile, the results cannot be considered as the effect of nursery school in general, but must be seen in relation to the type of nursery school achieving them, and the methods by which they were achieved. The American kindergarten must for this purpose be considered as a sort of pre-school in which a conscious effort is made to teach the subjects which will be taught in the first year of school.

A number of early studies of this type (Peters, 1923; Gard, 1924; Theisen, 1925; Goetch, 1926; Teegarden, 1932; Gates and Bond, 1936; Peterson, 1938; Brueckner, 1939; Sprinkle, 1948) all report that school beginners who have attended kindergarten all achieve higher test results in reading than the children in control groups, which is not surprising in view of the fact that they had all received special training. The far more interesting question of whether these children as a whole continued to do better is not answered, as there was no subsequent testing. Studies of the effect of nursery school on specific areas in which the children have been given conscious training, such as in reading or adding up, cannot, of course, be content with a short term effect on school beginners. Moreover, the question must be raised as to the possibility of a negative result of this early training: can there, for instance be a question of too much training, or can training of this sort have a negative effect in other fields?

Moreover the studies mentioned above all suffer from the defect of not having matched the children with regard to milieu, and since the kindergarten children are usually from a rather better off middle class milieu than those not attending kindergarten, it is not really possible to say whether the effect stems from the kindergarten training or from the fact that the children come from a milieu with above average intelligence. For these reasons no further attention will be paid to these studies.

The following studies, however, are concerned with effect of a certain duration, demonstrated after one year or several years at school. Voas (1940) compared 114 schoolchildren who had attended nursery school with a larger number who had not, and discovered that after between one and three years at school there was no difference between the two groups with regard to reading ability. An intelligence test of the two groups had found no difference between them, but as this study suffers from the same matching problems seen above, its results cannot be considered conclusive.

The same objections can be raised in the case of a study by Bergamini

153

and Swanson (1954) comparing school beginners with and without nursery school experience which found that those who had experience did better in a reading test designed to test readiness for school.

Kounin (1939) compared 26 nursery school children with 31 who had not attended. After they had been at school for between one and four years it was found that the nursery school children were achieving better results than the control group. The author himself states that he cannot make any definitive conclusion to the effect that this was because the children had attended nursery school, but that much points in that direction. This study has the advantage that the groups were comparable in intelligence when one group started nursery school at the age of three. Both the nursery school group and the control group were children with above average intelligence; the average I.Q. was 118.

Pratt (1949) also included a follow-up study. He studied 226 school beginners, of whom 72 had attended kindergarten, 26 had been kept down in the first class and 128 had previous experience of school. Although the nursery school children and those in the control group were of a comparable mental age, the nursery school children did significantly better in a test of their readiness for school. An assessment based on Gate's reading test carried out at the end of the first year showed an even greater difference between the two groups. It is, however, still questionable whether the two groups were comparable with regard to social background and parental attitudes.

Moreover the study shows that the tests used appeared to have different predicative values for nursery school children and control group children.

Fast (1957) carried out a study in which the group being tested and a control group were also matched with regard to social background and the parents' wish to have them attend nursery school (e.g. because their children were on waiting lists); 180 school beginners from three urban schools took part in this study, 134 had attended kindergarten, while 46 who had not attended kindergarten constituted a control group. By means of testing the two groups were matched with regard to intelligence and mental age. The children were given a test to judge their readiness for reading soon after starting in the first class, and they were subsequently also given other tests, including a reading test at the end of the school year. The kindergarten children did significantly better than the others in all fields.

By means of a reading comprehension test and a vocabulary test Fox and Powell (1964) compared the reading standard at the beginning of the second year in 179 former kindergarten children who had attended half-day nursery school for eight months with 115 other children who had not been to kindergarten. The two groups had the same, roughly average I.Q.

and were said to come from the same milieu.

The nursery school group did best in the tests, but the results were not significant. Here it must be pointed out that the period of influence was fairly short, while the effect was measured after that influence had ceased. It is, in other words, a question of after-effect.

The studies of readiness for school so far discussed all stem from American kindergartens, which all provide systematic training. Only three studies of this problem coming from other countries have been found: one Indian (Saksena, 1961), one British (Douglas and Ross, 1964) and one Swedish (Stukat, 1966).

Saksena's study, which has been referred to already, does not point to any difference between nursery school children and other school beginners as far as reading, writing and drawing are concerned, i.e. subjects in which training could be given, while the nursery school children were a little better at understanding what was said to them, and did better at arithmetic. As already pointed out, they showed a distinctly better personal development than the others.

Douglas and Ross (1964) found that former nursery school children did worse in reading than other children in the class at the ages of eight, 11 and 15; yet the study also pointed out that the nursery school children came from a poorer milieu. In this area, then, nursery school was unable to compensate for a poor milieu, in contrast to what was the case with children's general adaptability.

In his study, including a test for readiness for school and various reading and arithmetic tests, Stukat (1966) found no difference in the ability of children from *lekskola* and others to take advantage of basic teaching in reading, writing and arithmetic. On the other hand the children from *lekskola* did considerably better than the others in that part of the test which could be called a general knowledge test. This emerged both from the tests and from the teachers' reports.

Understanding of figures and readiness for arithmetic.

It emerges from several studies that nursery school children are better at figures than control group children, even if no direct training in arithmetic has been given them. However, none of the studies to date is sufficiently convincing.

By studying the reports of 1,123 school beginners, McLatchy (1929) discovered that those who had attended kindergarten had progressed twice as far in certain areas of figure work as the others. However, as the groups were not matched with regard to milieu, it can be taken that the kindergarten children came from a better background.

The same lack of a control group is, as already stated, to be found in a study by Bergamini and Swanson (1954). In this a comparison of tests to see whether children were ready for school showed that children from nursery school did better than others in arithmetic.

Trusal (1955) discovered that the apparent advantage which nursery school attenders have in arithmetic disappears when the groups are matched in pairs.

Mott and Martin (1947) did a comparative study which showed that the nursery school children were clearly ahead of the control group, but that the others soon caught up with them.

Saksena (1961) found that nursery school children did a little better in arithmetic.

Fox and Powell (1964) included in their study the children's ability to deal with figures and to add up. The conclusion reached is that nursery school attendance has not improved performance in arithmetic in the lower forms.

Stukat (1966) does not believe that the results of his work indicate any significant effect from attendence at *lekskola* on the children's ability to acquire basic arithmetical principles.

Some experiments with special training in the understanding of figure work do, however, show that a special training programme can produce effects.

Koenher (1948) compared four groups of nursery school children, with approximately 30 children in each group, of which two were given special training while the others merely took part in the normal nursery school activities. One of the experimental groups was given its training in the mornings, the other in the afternoons; the corresponding control groups attended in the afternoons and mornings respectively so that they could be taught by the same teacher. The aim was to obviate possible differences in teacher personalities. This procedure itself must be considered doubtful, as an even more dubious factor is the attitudes of the teachers to the two methods.

The groups were not matched, but an initial test showed that they were equal in average intelligence and readiness for school.

The training throughout the whole of the nursery school year (eight months) consisted of games with money, clocks and calendars, in the course of which a conscious effort was made to teach the children numbers, weights and measures. The pupils needed to be able to count and to divide into groups, and they learned to recognise and write figures.

A test carried out at the end of the programme showed the experimental groups to be significantly in advance of the others.

An East German test (Böttcher, 1966) gave similarly good results in developing an understanding of numerical concepts by means of games. The particular aim of this experiment was to compare the effectiveness of group games as opposed to the more openly educational individual acquisition of mathematical principles which is part of the prescribed nursery school programme.

36 children took part in the special programme of games with figures. A control group of 34 followed the normal nursery school course. The average age of the two groups was the same, about five and a half. No indication is given of intelligence levels or social backgrounds, but they were presumably similar, as both groups were nursery school children. An initial test showed that the two groups were similar in their readiness to deal with arithmetic.

The training period lasted three months. In it, the children, in pairs, played with a train which could be sent from one to the other. Each of the children had a box with five compartments and also had some pictures showing what ought to be in the compartments at certain times. In addition they had a box of miniature toys, such as toy kitchen utensils. Then they had to ask each other for the number of things shown in the picture, after which the other child was to send what was asked for by putting it in the train. Emphasis was thus laid on social cooperation as well as the connection between action and expression.

By systematic planning the children were trained to understand cardinal and ordinal numbers up to ten as well as to understand quantities and have the ability to make up quantities between two and six.

A subsequent test made after the experiment, which appeared to be scientifically carried out, showed the experimental group to be significantly ahead of the control group which had followed the school's normal programme.

Singing and music.

Jersild and Bienstock (1931, 1934) trained three-year-olds to sing notes and intervals which at that time were beyond their range. The experiment included 19 nursery school children who were given musical training and a corresponding control group which received no training. The training consisted of exercises and songs containing intervals both within and beyond the children's normal singing ability. They worked in groups of two or three in which the clever children were purposely put in with those who were less gifted. At the same time the composition of the groups was constantly changed so that the same children were not singing together all the time. The training lasted for six months, with forty periods of ten minutes each. In comparison with the control group, which was not given specific training, the trained group made obvious progress, and this progress was maintained and reflected in a test a year later. The authors stress that a child's mucical range is often below what it could achieve. The training extended the range beyond what could be expected by ordinary spontaneous processes.

The subsequent study reports that the early musical experiences which a nursery school can provide do not only have a momentary effect, but can have a permanent influence on a child's musical abilities.

Updegraff et al. (1938) carried out a similar experiment with nursery school groups aged three, four and five. An experimental group and a control group for each age were selected after a test of different aspects of their musical ability. The experimental groups were trained for about 40 days; they were divided into small groups, the composition of which was varied, and they were taught in such a way that they enjoyed themselves. They were taught to cope with intervals and given an understanding of high and low ranges and other musical accomplishments such as the understanding of and repetition of melodies. After the training period the experimental group was found to be far superior to the control group in musical ability. Moreover, the children in this group were much more interested in music, as was shown in the other activities in the nursery school. Possibly the training also increased the children's own confidence in their musical ability and gave them fresh motivation for learning to sing.

Smith (1964) examined the effect of teaching groups of three and four-year-olds to sing in tune. There were 20 children in the first group and 21 in the second.

The children were trained for about 20 minutes every day for a year, after which they were compared with two control groups of nursery school children who had not been given this training. The study concludes that the group training had improved the members' ability to sing in tune, even when no individual training was given.

However attempts to train the children in playing musical instruments did not, according to available studies, appear to have any noticeable effect. Jersild and Bienstock (1935) carried out an experiment aimed at increasing the children's rhythmical abilities. The experiment was carried out in the same manner as the song experiment by the same author referred to above. No significant improvement was here to be found in the training group.

Colby (1935), who used the same technique in an attempt to teach children to reproduce melodies on a flute, was also unable to see any significant improvement in the training group. This experiment has, however, been criticised (Fowler, 1966) for using an instrument which did not correspond to the children's physical development at the time.

All in all, it appears that attempts to improve children's playing ability are too few in number and insufficiently comprehensive to be of significance.

Ability to draw

Only one study of the effect of training in drawing has been registered, (Dubin, 1946). A group of 12 nursery school children was compared with a control group which was matched with regard to sex, age and interest in drawing. Throughout a period of six months the children in the experimental group had an individual discussion of all their spontaneous drawings with their teacher. The child was encouraged to talk about its drawings, to relate the whole to the individual parts and to develop concepts in connection with the drawings, and at the same time they were encouraged to reach the next stage in their development.

After six months the experimental group was again compared with the control group who had not taken part in such discussions. The drawings were classified and assessed after a system of points scored. After the six months both groups produced more, but while the two had been identical at the beginning of the experiment, the group which had received training was now seen to have developed considerably more than the other group. The experimental group was ahead in both the scope and complexity of the drawings.

No subsequent test was carried out, so it is impossible to decide whether this was merely a short term effect. Nor is there any indication of whether this gain had to be paid for in other ways, possibly by boredom.

Speech

In the chapter on intellectual development it is pointed out in the section dealing with linguistic development that the normal child's linguistic development does not seem to be improved by attendance at nursery

159

school under normal conditions. On the other hand it does look as though nursery school has a positive effect on the linguistic development of children who are either handicapped in some way or come from an unfortunate background. The following section will discuss some studies in this category, aimed particularly at preparing children for school.

Pendergast (1966) carried out an experiment which indicates that nursery school can prevent speech difficulties at school. 15,255 children in the first class in schools in Seattle were tested to see how many had speech difficulties. The children were divided into two age groups, the younger having attended nursery school since this had become compulsory in that particular year. The large amount of material can thus be seen as making up two comparable groups. A comparison of the group which had attended nursery school with the one which had not showed that the incidence of speech difficulties was roughly the same at the beginning of the first class. About a quarter of the children had pronunciation difficulties. Of these only the 25 per cent with the greatest impediments were sent for therapy.

A re-test after a year at school plus therapy showed that there was no difference between the children who had attended nursery school and those who had not. However, those children who had speech difficulties but had not received therapy were significantly inferior to the nursery school children after one year.

The study concludes that, apart from the children who were given therapy, it appeared that nursery school reduced speech difficulties during the first year at school.

A special aspect of nursery school teaching of language is found in the teaching of a second language, either, on the one hand, for children coming from abroad who have to learn the language of the country in which they now reside, as in the case of some Israeli and American nursery schools, or, on the other, in the teaching of a foreign language.

Ginsberg (1960) carried out a series of extensive experiments in Russian nursery schools in teaching five and six-year-olds to speak English, French and German. After some unsuccessful attempts, using standard methods of language teaching as used in schools, completely new methods, based on games, were devised. The children were not to learn single words, but were to use sentences connected with the game. These children were compared with others who only started learning languages in their fourth school year. It evolved that the nursery school children did far better. If a start on a foreign language is made at the age of five, the child can have a working knowledge of it by the time it is eight years old. The study comes to the preliminary conclusion that nursery school children learn a language faster, better and more permanently than school children. The reason for this is considered to be that, in contrast to older children, nursery school children learn a language merely by hearing it, not necessarily by saying it. They need not learn phonetics, but are immediately able to pronounce correctly by imitation.

Fuller (1936) studied the significance of nursery school for the linguistic development of school beginners who were handicapped by coming from milieus using a different language. Three groups of children were studied over a four year period, 30 pupils who had had two terms of speech training in nursery school, 13 with one term of this type of training and 29 without any nursery school training. The speech training in the nursery school was aimed at building up vocabulary by means of games, conversations and story-telling. Pupils with nursery school speech training made fewer mistakes in language in the first class and completed the syllabus in a shorter time; likewise they completed the second year syllabus in a shorter time and still read slightly better in the following classes. The teachers were of the opinion that the language training in nursery school had been efficient in preparing children with language handicaps for work in higher classes. However, the average age and I.Q. of the pupils who had attended nursery school were both higher than those of the control group. Nor did the study pay attention to possible differences in milieu.

Smilansky (1958) carried out a series of studies of the significance of nursery school for culturally under-privileged children coming to Israel from abroad. Preliminary results look promising. The results of a later report (Smilansky, 1967) will be dealt with in the next chapter.

Dawe (1942) studied the significance of nursery school for preparing children for school who came from an institutional milieu with little possibility of contact with adults. The experimental group was trained in nursery school according to a programme aimed at improving their linguistic development; this consisted of training in the understanding of words and concepts, the showing of pictures for discussion, reading stories and poems, going on short excursions with the aim of looking at things and discussing them. The main emphasis was not so much on teaching words to the children as on teaching them a real understanding of words and concepts. At the end of the training programme, which lasted for 50 hours, the experimental group was significantly ahead in vocabulary, information on everyday life and on nature study. They were also more ready for learning to read, and intelligence tests also pointed to a significant improvement.

In recent years this method of preparing socially and culturally deprived children for school has been taken up on a large scale in the USA under the name of Operation Head Start. These efforts, based on a series of systematic experiments, will be dealt with in more detail in the next chapter.

The time for beginning preparation for school

Some studies are concerned with the question of the right time to start preparation for school.

In connection with the comprehensive study of British primary schools (Plowden Report, 1967) teachers were asked for their opinion of nursery school. It must be remembered that infant school is obligatory for all children aged five and upwards, so that nursery school in Great Britain concerns children aged two to four.

95 per cent of teachers at all levels thought that nursery school should be available for all parents who wanted to send their children for educational reasons; 25 per cent thought that only children with special needs should attend, 80 per cent thought that nursery school should be available for three and four-year-olds, only 2 per cent that they should be available for two-year-olds. 70 per cent thought that half a day was sufficient for most children. The answers as to when full time attendance should begin are as follows: at three years—20 per cent; at four years—45 per cent; at five years—26 per cent. 77 per cent of the teachers considered that full time attendance should be compulsory from the age of five (as it is now), while 17 per cent thought six a more suitable age.

The question of whether it is an advantage for children to begin preparation for school as early as possible is still unanswered, as studies available come to different conclusions. Weiss (1962) examined the effect of putting highly gifted children into nursery school at an early age. 35 very young school beginners were matched against a control group of beginners of normal age, so that the groups were alike in intelligence, sex and personal adjustment. At the end of the school year the differences between the two groups were studied. The younger ones were less well adjusted personally and socially, and they did less well in school subjects than the control group. Both the experimental group and the control group were children of above average intelligence. When the experimental group was compared with a group of children of average intelligence who had also attended kindergarten but started school at the normal age, it turned out that the experimental group were not even on a level with them in the areas listed above. However, this study tells more about what

162

it is to be young among older children than about the actual time of starting education.

Meanwhile, Hobson (1963) came to a positive conclusion in his study. 550 schoolchildren who had started kindergarten at a particularly early age reached grammar school level at the same time as those who had started at the normal age. The children with the early start were significantly better than the others in the areas studied. A significantly greater proportion of the early beginners did particularly well when they were moved up to college. However, this study suffers from the drawback that the two groups were not matched in the relevant areas as they had been in Weiss's study. So this result should probably be interpreted in the way in which Tordrup (1961) interprets the results of his Danish study—that it is not because they start school early that they *become* better, but that they start school earlier because they *are* better, i.e. early beginners are of a higher intelligence than the normal, and if they are to be compared with children starting at the normal age, the control group must have the same I.Q. for the effect of an early start to be assessed.

Efficiency training and personality development

Taken as a whole the results of studies indicate that it may well be possible to achieve a certain effect by direct training and preparation for school undertaken at nursery school, but more especially they indicate that it is possible to achieve a more indirect effect by working with the personal and social development of the child.

It is possible to throw light on why indirect preparation for school, consisting in the development of the child's personality, is of greater importance than direct training in specific skills.

Brenner and Samelson (1957) studied the connection between personality factors in nursery school children and good progress at school. From a class of school beginners who had been assessed by their teacher with regard to how well they did in the first class and how far they were sufficiently mature to be put up into the next class, the five best and the five worst were selected for closer study. Various data were taken from observations made in the first six weeks of attendance at nursery school. The descriptions of the children concerned the way in which they treated material things, verbal symbols, other children, their teacher and other adults, and on the basis of these descriptions certain general patterns emerged which were characteristic of children who would probably do well in the first class at school and those who would do less well.

The personality factors in children likely to do best were: (1) self-assurance and easy relationships with others; (2) intellectual curiosity and the ability to undertake independent activities; (3) the desire to fulfil others' expectations and to do what is considered right; (4) an attempt to build up life according to the example of adults and to be accepted by adults as one of them; (5) a powerful urge to raise themselves above the other children, to compete with them and beat them.

The most noticeable personality factors in nursery school children likely to do less well in the first class at school were: (1) a strong feeling of fear and anxiety preventing contact with reality; (2) insufficient self-confidence and general immaturity in all areas of personal development; (3) restlessness and an inability to settle down quietly; (4) aggressiveness and difficulty in accepting the rules for social behaviour in school; (5) fear of competition and defeat and a desire to avoid situations which could lead to humiliation.

This analysis points especially to the indirect significance of nursery school for adjustment to school by forming the child's personality rather than through direct training in various skills.

The following study also indicates that preparation for school resulting from greater social and personal maturity also has its effect on the child's ability to acquire knowledge and to develop skills.

Herr (1946) took 300 six-year-old Spanish speaking school beginners in the USA, who had all had one year's pre-school training in a nursery school where the emphasis was on social and emotional adjustment rather than on individual skills. He compared them with a corresponding group of children with similar backgrounds and intelligence, but who had not taken part in the nursery school programme. The nursery school pupils' average I.Q. rose from 66 to 96 points, while that of the control group rose from 69 to 78. When the children started school the nursery school children scored 48 points in tests assessing their readiness for reading, whereas the average for the others was 8. At the end of the first year at school the nursery school group averaged 46, while the control group now had 16 on average. Thus the control group had not caught up with the nursery school group in the course of the first year at school. The basis for the better standing of the experimental group was not special training in reading, but a nursery school programme aimed at improving social and emotional adjustment.

The study of school beginners who could read when they entered the first class, carried out by Durkin (1964) showed certain characteristic differences in long term development between the children who had been systematically taught to read by their parents and those who had only received help from them when they spontaneously asked for it.

At the start of school the children who had been systematically trained were better than the others. However, in the second year the difference was wiped out, and in a test carried out in the third year at school the trained group did less well than those who had only been stimulated to the extent they asked for help. In the fifth class this difference was even more pronounced. Both groups, however, lay ahead of other children in all the classes concerned.

For training in skills to be considered as having a positive result, two conditions must be fulfilled. The training must bring about better results not only at the time during which it is taking place, but also in the longer term, that is to say an effect lasting for a shorter or longer period, as the price paid in the form of giving up more amusing occupations during the training period would otherwise be unreasonable. Secondly, a training effect must not be achieved at the cost of other spheres of development, so that the cost is only discovered later in the form of slower development in other spheres. Such results as there are from experiments in training nursery school children do not appear to fulfil these two conditions, and the sort of experiments which were particularly common in the 1930s have largely been discontinued.

Much of what experimenters have tried to teach children at a very early age would doubtless have come of its own accord and without much effort later on. This is perhaps especially true of the learning of skills which presuppose biological growth and maturity; here the possibilities of development should be present for the child to take advantage of when ready, just as influences working against the effect desired should be removed.

Perhaps the most famous is Hilgard's (1932) experiment with the motor training of nursery school children. Two groups of ten children aged from two to three were matched in respect of age, sex and previous motor ability in the three spheres to be tested: buttoning and unbuttoning, using scissors for cutting, and climbing, three areas of motor development which are particularly relevant at that age. The experimental group was given 12 weeks of training in these fields, during which time they were tested every fortnight. The control group, which was not given any special training during these 12 weeks was also tested again at the end of the period. After the 12 weeks the experimental group was far ahead of the control group in every sphere. Then, the control group was given one week's training, after which both groups were re-tested, and it evolved that the control group had only taken one week to achieve what the other group had been twelve weeks in doing. The result is interpreted as being due to the maturation processes which had taken place in the control group during the 12 weeks, and also to the fact that they had had a certain amount of general practice so that they had a much better basis on which to begin than they had had twelve weeks before.

This may contain the explanation of why, despite the facilities offered, nursery school often does not appear to improve children's motor development beyond what is normal, while, on the other hand, institutions not offering the right facilities are inclined to retard motor development.

As for social, emotional and personal development and adjustment, that is to say the cultural superstructure of biological growth (cf. Piaget, 1950), it does not appear to be sufficient merely to provide plenty of facilities.

A French study (Lézine, 1964), which was discussed at length in the chapter on day nurseries, and which is concerned with the significance of toys and games in day nurseries, concludes that it is not sufficient to provide the child with toys for it to use spontaneously, but that it is necessary to organise the child's activities.

Henry and Sharpe (1947) find in their study that nursery school children whose access to toys has been limited must be encouraged and stimulated to use them.

A series of experiments undertaken in nursery schools, and which will be discussed in Chapter 16 on laboratory studies, proves the significance of adequate educational stimulation in connection with a child's play and its life in a group, for the sake both of its constructive and creative personal development and of its social and emotional adjustment.

In general it can be said of this question that on the one hand there is little to indicate that the child's development is helped by direct training, while on the other it is not sufficient to leave the child to its own spontaneous activities, even if it provided with ample facilities. A relevant stimulation is necessary.

PART IV

Studies Concerning Special Categories of Children

11 Readiness for School in Culturally Deprived Children

American sociological studies have indicated that schools in the USA are traditionally orientated to promoted middle class standards and conform to middle class educational ideas. In a society such as the American, where patterns of behaviour vary considerably from one social sphere to another, this can produce adjustment difficulties for children from the lower social classes. As these milieus are normally less interested in reading or in culture generally, the children coming from them are also handicapped in this respect. An awareness of this state of affairs has led to the launching of an ambitious educational programme aimed at putting children from culturally deprived milieus on a level with middle class children by means of what is known as a programme of pre-school enrichment, which takes the form of nursery school attendance of varying periods. The project, called Operation Head Start, is now of considerable dimensions and, of particular interest in the present context, a series of experiments dealing with the effect of nursery school has been incorporated into it. The project is very popular with parents, and within a few years the number of participants has risen to approximately 600,000 children, and the cost per year to something like 100 million dollars.

The basis for the start was the annual meeting of the American Association on Mental Deficiency 1961, at which a number of experts on child development discussed the educational problems associated with culturally and socially deprived children. The result was a recommendation that a programme of educational training before school age should be launched in order to make good the intellectual shortcomings with which deprived children start school (Weikart, 1967 a and b).

The following year the Arden House Conference on Preschool Enrichment took place, at which attention was paid to the theoretical problems concerned with creating an enriched pre-school period for the deprived children (Hunt, 1964 a and b; Deutch, 1965). It was decided that the cognitive aspect of development, especially language and the formation of basic concepts, would have to be the principal area dealt with.

Hechinger (1966) describes the difference between a middle class home and one from the lower social strata. It emerges from this how difficult it is for a child from the poorer classes to be on a level with a middle class child educationally. A home from a poor social background does not give the smaller children the opportunity to talk, ask questions and receive answers. In an overcrowded apartment curiosity is a nuisance. During the day the parents are concerned with earning a living, and older brothers and sisters are left to look after the smaller ones, or else they are left with some woman who is so badly off that she cannot find work herself. When the parents come home tired from work the atmosphere is not conducive to providing much care for the children, and there is no desire or urge to talk to them. The passive child is considered to be a good child.

Studies made of the effect of the Head Start project show varying results. Allegato (1966) analyses the data provided by the leaders of the project, which indicates that the children on average rose by nine points in their I.Q., that they were better prepared for learning, more intellectually curious and better adjusted at school. A standard test showed significant improvements in school work and mental capacity in the children who had taken part in the project over the entire country. This sounds impressive in consideration of the fact that the entire educational programme only lasts between six and eight weeks in the summer, and that the teachers themselves need not be trained, but would have attended special courses of at least a week's duration. However, it appears that no use was normally made of control groups, and so the results can easily be due to the very enthusiastic way in which the programme was carried out simply having given the children training in managing the tests better the second time than the first.

However, there are other, more carefully controlled tests carried out as part of the project. The entire Head Start programme is aimed at the start of kindergarten, which is the first class in American schools (i.e. for four-year-olds), so that we are in fact concerned with a nursery school programme. As the effect appears to be closely related to the duration of the programme and to the quality of the teaching in general, differences in these areas will be pointed out in the following summaries.

Henderson (1965) carried out an educational research programme in which he studied over 1,000 children, some of whom took part in the short summer programmes, some in programmes lasting a year. An educational programme for parents was also arranged in which the teacher visited the home twice a month. Social workers also paid visits to certain homes. The course lasting a year placed special emphasis on linguistic development and consisted of a more carefully devised programme aimed at introducing new materials and the opportunity for the children to broaden their experience. Most teachers stressed social, emotional and

170

motor development, and only a minority of them considered intellectual development to be most important. The results were worked out in intelligence quotients and linguistic quotients. In the case of the children who had taken part in the summer programme there was no significant difference between them and the control group. The children who had taken part in the one year course were found to have a higher I.Q. than the control group, and this difference was significant. Their linguistic development was also higher, but here the difference was not significant. When the children started in the first class in school they were compared by means of a test of readiness for school. The result here was that although the experimental group was better than the control group, the differences were not statistically significant.

Strodtbeck (1963) carried out an exercise concerned with readiness for reading in four-year-old nursery school children. The programme lasted for three months. The children were tested three months before the start, at the start, and at the end of the course. There was no control group, and the individual children's results were compared with the results they had achieved three months before the start of the course. Two of the groups, each containing about 10 children, followed the normal nursery school programme which aimed to stimulate spontaneous activity in the child and improve its social relationships. Three groups of a similar size were given a different and more carefully controlled form of teaching. The teachers consciously took more part in the children's free activities and showed them how to do different things. They were encouraged to talk to the children, and in particular conversation during mealtimes was cultivated. The test showed that the children in the last three groups gained 4.3 points over the others in mental development.

Beller (1965) carried out a study which showed the importance of the teacher's own training. The children taking part in the nursery school programme, which lasted for a year, ended with an I.Q. six points higher than when they started, and were on average eight points above children who had not had this nursery school training. The nursery school group was better in all verbal intelligence tests, but not always in individual non-verbal tests, which might indicate that their progress was in the field of verbal expression. In one of the groups the teacher was an experienced nursery school teacher, but not in the other two groups. On average the first group did better than the other two.

Gray and Klaus (1965) carried out a programme in which the children took part for ten weeks in the summer for two or three years. In the intervening period between the courses the teacher visited the homes once a week. There were corresponding control groups. The aim of the programme was to prevent the accumulation of shortcomings which is thought to arise during the development of a deprived child. Emphasis was laid on two fields in particular. The first was the attitude towards achievement, especially the activities necessary at school, interest in school materials, concentration and the ability to work for a reward which would come in the future rather than on the spot. The other point emphasised was the preconditions necessary in order to be able to achieve something, especially linguistic, cognitive and perceptual development. Within the two-year period the I.Q. of the experimental group rose by an average of seven points, while that of the control group fell by an average of five. This difference is statistically significant. The study, which has not yet been concluded, reports that the children taking part in the experiment appear to be doing considerably better than the control groups.

Goldstein (1965) reports the preliminary results of a number of wide-ranging projects being carried out in the Wakoff Research Center in New York City. The theoretical background is treated in detail by Deutch (1965). The educational content of the programme is discussed by Feldmann (1964). The emphasis is placed on linguistic development, which is encouraged by means of activities aimed at producing verbal responses. Training in auditive and visual distinguishing abilities is stressed. The activities included in the programme also aim at training in the formation of concepts and in passing on knowledge. The classroom used is arranged with a view to building up the child's understanding of space and order. Attempts are made to strengthen the child's self-awareness and self-assurance. Two experimental groups of 100 children in all, and divided into two groups, took part. The author reports that within a five year period their I.Q. s went up by an average of five points, while the control groups showed an average decline of seven points. The differences are statistically significant.

Wilderson (1965) reports on the first 60 children to take part in a large research project in Baltimore (Baltimore Public Schools, 1964). Emphasis was placed on cognitive ability and on the development of a child's self-awareness. The experiment, lasting five months in all, showed a rise in both mental and verbal maturity in comparison with the levels of the same children at the beginning of the experimental period. There was no control group. Certain differences were statistically significant. Progress was also found in the ability to discriminate auditively and visually, in the ability to express and accept new ideas, to talk to others and to work together with others. When they started kindergarten, it appeared that the children who had taken part in the programme found it easier to adjust than other pupils, and they were freer in their manner and more ready to

172

express themselves. The next phase of this experiment concerns 140 children; half of them are taking part in a full day programme, and the other half in a half day programme, and each half is matched with a control group. The idea is to measure the results right up through school.

Kohlberg (1966) has carried out an experiment to compare the effects of courses of varying length. It comprised a summer programme of a few weeks on the one hand, and on the other a programme lasting a year. At the same time tests were carried out to study the effect of mixing classes so that they included children from different milieus. In addition the experiment was linked to a study of various educational techniques.

In the summer programme, which lasted for a few weeks, three nursery school classes took part; two were integrated by bringing together equal proportions of children from middle class homes and poorer milieus. Of these two classes, one carried out a programme seeking to improve readiness for school, while the other had a Montessori programme. The unintegrated class had what was called a 'free' programme. The children underwent intelligence tests before and after the programmes. The two integrated classes rose by an average of two to three points, while the unintegrated class showed a significant fall in average intelligence of five points. From a behaviour report which the teachers compiled it emerges that the differences were particularly noticeable on a scale measuring distraction, as the children in the unintegrated and free nursery school class rose on the distraction scale, which means that their attention was easily taken from their work, while the children in the integrated, more rigorously taught groups fell on this scale. The combination of free teaching methods and the lack of middle class children to serve as models for behaviour and work was, it appears from the study, the most important factor contributing to differences in class as well as the test results.

The one-year programme consisted of a single integrated class, and the preliminary results indicate that the children from the poorer social background rose by an average of 17 points in contrast to the middle class children, who rose by 10 points. This considerable average rise, in contrast to the much smaller one resulting from the summer programme, is explained by the difference in duration of the stimulation provided and, to some extent, by the fact that throughout the year the teacher was able to devote more attention to the children than was possible in the summer programme. A similar difference between the short summer programme and the one-year programme can also be measured in the children's social attitudes. Unfortunately, the study does not indicate whether it was because of the mixed groups or because of the teaching that the children from the poorer social milieu made progress in integrated classes, but not in the others.

A comprehensive study is concerned with the best time to commence intellectual training. Bloom (1964), on the basis of his research into children's development, pointed out that four is the age at which the greatest intellectual growth takes place, and argued that this must be the best time for beginning training. His review of long-term projects shows that 50 per cent of all intelligence changes occur before the child reaches four and a half, the next 30 per cent between four and a half and eight years, and only 20 per cent in the years between eight and 18. Bloom concludes that as the changes for the better take place in a stimulating milieu, it must be assumed that nursery school can bring about especially significant changes in children from underprivileged homes.

Caldwell et al. (1964 and 1965) carried out a programme with an enriched milieu for children under the age of three, aiming to improve their chances of benefitting from teaching. The children came from a poor social milieu, and all the mothers went out to work. The experimental group consisted of 30 children, 20 boys and 10 girls, while the control group was taken from a similar social milieu but was not matched in pairs with the children in the experimental group. The children took part in the programme for between three and 18 months. The leading programme was aimed partly at improving the children's personal and social development, partly at enabling them to extend their intellectual growth through their own experiences. The children were examined by means of intelligence tests. The results are a rise averaging about six points. When the children are divided up into those below two and those over two at the start of the experiment, there is no great difference in the rise in intelligence in the two groups. However, those taking part in the programme for up to six months only rose by an average of three points, while those who took part for longer rose by eight points. If the material is divided into more and less deprived, it is shown that the children who have suffered the greatest cultural deprivation rose by an average of seven points, whilst the less deprived only rose by an average of four points. No indication of significance is given, however, and the amount of material upon which the results are based is small.

Goldstein and Chorost (1966) studied school beginners, some of whom had kindergarten experience, some nursery school experience and some neither. The children studied came from the first, second and third forms of a large school, and were selected from among 418 children in these age groups. 32 of the children had attended nursery school, 57 kindergarten and 28 neither. The nursery school group and kindergarten group were

174

matched with regard to social background and sex, while the control group was not matched against these, but appeared to have come from slightly less poor milieus, as fewer of them had free dinners at school than was the case in the other groups. No children with adjustment difficulties were included in any of the groups.

By means of intelligence tests carried out at different times, three aspects of the children were examined: cognitive development, achievements at school, and personal and social adjustment. The results of the comparisons showed that the children without experience of pre-school training were less able to reason logically and were inferior to the other two groups in non-verbal intelligence. The difference was statistically significant in the first form, but in the second and third forms the differences were no longer great as to be of significance. The children from nursery school and kindergarten did better at reading than the control group in the first form, but not in the second form. The control group was less successful than the experimental groups in arithmetic in all forms. As for behaviour, it appeared that the control group showed signs of being more passive than the two pre-school groups, a difference which was statistically significant in the third form. The author concludes that children with experience of some pre-school training, whether it be nursery school or kindergarten, do better in school than children from a similar milieu without experience of pre-school training; these latter are especially badly off when it comes to reading and arithmetic.

The children's milieu seemed to play some part in the individual child's ability to get on, and the study showed a number of areas in which nursery school could make a contribution. On the other hand, much to his surprise, the author finds no difference between children who had attended kindergarten and those who had gone to nursery school, but he is of the opinion that the reason why the nursery school children did not do better was to be found in its mediocre educational standard, which made it rank rather as a daycentre for minding children.

The author himself points out a number of weaknesses in his study; the control group was too small, and it was not matched with the other two groups, and when children of different ages are included in a study it is necessary to have a complete control of background factors. Moreover longitudinal studies are to be preferred.

Only few studies have so far been able to produce any long-term report. Weikart (1967 c) started a series of studies in 1962, and some preliminary results are now available. The aim was to complete the study in 1967. Small groups of children belonging to four different age-groups are being carefully studied. The children chosen for this experiment are coloured,

175

come from a culturally deprived milieu and have been diagnosed as mentally retarded. They are being compared with corresponding control groups with regard to cultural deprivation and average intelligence. This nursery school experiment is based on a free but carefully planned teaching programme which seeks to improve the children's cognitive abilities. The main emphasis is placed on verbal stimulation, dramatic games and walks and visits more than is usual in nursery school programmes. The children attend three hours daily for five days a week. They first take part for two years in the experimental programme, then attend kindergarten for one year, after which they enter the first class at school.

The results for the first age group are now complete up to the end of the first class, for the second up to the completion of kindergarten, for the third up to the end of the experimental programme, and for the fourth until the end of the first year of the experimental programme. Three tendencies become clear from the tables: firstly, all the groups show an increase in intelligence. This the author puts down to the regression phenomenon. Secondly, the control group, which has no pre-school training, shows a rise in intelligence at the beginning of school, but then a tendency to stabilise. The third tendency is a very marked rise in intelligence, as much as 20 points after one year's pre-school training, followed by a slight drop in the second, whether the child continues in nursery school or moves into kindergarten. However, there are statistically significant differences throughout between the experimental group and the control group. The average rise for the experimental group is 15 points and for the control group three points.

Nevertheless, once both the experimental group and the control group have attended kindergarten for one year, there is no longer any statistically significant difference in their test results. A difference re-emerges after one year at school, by which time the experimental group is again significantly ahead of the control group. While the control group settle on the average level for this social milieu, the experimental group has risen significantly above it, which the author finds to be a result of importance both for the experimental group and for the nursery school.

Larson and Olson (1965) and Olson and Larson (1962) carried out another programme lasting a year in which the experimental group was noticeably better than the control group in linguistic development. The nursery school programme was described as well organised, but after one year at school there was no longer any difference between the control group and the experimental group, so that the question of long-term effects is left open.

So far, all the nursery school programmes for culturally deprived children

176

have made use of more or less traditional nursery school programmes. Experiments have, however, also been made with programmes for children of pre-school age which are more like those offered by schools. In this connection it should be pointed out that a tendency has been observable in the authors so far dealt with to see more rigid methods as being most suited to culturally underprivileged children.

Bereiter (1966) undertook a study which included 15 culturally deprived four-year-olds together with a corresponding control group. The children took part in a pre-school programme for three hours daily. Every hour included 20 minutes of direct training in speaking, addition and reading, followed by half an hour of more relaxing activities, and 10 minutes of relatively free play. Each teacher has his own activity, and the groups of children change teachers constantly, as happens, for example, in grammar school. The programme is academically orientated and based on two basic principles. First the idea that mere enrichment of experience is not sufficient to enable the culturally deprived child to overcome its shortcomings in the fields necessary for future success at school. Secondly the idea that training in formal structural aspects of language will be of greater value in developing a suitable attitude to school subjects than a training seeking to develop social communication. In this programme emphasis is placed on direct instruction in order to give the child the knowledge necessary for being able to think. The experiment is not yet concluded, but great success is reported in achieving cooperation with the children, with which goes a general increase in mental capacity and scholastic progress. No numerical data are yet available.

Alpern (1966) records the results of a programme even more narrowly designed to prepare children of pre-school age for school. The experiment included 22 children aged four years and a control group matched so that the groups were identical with regard to sex, intelligence and readiness for school at the time when the experiment began. The teaching programme aimed at increasing the children's linguistic abilities, at developing a positive attitude in them to concepts such as teacher, school and learning, and at increasing their acquaintance with the middle class values stressed at school. The experimental group attended nursery school three times a week, on average 72 times during the year. Both groups showed a slightly improved I.Q. between the first and second testing, but the rise was not significant, and there was no difference between the experimental and control groups. On the other hand readiness for school had increased in all spheres in both groups. The rise was significant for both groups, but the experimental group was a little ahead of the control group. This difference, however, was not significant, and a fresh study carried out 17 months later, including a fresh test of readiness for school, showed no distinction. Nor was there any difference in teachers' reports on school motivation and progress.

While there is nothing to show that direct training in school subjects is a more effective help to the children's achievement and development at school than the traditional nursery school programme, it does emerge from these studies that there is a slight difference in results according to how consciously the nursery school teaching has been planned in order to achieve a specific objective. It is possible to distinguish between programmes giving the child the opportunity to develop very largely at its own pace, and others in which the nursery school arranges specific activities with a view to accelerating development in certain areas. In the studies discussed the stress has been on verbal and cognitive activities, and it appears that nursery school programmes of this nature have a greater effect on culturally deprived children than on others.

A theoretical discussion (Getzels, 1965) argues that the teaching methods employed must be related to the kind of cultural deprivation at which they are aimed. Three main ideas emerge: (1) that cultural deprivation is only a matter of degree, and therefore an ordinary nursery school programme such as that used for middle class children must be the solution; (2) that culturally deprived children lack a sense for school subjects and activities, and therefore some preparation for school should be included in their nursery school experience; and (3) that culturally deprived children are fundamentally different from middle class children in the way in which they see themselves, in their language, cultural values and perceptual processes, and therefore a nursery school programme with compensatory teaching methods is necessary in order to moderate these effects of milieu.

In Israel studies have been made over a number of years of culturally underdeveloped children whose parents have emigrated to Israel from the Arab countries, and there even better results have been achieved by means of compensatory teaching in pre-school years. Smilansky (1958 and 1967) reports a rise in I.Q. in children taking part in the experiments of as much as 30 points for children under school age and 15 points for children of school age. The experimental groups have been children aged between three and five years whose parents have immigrated from countries such as Morocco, Yemen and Iraq, while the control groups have been ordinary nursery school children. A subsequent testing of the children in the experimental group shows that the progress was not only short term, but that it continues at school provided the teaching continues to build on the foundation laid by nursery school. Experiments are now being carried out

178

to determine whether a two-year programme would have ¡a noticeably better effect than a one-year programme. Moreover attempts are being made to discover which methods seem to achieve the best results, and whether it is advantageous to start at an early age. Smilansky points out that it is not sufficient to give children from culturally underprivileged milieus an equal chance of cultural activities, but that they must be given preference, not least by means of compensatory teaching. Culturally under-developed children need modified teaching and a special programme if they are to catch up with other children and not end in a remedial school.

Problems of how to teach culturally deprived children are perhaps not of such immediate interest in Danish nursery schools, although Sofie Rifbjerg (1967) draws attention to Greenland in her discussion of Head Start. Nevertheless, the results are still interesting, as they give an indication of what can be achieved by nursery schools. Moreover the idea of a compensatory programme in Danish nursery schools is possibly not completely irrelevant for children from non-academic backgrounds, not particularly with a view to developing their ability to read, but in order to improve their understanding of verbal concepts and thereby their ability to think. With this we reach the question of what nursery school can do and how it best can achieve the effect desired.

12 The Significance of Nursery School for Physically Handicapped, Mentally Abnormal and Mentally Retarded Children

Mention has been made in earlier chapters of the significance of nursery school for children who are handicapped either as a result of growing up in an institution offering little stimulation, 'institutional deprivation', or in their own homes which also for one reason or another provide too little stimulation, 'cultural deprivation'. This chapter will now deal with the small number of studies available on the significance of nursery school for other groups of handicapped children.

Deaf children

The first two reports do not describe the effects of experiments, but are rather concerned with possible practical methods. Wagner (1935) carried out an experiment seeking to discover what sort of teaching programme was most suited to the needs of deaf children in nursery school. The experimental group consisted of six deaf children aged between three and a half and five years; the premises were well equipped with the necessary materials, and speech training made use of these as well as of group experiences.

Benning (1938) produced a number of arguments in favour of providing nursery schools for deaf children and made various suggestions for buildings, teaching staff, daily programmes and curriculum.

Lane (1942) wrote a report on the first study of the effect of attendance at nursery school on deaf children. 27 children who had attended nursery school were distinguished from similar children who had not been to nursery school in the following ways: the deaf children who had been to nursery school were not as far below normal mental capacity and school achievements as deaf children who had not attended nursery school; they were better at lip reading, developed a larger vocabulary and were able to express ideas verbally sooner. Moreover, they produced fewer of the behaviour disorders which can arise as a result of frustation caused by the inability to express oneself.

Stone, Fiedler and Fine (1961) studied the effects of various nursery school programmes designed for deaf children. An experimental group of 12 children took part in a programme for deaf children which was based on what were considered to be good nursery school methods for normal children, but with the early addition of individual hearing aids; the control group of 15 children, who were matched with regard to sex, deafness and intelligence as well as social and financial backgrounds, were given a more formal training process for deaf children. The groups were assessed in various linguistic fields and in 'personal development'. The experimental group did better in all the tests than the control group. However, as the children were only tested a couple of years after the experiment, this is really a retrospective experiment.

Craig (1964) studied the effect of more formal training on deaf children in nursery school; the children were taught both reading and lip reading. They were aged between six and 16 years, and were studied by means of various tests while at school. There were 243 altogether, and they were divided into groups according to whether they had attended nursery school or not, and by statistical calculations they were made comparable in mental age, chronological age, degree of deafness and sex. Four areas of lip reading were studied, and in none of them was any difference to be seen between the groups, though the nursery school children were significantly better in language tests. A test of vocabulary showed that they were significantly better, and they managed one area of Gates' reading test significantly better.

Children with speech difficulties

Sommer (1932) carried out a controlled experiment to test the possibility of developing and improving linguistic ability in nursery school children. The experiment showed a 57 per cent improvement on the norms laid down in the case of the group which had undergone special training as opposed to a 28 per cent improvement in the control group which received no training, and where the improvement was entirely due to spontaneous development. The final traces of speech difficulties were more difficult to overcome in the children who had not had previous training.

Wilson (1954) studied the significance of special training in nursery school with the aim of overcoming speech defects. 242 nursery school children took part in the experiment which lasted for twelve weeks. Half of them took part in the speech training programme, while the other half, which did not take part, constituted a control group. The aim was to study how well the children pronounced some of the most difficult consonants before and after the 12 week training period. The study showed a statistically significant reduction in the number of pronunciation difficulties in the sounds included in the training programme. The experimental group also made more progress with sounds not included in the training programme than did the control group. On the other hand this training programme did not lead to any significant improvement in readiness for reading.

Pendergast (1966) studied no fewer than 15,255 school beginners and, with a view to speech difficulties, divided them into two groups, one of which had attended nursery school while the other had not. The incidence of pronunciation difficulties was roughly the same at the beginning of the first form at school. Experience of nursery school, however, appeared to play its part in making it easier to remedy speech difficulties, as the children who had been to nursery school overcame them more quickly than the other children.

Blind children

No studies of the effect of nursery school on blind children have been registered.

Children with brain injuries

Yum (1954, 1955) described a nursery school programme for children with brain injuries. These children need more definitive instructions and more direct guidance in creative activities and play. The emphasis must be placed on a teaching method which is described as help to self-help. The parents must be drawn into the work.

Koch (1958) carried out a follow-up study of 13 children suffering from brain injuries. They had attended nursery school between the ages of eighteen months and three years, and were studied five years later to see how well they had done. Note was also taken of parental assessments of the value of nursery school, but the study does not provide a precise report. Nor did the author include a control group.

Argy (1965) studied the effects of various nursery school programmes on children with brain injuries. 71 children took part in the experiment; of these 40 were divided into two groups and taught by the Montessori method, while the remaining 31, also divided into two groups, were taught by a more 'orthodox' method, class instruction.

After two years in nursery school the groups being taught by the Montessori method had developed better with regard to social maturity, motor development and linguistic ability. The authors stress that the Montessori method, which aims at more individual training, seems to be particularly well suited to children suffering from brain damage.

Physically handicapped children

Denhoff (1954) stresses the significance of cooperation between parents and teachers when the child concerned is 'different'. He provides a series of examples of common problems and suggests ways of dealing with them.

Gordon (1966) discusses a study of various methods of helping handicapped children. The nursery school is linked with a rehabilitation centre, and every child attends nursery school for six weeks. Preliminary results look good, but no final report is yet available.

Children with behaviour difficulties

In studies already discussed, various examples have been seen of how nursery school can prevent the appearance of adjustment difficulties and behaviour difficulties, e.g. Schmidt-Kolmer (1964) and Stukat (1966). Nursery school can, however, also have a therapeutic effect on children already suffering from behaviour difficulties. It is to be supposed that nursery school is often used for this purpose by parents who feel that their children 'are ready for nursery school', while psychiatrists and psychologists use the therapeutic effect when trying to help a child to adjust to other children in a nursery school group.

Beer (1936) stresses the significance of cooperation between psychiatrists and nursery schools. Potential psychiatric cases can be diagnosed in nursery school, and other children who are not sufficiently adjusted to attend nursery school can be sent there after the necessary psychiatric treatment. In this way psychiatric guidance can be of benefit to a nursery school.

Ackerly and Meller (1941) describe the cooperation between a nursery school and a clinic for mental hygiene. The nursery school sent many children to the clinic who would otherwise not have been sent for treatment in time. Through the nursery school's intervention the parents were better able to accept the necessity for psychiatric treatment, and a counselling service for parents was started.

Rexford (1949) describes cooperation between a nursery school, psychiatric treatment and family guidance. The nursery school is consciously used to re-adjust emotionally disturbed children into a group situation, and it is emphasised that this sort of psychiatric treatment for children must become more common in future.

Washburn (1944) provides a more accurate description of how children with behaviour difficulties were placed in groups of four or five carefully chosen well-adjusted children. The treatment was carried out with close cooperation between psychiatrists, psychologists and nursery school teachers, and this work was accompanied by a weekly discussion with the parents. The significance of the well-adjusted children grew throughout the year. Their ability to accept the rules of the nursery school, and their use of the materials provided formed a pattern which the maladjusted children copied. The parents were able to watch their children in the groups through a window without being seen themselves, and this formed the basis for an understanding of many problems and made it easier for the parents to understand the general principles. The study showed that the more use that was made of parental cooperation, the more successful was the therapy.

Bender and Yarnell (1941), also writing on an observation nursery school, in which the most common reason for placing a child was some emotional crisis in the mother, report that many children made favourable progress as a result of the social education resulting from group work. The children concerned largely overcame their fear; their neurotic symptoms diminished, and it was possible to conclude the treatment.

Bernstein et al. (1954) describes the individual treatment given to a three-year-old child before it could be sent to nursery school, where further treatment was continued in close cooperation with the clinic.

Alpert (1955) describes work in a special nursery school with children suffering from emotional disturbances. 30 children attended the school in which therapy and teaching were balanced according to the children's needs. The relationship between the teacher and the child was of prime importance. By means of such techniques as guided regression, persistent stimulation, carefully measured and structured new experiences, the children were induced to act in a healthier fashion.

185

Mentally retarded children

In the chapter on the significance of nursery school for the child's intellectual development the conclusion reached was that the poorer the child's start, the greater did the positive effect seem to be, so that children starting below normal made relatively greater progress than those who were above average to begin with. But these were studies of children who could be considered as normal. In this chapter the interest centres on studies of children whose intellectual development is below normal, and who can thus be called children of very low intelligence.

Skeels and Dye (1939) carried out an experiment in which 13 mentally retarded children were moved from the institution in which they had been placed to private care by women who themselves were of poor intelligence, and at the same time the children started attending nursery school. They were aged just under two years, and varied in intelligence from 35 to 89, with a group average of 65. They were compared with a corresponding control group of the same age, but with an average I.Q. of 87, who remained in the institutional milieu until they were four years old.

The result of the experiment was that the I.Q. of the mentally retarded children who were put in care and sent to nursery school rose by an average of 27 points, so that they now averaged 93 points, while the control group, who remained in the institution, dropped by an average of 26 points and now averaged out at 60 points.

As the children chosen for the experiment were those with the lowest I.Q., while those with the higher I.Q.s were kept in the institution, a regression effect is to be expected in the re-testing, but the change is so great (in fact the two groups exchange I.Q.s) that regression effect alone cannot explain it. Whether it was due to nursery school attendance or to the emotional relationship established with their foster-mothers, cannot be said on the basis of the facts reported. Since this study others have indicated the importance for mental development of a close contact between the child and its mother or mother substitute.

Kirk (1958) carried out an extensive and thorough study of mentally retarded children throughout a five year period. The study included two experimental groups and two control groups. One of the experimental groups consisted of 15 children from a children's home, with a corresponding control group of 12 children. The other experimental group consisted of 25 children of low intelligence being brought up at home; their control group consisted of 24 children. The experimental groups attended nursery school for between one and three years before going into the first form at school; the control groups did not. All the children were retarded.

The experimental group from the residential home had an average I.Q. of 61 points against 57 for the control group. The other experimental group had an average I.Q. of 73 as against 76 in their control group. In some cases the retardation was due to organic disturbances, in others to cultural influences and in some cases to both. The two experimental groups took part in a nursery school programme based on the usual nursery school activities, but adapted to the individual needs of the children. In addition they were given individual guidance in areas where they had specific mental shortcomings. The result of the experiment was that the experimental group of institution children rose 12 points, while the corresponding control group was further retarded by 7 points. The experimental group of children brought up at home rose 11 points, while their control group remained unchanged. A subsequent test after one year's schooling showed that this progress was maintained. Meanwhile the control group of children being brought up at home had now reached the same level as the experimental group. However, the control group of institution children were still far behind, while the experimental group from the home maintained the level it had reached in nursery school. As for readiness to read, which was measured both by a test and by teachers' assessments, there appeared to be no difference between the experimental groups and the control groups.

The experiment carried out by Skeels and Dye (1939), to which reference has already been made, illustrates the significance of this acceleration at an early age. The experimental group were tested again after 21 years (Skeels, 1965). The 13 mentally retarded children from the institution who attended nursery school developed to the extent of being at the very bottom of the scale for normal intelligence, while the control group, who did not attend nursery school, were further retarded to the extent that they could be classed as feeble minded. The nursery school group reached the level of twelfth grade on average, and four even moved on to college, while the control group on average only reached the third grade. Since leaving school the experimental group have become skilled workers or gone to some form of further education. Half of the control group are without work, and only one has a job which can be classed as more than unskilled labouring; four are still in the institution. 11 of the 13 in the experimental group have married, and nine of them have children, while only two in the control group have married. In evaluating the relative significance of nursery school, however, it must be noted that 11 of the 13 nursery school children were adopted, while all the children in the control group remained in the institution for many years.

Ikeda (1955) writes of an experiment based on an expansion of the usual nursery school programme for the use of mentally retarded children. Special emphasis is placed on awareness of difficulties in learning, more systematic teaching and more individual teaching, especially clinical teaching and intensive work by the parents. However, no study has been made of the effect of this programme.

Fouracre (1958) describes a study of the effect of group training on four and five-year-old mentally retarded children. The experiment compares the effect of nursery school attendance and staying at home under specialist supervision. 30 children were in each group, together with a similar number of children constituting a control group. This latter group was neither sent to nursery school nor given parental guidance. Each year throughout the following five year period three similar groups were brought in, so that altogether there were five nursery school groups and five supervised groups at home plus five control groups. No results are yet available.

Lithauer (1932, 1933) studied the effect of leaving children of low intelligence in nursery school for an extra year, until they had the same mental age as other school beginners. Lithauer (1932) studied 73 children attending an experimental nursery school for children of school age who were not sufficiently well developed mentally to start normal school work. For most of them the start in the first class was a failure. After a year in the nursery school, most of these children did satisfactorily when they again started normal schooling.

A subsequent examination (Lithauer, 1933) of 25 of these children who stayed at nursery school until they had a mental age of six, after which they were placed in the first form, showed that 16 made normal progress throughout the five years studied.

The West German study by Schütter-Janikulla and Krohne (1966), to which reference was made in Chapter 10, indicates that good results were achieved by placing retarded school beginners in a sort of remedial nursery school where they were given special training to prepare them for school. This put them on a level with other children, at least at the time when they began school. The study does not indicate whether there are any long-term effects.

The East German study of training in understanding numbers, referred to in the same chapter (Böttcher, 1966) included 14 retarded children as well as children of normal intelligence. The results showed that after special group training the retarded children made the same progress as did the normal children.

13 Children whose Mothers go out to Work

The effects of nursery school attendance

Apart from remarks on certain differences in American studies between children in day care and children either in nursery school or kindergarten, no distinction has been drawn in the studies discussed between the effects on children whose mothers go out to work and those whose mothers stay at home. In general a more positive effect is found in the case of nursery school and kindergarten than in day care. At the same time the position is such that mothers going out to work are inclined to put their children in day care, whereas mothers at home tend to send their children to kindergarten or nursery school. The differences noted are probably more due to the differences in quality between the various institutions than the result of the mother's going out to work or staying at home.

It may well be, however, that nursery school will have different effects on the children according to whether the mother goes out to work or is at home all the time, as it can be assumed that their children will have different backgrounds and needs when they start to attend nursery school. The fact is that mothers at home will normally send their children to nursery school for educational reasons, while those going out to work will do so rather out of social necessity.

Meanwhile no studies have so far been registered which take heed of these variables. Those so far discussed have compared nursery school children with children brought up at home without any attention to whether the mothers went out to work or not. The few studies available in which the mothers of all the children at nursery school go out to work make the comparison with children whose mothers are at home and who themselves are brought up at home (Koshuk, 1947; Glass, 1949; Douglas and Blomfield, 1958; Yudkin, 1963; Moore, 1964; Hansson et al., 1967). In studies of this kind, in which nursery school children whose mothers go out to work are compared with children brought up at home and whose mothers are at home with them, it is impossible to see whether the difference in effect is due to the influence of nursery school or whether it stems from conditions at home.

There are, however, a few studies in which a comparison is made between a group of nursery school children whose mothers go out to work and another whose mothers are at home. The results of these studies, however, are of very limited value.

Siegel et al. (1959) compared two groups of nursery school children, each of 10 girls and 16 boys aged between five and six, and all coming from unbroken homes. The mothers of one group went out to work, while those of the other were at home. The study aimed especially at evaluating a number of psychological traits. Only in the case of one of these, the urge to dominate, did the children of mothers going out to work come significantly above the others. Yet even here the authors are inclined to ascribe this difference to coincidence, as no difference was found in other areas. The authors conclude that the mother's going out to work or remaining at home has no effect on the children. But it is not possible to draw this conclusion, as both groups attended nursery school, and nursery school might well have eradicated any differences there might have been between them from the start. The only conclusion it is possible to draw is that there is no difference between the two groups once they have been in nursery school for a period. Indeed, if a distinction is made between boys and girls it will be seen that in eight of the ten behaviour variables studied the difference between children with mothers out at work and children with mothers at home points in opposite directions for the two sexes.

Nye et al. (1963) studied the deprivation effect on 208 three to four-year-olds who attended nursery school; the mothers of half of them went out to work, those of the other half were at home. The two groups came from identical milieus. The effect was studied by means of interviews with the mothers, whose views were sought on a number of points related to anti-social behaviour, excessive reserve and nervous symptoms; there were 35 questions altogether. The study comes to the conclusion that there was no difference between the groups. However, as the basis of the study was the mothers' views on their children's behaviour it is strictly speaking only possible to conclude that there is no difference in what the two groups of mothers say about their children's behaviour (and as they came from the same social milieu, it can be imagined that their yardsticks were similar).

A Danish study of 100 school beginners who had all attended nursery school (Sjølund, 1964) found in comparing those whose mothers went out to work with those whose mothers were at home, that while it was impossible to point to any differences in social adjustment at school, the children whose mothers were at home adjusted more easily to work at school. Meanwhile it was not possible to match the two groups with respect to social background, though there was a tendency for the

190

mothers who stayed at home to be socially better off.

Studies taking the opposite point of departure and examining the effect on children of their mothers' work outside the home have, on the other hand, not so far considered nursery school as a possible compensatory factor as distinct from other ways of helping the child to adjust. This is the case, for instance, on the comprehensive Plowden Report, 1967, which finds that 21 per cent of children experiencing starting difficulties at school have mothers out at work, while 27 per cent have their mothers at home, but is not possible to discover whether this is due to nursery school attendance or not.

Douglas and Blomfield (1958) studied the incidence of serious symptoms of emotional disturbance such as bed-wetting and finger-sucking, but found no difference between the children of mothers going out to work and those with mothers at home.

The results of the most important of these studies are summarised in the article by Sjølund (1964) referred to above, and the conclusion reached is that the question of the mother's going out to work or working at home is not in itself decisive for the child's adjustment and development.

Lebovici (1964) notes that mothers who go out to work can give their children more attention in the time they spend with them, and Stoddard (1940) finds that mothers going out to work look after their children better in the few hours they spend with them than do mothers who are at home all the time. In this case, however, the mothers going out to work had only part-time jobs.

On the other hand several studies indicate that there may be differences in ideas on upbringing between mothers out at work and mothers working at home. Sjølund (1964) noted that the group of mothers at home were inclined to be more strict, more often made too great a demand on the child, more often give it duties to carry out, often paid less attention to the stage of development reached by the child, and more often were the cause of a bad emotional climate in the home, while the group of mothers out at work all day were less authoritarian, more often made too elementary a demand on their children and more often lacked contact with them.

This corresponds to the discoveries made by Moore (1964), who finds that the greatest difference between the children of mothers going out to work and those whose mothers are at home is in the development of the ego and super-ego. Children whose mothers went out to work were less bothered by a stringent super-ego, while a mother constantly present appeared to cause a child to learn to control its ego at an early age, often leading to ego-restriction.

The effects of alternative arrangements

In a study of the effects of nursery school on children whose mothers go out to work, it is more reasonable, instead of comparing a group of children with mothers out at work with another group with mothers at home, to compare it with the alternative forms of care available for mothers who are either forced to go out to work or who wish to do so. In the section on the effects of day nurseries mention has already been made of how there has been a policy in Great Britain and West Germany of persuading the mothers of small children to stay at home by simply making it difficult to open day nurseries, which, however, led not to the mothers' staying at home, but to their finding less suitable methods of having their children looked after. In the Plowden Report (1967) it is said that as it obviously is inevitable that mothers will go out to work, suitable ways of looking after the children must be found.

In this case the alternative to nursery school will be some form of private care, and there are a few studies comparing the effect on children of nursery school and private care respectively. Moore (1964) did a study of 167 children of school age and compared the children of mothers going out to work in an effort to trace the effects of nursery school and private care on them. He discovered that the nursery school children had found it easier to adjust to school and were relatively less nervous, which may have been the result of playing in a group. At the same time they had fewer feelings of guilt and were more careless in their manner, which may have been the result of greater freedom from supervision.

These differences correspond roughly to those already seen between the influence of home and nursery school. In other words private care has much the same effect as a home upbringing. This becomes even more apparent from a more thorough Swedish study of just this question (Kihlblom, 1953). From a large amount of material the author chose to compare 30 boys and girls from all-day nursery schools and 30 boys and girls in private care (under the supervision of the child care service); they were comparable in most respects. The children were aged between four and six years. The effects were studied partly by means of interviews with the mothers and the nursery school teacher or registered child minder as the case may be, and partly by means of observations of the children at play; in addition psychological tests were carried out. The amount of material resulting from this study is very large, but special mention should be made of the difference in attitude towards upbringing in nursery school and private care. This was measured on a scale ranging from a liberal attitude to a restrictive attitude. While two thirds of all the mothers were in this latter category as opposed to one third in the first, only about half of the child minders were in it and one eighth of the nursery school teachers. The study suggests that the difference between the child minders and the nursery school teachers might be due to age, as most of the child minders were appreciable older. On the whole the advantages of nursery school appear to be of a more educational nature, while it is stressed that private day care gives the child a milieu which corresponds more closely to the home milieu.

Barbiero and Galdo (1960) compared 200 nursery school children from Naples whose mothers went out to work with 40 children (also with mothers out at work) who were looked after at home by relatives, for instance their grandmothers. They found that the longer the children had been at nursery school, the more retarded they were in comparison with the children looked after by relatives. The nursery schools were described as having suitable premises and good hygienic standards, but insufficient staff and material. It is not possible to decide whether this difference is due to the particular family structure.

Differences in the effect on boys and girls (the pattern of sex roles)

The mother's absence from home

Studies of the effect of the mother going out to work show certain differences in the effect on boys and girls, which are ascribed to the development of the children's pattern of sex roles. Nye and Hoffmann (1963) sum up the differences in American studies by saying that it looks as though the mother's absence results in the boys' becoming more dependent and reserved than girls (and also more than boys whose mothers are at home), while girls on the contrary become more independent and confident than boys (and also more than girls whose mothers are at home). The authors designate this as a negative effect on boys and a positive effect on girls. Dependence and reserve are symptoms resulting from their missing their mothers, and appear to be more serious in boys than in girls.

The Plowden Report (1967) indicates the opposite. A survey of school beginners in need of special help included equal numbers of girls with mothers out at work and at home respectively, 10 per cent in each case. At the same time 20 per cent of boys with mothers at home needed special help as opposed to only 15 per cent of those whose mothers went out to work. However, more girls whose mothers were out at work had slight adjustment difficulties on starting school.

Stolz (1960) merely concludes that boys whose mothers go out to work appear to be less aggressive than other boys, while girls appear to be more aggressive than others, so that the pattern of sex roles is evened out as a result of nursery school attendance.

Age and situation respectively appear to be important factors in boys' and girls' ability to adjust. Burchinal and Rossman (1961) find that at nursery school age girls whose mothers go out to work are inclined to react to this by introspective reactions such as dejection and daydreaming.

A Danish study (Sjølund, 1964), observing the same children's ability to adjust to first nursery school and then school, showed that girls were less well adjusted in nursery school than at school, but that the opposite was the case with boys. It could not be determined whether this was due to age or to the different situations.

Differences in the effects of nursery school on boys and girls

What significance have these problems stemming from the pattern of sex roles on the one hand for the children's behaviour in nursery school and on the other for the nursery school's effect on their ability to adjust?

Moore (1964) found that taking the groups of children as a whole there was no discernible difference in the ability to adjust whether the children had attended nursery school or not. However, if a distinction is made between boys and girls, the tendencies appear to be contrary, in that boys appeared to be better adjusted in nursery school than at home, while girls seemed to be better adjusted if looked after by their mothers.

A tendency to the same sort of thing is found in the Danish study (Sjølund, 1964), where a distinction is drawn between social adjustment and adjustment to work. Social adjustment was better in girls whose mothers were at home and boys whose mothers went out to work. On the other hand there was no difference in adjustment to work. All the children concerned attended nursery school.

Hansson et al. (1967) also found a difference in the pattern of sex roles in boys and girls according to whether they went to nursery school or stayed at home. Girls in nursery school had more difficulty in adjusting to reality than girls brought up at home, while the opposite was the case with boys. Boys brought up at home were more inclined to see their fathers as figures of authority than were boys attending nursery school. Girls attending nursery school had difficulties in identifying their roles which were not experienced by girls at home, a state of affairs found in other studies.

Boys have greater difficulty in identifying their roles when they spend too much time alone with their mothers, girls when they spend too little time with their mothers.

Siegel et al. (1959) compared 26 pairs of children attending nursery school, boys as well as girls; one child in each pair had a mother going out to work, the other a mother at home. The tendencies found in boys and girls went in opposite directions. The boys with mothers at work were less aggressive, less willing to conform or comply, less sociable and less self-sufficient, while girls in the same circumstances were less obedient, less inclined to seek comfort and less dependent on adults than girls whose mothers were at home.

All in all, these short studies are not sufficient to do more than point to a problem. Nothing conclusive can be said on this important question.

14 The Children's Upbringing

The significance of parental attitudes for children's adjustment to nursery school

Parents' attitudes towards their children and their feelings on nursery school seem to be important factors in judging the effect of nursery school on the child.

Hattwick (1936 b) studied behaviour patterns of 335 nursery school children aged between two and five years and visited their homes to assess home influence. He found that parents whose children paid too much attention to them were inclined to develop infantile and reserved reactions. Conversely, insufficient attention in the home appeared to be related to aggressive behaviour. Homes in which there were signs of physical or mental tension resulted in poor emotional adjustment and a lack of ability to cooperate with others. A share of responsibility in the home developed a child's self-confidence and put an end to more infantile habits. If the parents played with the children, they helped to develop a sense of emotional security in them.

Chadwick (1928), in a study of a nursery school in a poor district, found that almost all the parents had unhappy home relations which harmed the children.

Hattwick and Stowell (1936) produced a study of 500 nursery school children and found that children who were either treated as babies or on the other hand had too much expected of them developed far more social difficulties and poorer work habits than children from balanced homes.

A number of studies from the Iowa Studies in Child Welfare (Baruch, 1937; Grant, 1939; Trumbo, 1945; and Witmer, 1937) show that children from homes with a good emotional climate are better socially adjusted and more willing to cooperate than children from homes with emotional tensions between parents and children or between the parents themselves.

Gottemoller (1939) studied 22 nursery school children and discovered, partly on the basis of his own observations and partly from teachers' reports, that there was a close relationship between parents' behaviour and attitudes towards the children and the children's adjustment to nursery school. Reeves (1941) also found that adjustment was related to parental attitudes.

Farquhar (1942), who studied 20 former nursery school children at school, four years after they had started nursery school, found that the factor which had played the greatest part in their adjustment was their relationship with their parents.

Lafore (1945) visited 21 homes in order to study the way in which parents treated their children before school age. He evaluated the incidence of positive and negative approaches in order to reach a specific goal, and found that parents most inclined to dictate or interfere, scold, punish or humiliate produced the highest incidence of inimical behaviour, crying and teasing.

Glass (1949) found that children's adjustment problems were related to the parents' attitudes and personalities, and that this was far more important to the child's adjustment potential than attendance at nursery school.

Baldwin (1949) noted that parents' attitude do not only have an effect when they themselves are present, but have a lasting effect on the child. A study was made of 45 aspects of behaviour in 56 nursery school children aged between three and five years, while parental attitudes were classed as warm, democratic or inclined to spoil. Democracy, usually allied to warmth, was found to be the most important variable in producing free and active participation in family life, successful self-confidence and self-assertion, while it also encouraged creative and constructive behaviour. Spoiling a child, on the other hand, tended to make it timid and to inhibit gross motor development.

Lévy-Bruhl (1956), in a French study, found a connection between a child's initial adjustment and the mother's attitude. Kalinina and Chepeleuts (1962), in a Russian study, also found that children of nursery school age who have adjustment difficulties have been exposed to the wrong sort of treatment and upbringing by their parents.

Kaffman (1961), studies 219 kibbutz children of nursery school age and compares the incidence of behaviour disturbances with the American norms for the same ages. He finds that the kibbutz children only differ from American children of the same age in two ways: the incidence of finger sucking is three times as high in the kibbutz children, while eating problems are three times as common in American children. A further comparison of 108 finger-sucking children from with kibbutz group with others from the same group indicates that finger-sucking is due to a more permissive upbringing on the part of the parents.

The sooner a child is studied after starting nursery school, the closer is the relationship discernible between its behaviour and parental attitudes. A Danish study (Sjølund, 1963) of 40 beginners at nursery school, describing them on the basis of Nordland's evaluation scale for social behaviour, indicated that of the 13 children who on the basis of a description of their behaviour had the greatest adjustment difficulties, nine had mothers among the ten whom a test of attitudes showed to be most negative on questions of upbringing.

Only in one of the studies (Highberger, 1955) was it impossible to find any connection between children's behaviour and parental attitudes, but Hartup (1959) demonstrated that the evaluation scale used was unsuitable.

The close relationship between parental attitudes and children's behaviour becomes even more obvious in cases of nursery school children with adjustment difficulties. Bender and Yarnell (1941) found in their study that the most common cause of children being placed in the observation nursery school was some crisis in the mother's emotional life. Nursery school attendance and group influence were often sufficient to improve the condition of many of the children.

Koshuk (1947) found that the greater the difficulties experienced at home, the more obvious was the positive effect of nursery school. In general the mothers concerned indicated that the children's improved emotional and social adjustment also had a positive effect on family life.

A few studies are concerned with differences between boys and girls starting in nursery school, and any connection between these and parental attitudes. Blomart (1963) studied a group of children starting nursery school and found that as a rule girls were more mature, found it easier to join a group and were more willing to play with other children. Parental attitudes were of great significance for their children's ability to adjust. Over-protectiveness or an inimical attitude on the part of the mother inhibited a child's maturing process and its growing sense of independence, and influenced its group identification.

Cummings (1944) studied 239 nursery school children aged between two and seven years. The boys showed significantly more symptoms of emotional disturbance than girls. Over-protected children showed more nervous symptoms than neglected children. Neglected children were more commonly described as aggressive, cruel, lying and so on.

A few more recent studies have been concerned with the connection between specific modes of behaviour in the child and specific parental attitudes.

McDavid (1959), studying children's behaviour both in nursery school and at home, together with parental attitudes and behaviour, found that the child's ability to take part in make-believe games with other children was connected with its experience of adults in the home and showed a

199

negative connection with parental attitudes such as suppression, punitive methods or excessive permissiveness. The greater the child's possibility of extending its horizon through conversation with the parents, the greater was its social acceptance in a group.

Sjølund (1967 a) examined the connection between independent and conformist behaviour respectively and the parental attitude to questions of upbringing. The most conformist and the most independent children were selected from 40 nursery school groups, after which the mothers of these children answered a questionnaire on their attitudes towards upbringing. By and large the mothers of the most conformist children expressed a more dominating attitude, either in the form of authoritarian discipline or of domineering over-protectiveness. An analysis of the children's social background showed that the two groups were roughly similar with regard to the fathers' professions; but two thirds of the children whose mothers were at home belonged to the conformist group, and two thirds of the children whose mothers went out to work belonged to the independent group. Most of the eldest in a family of children were among the conformist group, and most of the youngest among the independent ones, corresponding to Adler's theories on the significance of a child's position in a group of brothers and sisters.

Another study (Sjølund, 1967 b) on similar lines dealt with the connection between parental attitudes towards upbringing and on the one hand constructive imagination (creativity) and on the other inhibition in the child. The most creative and the most inhibited children were selected from 60 nursery school groups, after which the mothers answered the questionnaire. The parental attitudes most closely related to inhibited creativity were excessive demands on the child and too powerful emotional ties with it. An analysis of the children's milieus showed that there was a majority of children of academics and teachers in the creative group and a majority of officials and tradespeople among the inhibited.

Differences between home and nursery school with regard to upbringing

The differences in attitude to upbringing between home and nursery school, to which reference has been made in several studies, has been the subject of a closer analysis in an American project (Prescott, 1964, 1965). As a part of her very extensive programme she asked 250 mothers from different social backgrounds, but all of whom went out to work, about the sort of behaviour they expected of their children and about the methods they used to bring them up. They all had children between the ages of two

200

and five years, and these children were dispersed in 30 different nursery schools. The principals of these schools and the children's teachers, 67 in all, were interviewed and asked the same questions. The survey showed that the teachers were more inclined than the mothers to look for behaviour of a sort which enabled good order to be maintained and which enabled social intercourse to develop smoothly. The parents, for their part, made greater demands on their children's behaviour in the 'moral' sphere. They had stricter ideas as to what was fitting for boys and girls to do respectively, and they demanded behaviour more in accordance with the sex roles. They were less prepared to answer questions such as 'where do babies come from' or to accept sexual games or masturbation. Nor were they so prepared to accept that their children used 'naughty' words or showed aggressive tendencies towards adults. In these respects there was not much difference in parents' expectations of younger or older children, whereas the teachers did not demand the same of the smaller ones as they did of the older ones. There were certain differences in expectations in parents of different financial status. Those with a higher financial status were more inclined to stress good manners in their children, while those with a lower income tended to be stricter in other fields, but less demanding in this respect. Moreover the attitudes of the teachers themselves were analysed. Divided up according to the children's milieus, the teachers on the whole made fewer demands in the areas in which the parents were strict, and vice versa.

The study included a comparison of disciplinary methods in parents and teachers, a distinction being drawn between two groups of methods: verbal methods such as explanations, reminders, reprimands etc., and restrictive methods such as isolation, loss of rights and other forms of punishment. The parents were much more inclined to resort to punishment than were the teachers, while teachers made more use of verbal reprimands. If the teachers dealt out punishments, they were in the form of the loss of some right, while the parents often resorted to smacking. Here, too, parents treated children of all ages in the same way, while the teachers reported greater differences in methods, according to the age of the child. Differences in milieu also played their part, and parents from lower social strata were stricter than others. Again, differences were to be observed among teachers, as those from private nursery schools were stricter than those in local authority or state nursery schools, and similarly the less well qualified teachers were stricter than those with a more thorough training.

The effects of different attitudes on upbringing in home and nursery school emerge indirectly in a study of the reasons for childrens' crying

(Landreth, 1943). A daily study for eight weeks of 32 nursery school children and 25 children being brought up at home showed that the cause of crying in the first category was usually conflicts with other children over toys or materials, while children at home usually cried because of conflicts with their parents, especially in connection with routine activities such as having to sleep, wash, eat and so on.

A Danish study (Sjølund, 1962) compares the attitudes of mothers and of nursery school teachers with various qualifications. Answers to the questionnaire on attitudes towards discipline, plotted on an authoritarian-democratic scale, showed nursery school pupils and their mothers at the authoritarian end of the scale on first starting nursery school, while those at the end of their nursery school career had shifted towards the democratic end. The furthest towards the democratic end were the most experienced nursery school teachers.

Similar differences between mothers and teachers with varying qualifications were also discovered in an American study (Dreyer and Haupt, 1960).

Cooperation between home and nursery school in the upbringing of children.

The above studies of the interrelationship of parental attitudes towards upbringing and the child's development and behaviour are of great practical significance for the nursery schools' work with the children. If the nursery school's task is to contribute to achieving the optimal development of the child, it will be necessary to try to change any unfortunate attitudes on the part of the parents. Various studies do indeed indicate that nursery school is more beneficial if it succeeds in involving the parents in cooperation concerning the methods of upbringing being employed.

Dragan (1935) found in an extensive survey involving 2,282 nursery school children that conditions at home appeared to have great influence on the development of the child's personality, while nursery school and the personality of the teacher were also of importance.

Washburn (1944) carried out an experiment in which children with behaviour disturbances were placed in small groups of normal children and took part in normal nursery school life. During this time the parents had the opportunity to watch the children in the groups without being seen themselves, which provided a basis for discussions with them on the more general principles of upbringing. The therapy was more successful when parents were positively inclined to it and could thus correct their more unfortunate attitudes.

In a more systematic experiment, including a control group (Rhinehart, 1949), a study was made of 21 three-year-old children in nursery school, whose parents took part in a specially designed programme on upbringing, compared with others who did not attend nursery school and whose parents did not take part in the course. The children whose parents took part in the training course made better progress than the control group in the formation of good habits and emotional stability. The study does not, however, make it clear whether the effect was the result of the children's attendance at nursery school or the course for parents.

In another study (Rhinehart, 1945) a comparison is made between the effects of two difficult courses for parents with children in nursery school.

The experiments with children from culturally deprived milieus, to which reference has already been made, place great emphasis on parental cooperation as a means of improving the level of their children's achievements.

A special American type of nursery school, the cooperative nursery school, in which the parents take it in turns to act as assistants to the nursery school teachers, appears to have had a beneficial effect on the attitudes of the parents concerned (Boulding, 1955). When supplemented with a more systematic training (Taylor, 1962) parents' attitudes can be developed even further along the right lines.

A few studies have been made of the effect of this. Gottsdanker (1952) found that parental attitudes had changed significantly as a result of his experiment. Some mothers took part in it because they had special problems in bringing up their children; they reported a vast improvement. Others said that they had become aware of problems they had not recognised before, and would probably be able to cope with them. Most of the mothers derived a more general benefit from the course. Some of them were said to have awakened to a completely changed attitude. In this experiment the mothers were under the effective guidance of teachers and psychologists. Each mother assisted one morning a week, and one evening a week took part in a discussion under the chairmanship of the principal on problems of bringing up children. The fathers also took part in this. The study concludes that the idea has both advantages and disadvantages. Among the disadvantages are listed the lack of professional training and uncertainty in the relationship between the mother and child when the mother had her own child in her group, while it was seen that the constant change of assistants created insecurity in some children. Advantages listed are the fact that the mother and her child take part in a common experience, the close contact on concrete problems between mothers and teachers, the opportunity for mothers to observe normal behaviour in other children and to discuss with other mothers problems resembling their own, which builds up their self-confidence and gives them a more relaxed attitude. When there is a need for help from the teachers, it is easier to talk straightforwardly with the teachers in the course of the day-to-day contact, and moreover a positive effect is derived from the parents' getting to know the nursery school so well.

Marshall (1961), studying a statistically selected group of 42 children who had taken part for a year in a nursery school course in which the mothers had participated, found that most of the mothers had an increased insight and understanding, and that an improvement could be noted in the children's behaviour.

PART V

The Connection Between the Quality of the Nursery School and its Effect Upon the Children

15 The Nursery School Structure and Equipment

A theme common to many of the studies of effect so far reviewed is that the appearance of a positive effect is dependent on the quality of a nursery school. The better the nursery school, the better the effect. It also emerges that the appearance of a positive effect varies according to the particular field under review. In certain cases nursery school has an almost exclusively positive effect, in other cases only under certain conditions. In the general studies comparing children attending nursery school with others who do not, however, it is extremely rare for the author to have paid attention to the role played by the quality of the nursery school, simply because most are only concerned with a single group of nursery schools or even a single nursery school.

However, some studies (for instance Jones and Prescott (1964) who compare several hundred nursery schools in California) indicate that the quality of schools varies enormously. Another study (Prescott and Harris, 1964) shows great variations in the teachers' ability to work with the children, and a third (Prescott and Harris, 1965) shows great variations in the qualifications of nursery school teachers. It is reasonable to assume that such variations must play their part in deciding whether a nursery school will have a positive effect on the children or not.

Although there is no scientific basis for defining a good nursery school, and although teachers themselves can scarcely agree on what constitutes a good nursery school, it would still be possible to study the effects of good and bad schools by making use of comparison of extremes, for example by choosing the ten nursery schools in a city which were acknowledged by specialists as being the best, and the ten considered the worst, and studying how they worked and what effect they had on the children. So far, however, no such studies are available.

There are, meanwhile, studies on the effect of certain aspects of a nursery school's functions and the approach of the staff. Such studies are usually based on two groups of children from the same school and matched as closely as possible. One group is subjected to a number of experimental variations in which the other group, the control group, does not take part, while everything else remains identical for the two groups. If the experimental group undergoes some change, while the control group does not, then this is ascribed to the effect of the experimental method.

A number of studies of this nature are reviewed in this and the next chapter. Each of these will in its own way help to throw light on certain aspects of nursery school, beginning with studies of the material structure of the nursery school and then proceeding via the educational programmes to studies of the teachers' personalities. It must, however, be pointed out that the results of these studies are taken at their face value; only effect studies are made the object of methodological evaluation. Here, then, the analysis confines itself to a comparison and evaluation of results communicated, and only on occasion to an analysis of whether the study was 'done properly'.

Space

Plenty of space is of importance not only for the well-being of the teachers. Numerous studies have indicated that the amount of space available has an indirect effect on various aspects of the children's behaviour. It goes almost without saying that a lack of space leads to more conflicts, but Murphy (1937) was able to demonstrate that the number of conflicts per unit of time was inversely proportional to the area of floor space.

Jersild and Markey (1935), in a comprehensive survey of conflicts between nursery school children, found that the incidence was least where there was the greatest amount of outdoor playing space, and greatest where there was insufficient space.

Body (1955) found the incidence of aggressiveness greater in children from a nursery school with a small amount of space than in a group coming from one with ample room to move about.

Henry and Sharpe (1957) compared a nursery school almost without space for outdoor play with another with plenty of space. During a period of observation the children in the first of these behaved aggressively on twice as many occasions as the others, and were only half as prepared to act together with other children.

Markey (1935), studying conditions playing a part in improving children's creativity, compared three groups of nursery school children and found that the greatest amount of creativity was found in the group with five times the amount of space enjoyed by the others.

A Swedish study, (Bendz-Sandell, 1964), using symptoms of tiredness in three-year-old children as an indicator, found a connection between them and the amount of space available both indoors and outdoors: the less space, the more signs of fatigue, whether caused by positive or negative experiences. This latter question will be discussed later.

Prescott and Harris (1964), in their large-scale comparison of Californian nursery schools, found that the amount of space available has a very wide significance in that it both regulates and decides the extent of activities available, and sometimes even influences the entire teaching programme.

In Danish nursery schools it is not unusual for the amount of space available to decide such important educational questions as the division into groups.

Green (1933 a), studying animosity and quarrelling in children, found that insufficient space was connected with the incidence of quarrelling.

The size of the nursery school

Teachers usually maintain that it is of advantage to the teaching climate of a nursery school that it should not be too big. From studies in other fields it is known that the bigger a social system becomes, the more social patterns become stylised, as would naturally be the case with nursery schools as well. However, little attention has been paid to this question.

A French study (Lebovici, 1964) argues that the institution must not be so big that the personal element disappears. The British Plowden Report (1967) suggests that a 'nursery centre' should consist of two or three groups of children of at most 20 children aged between three and five. The East German study by Schmidt-Kolmer (1964), which is based on an extremely thorough study of experimental data, suggests the same optimal size for a nursery school. An institution with fewer than 15 or more than 100 children is not to be recommended, according to this report, on account of the organisation of everyday educational activities. It sees an institution of between 50 and 70 children as creating the best conditions for work and social activities.

Prescott and Harris' study (1964) points to some direct effects of size, one of which is that size has an effect upon the teaching programme of an institution. An increase in size means that many aspects of a nursery school's tasks have to be regulated, and many more relationships and procedures formalised. Once a nursery school reaches a certain size, it means a change of role for the principal, who becomes first and foremost an administrator and head of staff. It is more difficult for the principal to maintain an informal manner when the institution becomes bigger, and this in its turn affects the teaching.

The lay-out of a nursery school

Although this question which must be taken as being of prime importance for a nursery school's social processes, the significance of the positioning of the individual rooms in a nursery school in relationship to each other appears never to have been studied.

The siting of a nursery school

No studies have been made which are directly concerned with the siting of a nursery school. The main question is whether it should be in the proximity of the home or place of work.

There are, however, some studies which indirectly touch on this subject. Moore (1963), in his study of British nursery schools, concluded that a changing milieu was the most unfortunate of all negative factors. A stable milieu was important for the child. David and Appel (1961, 1962), in their study of French day nursery children, suggested that too many changes in staff were undesirable. A stable relationship with an adult was important.

As the mother's home milieu is far more stable than her place of work, this indicates that the nursery school ought to be situated near the home. In addition, it is to be expected that the child's relationship with other children, which will become of increasing importance as it approaches school age, will benefit from stable conditions while the child is at nursery school.

The Russian system is to situate nursery schools near the home and day nurseries near the place of work. The mother then has access to the baby to look after it and feed it. It might well be that at this early stage, when other children are of no importance, it is an advantage to have the child near its mother. Here it should be mentioned that Russian day nurseries are only for small babies, while toddlers are put into nursery school.

Equipment

The importance of having sufficient stimulating material available is usually stressed by nursery school teachers, and this is confirmed in various studies, including a French one carried out by Lebovici (1964).

Body (1955) finds a greater incidence of conflict if there is insufficient equipment in the nursery school. Landreth (1941) found in his study of the causes of children's crying that in 75 per cent of the cases the reason was a conflict with other children over toys or playground equipment, while in his Danish study Simonsen (1947) found that the group of children achieving least was unused to having the necessary amount of toys to hand.

Gutteridge (1939), who carried out a large-scale study of motor development in 2,000 nursery school children aged between two and seven years from 33 different nursery schools, found that the development graph fell when there was not sufficient material for motor activities at hand. The same was found in a study by Blackhurst (1929).

The lack of suitable equipment is possibly the explanation of the suggestion mentioned earlier that nursery school has a negative effect on children's motor development. A Swedish project (Sandels, 1963) is at present making a more thorough study of this question.

Murphy, Murphy and Newcomb (1937) discovered that the presence of a large number of toys, but only one or two of each kind, produced more competition and quarrelling among children than a corresponding number composed of fewer kinds but more of each kind.

Johnson (1935) carried out an experiment with nursery school children in which she periodically furnished two playgrounds with large amounts of play equipment in addition to the standard equipment, such as sandpits and climbing frames. When the additional equipment was there, the amount of fighting, quarrelling, crying and teasing diminished, and when it was removed, these forms of behaviour increased and the teachers were more often forced to intervene.

Lézine (1964) stresses that it is not sufficient merely to ensure the presence of sufficient material to occupy the children, but they should also be encouraged to use it to the best advantage. Henry and Sharpe (1947) noted that especially in the case of children who have not been used to a sufficient quantity of toys it is necessary to encourage them and set them going at first.

Other studies also point to fields where the mere presence of materials is not enough and a little more stimulation is needed. Alper, Blane and Abrams (1955) found milieu differences in children's use of finger paints. Children from middle class homes preferred coloured chalk to finger paints and were more afraid than other children of getting dirty.

Corcoran (1954), studying nursery school children's use of colours, discovered that their choice of colours was less a conscious choice than the result of the order in which the colours happened to be placed.

Several studies have shown that certain types of equipment produce specific forms of behaviour. Green (1933 b) found that playing with sand led to more conflicts than any other form of occupation studied. Building bricks also led to conflicts. Updegraff and Herbst also noted that building with bricks caused the greatest number of refusals to cooperate, while playing with plasticine on the other hand led to the greatest degree of cooperation. The study only looked at these two forms of activity, however.

Parten (1933), looking at the entire spectrum of nursery school activities, found that playing with plasticine, drawing and so on produced social actions which ought really to be regarded as parallel actions rather than social cooperation. Play houses engaged the children in more directly social activities. Green (1933 b) found the same in connection with play in the dolls' corner.

Markey (1935), studying children's creativity, found that sand and building bricks were most often used in imaginative play.

Johnson (1935) found that the more materials there were available the more was the tendency to individual games, while social activities increased when the material was removed.

Van Alstyne (1932) found that certain materials caused children to talk to each other more and had what he called a greater conversational value than others. Games with dolls, building bricks, coloured chalk and plasticine gave rise to a lot of conversation between the children concerned, while painting, cutting paper and reading had the opposite effect.

Murphy (1937), in his study of sympathy between children, found that materials which actually demanded the cooperation of several children led to cooperation and stimulated sympathy among them.

These studies show how easy it is for the teacher to stimulate certain forms of activity. None of these forms can really be considered better than others, but must first and foremost be put in relation to the needs of the individual child. For instance a child with only limited possibilities for playing with other children at home is in greater need of taking part in something to bring about group activity, while a child from a large family may well be in need of some activity that can give it a chance to work alone and immerse itself in something.

Division into groups

One question much discussed by teachers is whether it is best to divide the children into groups according to age, or whether the groups should consist of children of varying ages. Is it better to have the children as close to each other in age as possible, or as different as possible? An analysis of replies to questionnaires sent to nursery school teachers on the question of advantages and disadvantages in mixed groups (Sjølund, 1964) shows that the advantages are concerned with the greater personal stimulation resulting from mixing, while the disadvantages are connected with the practical problems of teaching. Many of the activities taking place under the guidance of the teacher must necessarily be most suited to one specific age at a time. External circumstances, such as the design of the nursery school and the number of children per teacher are however really the factors deciding which form is practicable. In practice the problem is solved to some extent in schools containing mixed groups by re-arranging them into other groups for certain activities and allowing the children to play with others at the same stage of development. Few studies have been made of this question, but they all seem to indicate that groups that are too homogeneous narrow the children's horizons.

Markey (1935) found that younger children in a group containing a variety of ages showed greater imaginative gifts than children of the same age and sex in groups exclusively made up of children of the same age. The presence of the older children led to an increase in the imaginative activities of the younger ones.

Murphy (1937) found that the presence of the younger children led to more social behaviour and sympathetic attitudes on the part of the older ones who looked after the little ones, tried to entertain them and showed them how to use things. In the groups made up of children of similar ages she found a greater sense of competition in the individual children, and there was a much higher incidence of conflict.

Body (1955) noted a much greater incidence of aggressive behaviour, both verbal and physical, in the groups composed of children of much the same age.

Landreth (1941) on the other hand found that the incidence of crying as the result of conflict was greater when there was a particularly large difference in age between the two quarrelling.

Markey (1935) found that a child whose age was very different from the average age of a group made far fewer social contacts at play than the other children, while the same child, when placed in a group of varying ages, made far more contacts.

Murphy, Murphy and Newcomb (1937) found that groups of 20 two-year-olds with the same interests but with insufficient maturity to work and play together produced a high degree of tension and competition as a result of their inability to supplement each other.

These results are really all only by-products of other studies, but they are supported by a major Russian experiment. Nechaieva (1963) carried out a series of experiments in which children in different age groups were brought together with the object of stimulating the development of the younger ones and imparting a greater sense of sympathy and social responsibility to the older ones. The experiment lasted for several years, and the author concludes that it was successful, but that it demanded the careful guidance of a teacher: it was of no use leaving the children to themselves. The older ones had to learn to set a good example to the younger ones. The implications for two-year-olds appeared to be particularly great: if they were put with day nursery children, their linguistic and intellectual development was retarded, but when they were put with nursery school children, i.e. children older than they were, the stimulus they received was greater than normal. Since then the practice has been introduced of moving children from day nurseries into nursery school as soon as they can walk.

Apart from the question of age difference the way in which individual personalities act upon each other is of significance when deciding upon a suitable composition for the groups.

Hetzer and Noelle (1936) were interested in the functions of different types of children within a group and stressed the importance of maintaining a balance within a group (by which is meant that the group should function without too much friction). In particular they were interested in the effect on the group of including physically or mentally handicapped children, and also in the question of how many such children it would be possible to place in the group without spoiling the other children's chances. Problems of this nature have been discussed in the section on the effects of nursery school on handicapped children.

The importance of this question can be seen from some experiments in group psychology (Sjølund, 1965), although they were not concerned with nursery school children. If a poor worker was placed in a group of good workers, his daily production increased without any decrease in the achievements of the others. However, when the percentage of poor workers was increased, so did their influence, and when the majority of the group were poor workers, those who had previously worked well began to produce poor results.

The size of the group

No studies have been registered concerned with the question of the optimal size of groups composed of children of the same age or of different ages. It is to be supposed that the optimal size will also vary from one activity to another. Many genetic studies, however, show that children's tendencies to form spontaneous groups increase at a more or less constant rate, in harmony with their age until they are half way through school. Parten (1933), Green (1933 b) and Salusky (1930) found that both the size and durability of these spontaneous groups increase with the individual's social experiences.

It has already been mentioned that the size of the group can be of importance for the children's linguistic development. Williams and Mattson (1942), comparing groups of two, three and four children respectively, all of the children being grouped according to age, found that, with the increasing size of the group, the language used by the children became more friendly and social, and less egocentric. This corresponds to the findings of Sjølund (1965) that the impact of the personality increases in small groups, while social processes emerge more clearly in larger ones.

Dawe (1934 b) studied the effect of the size of the nursery school group in relation to how much children derived from a story being read to them, and how great a contribution they made to a discussion of the story. 433 children were included in the study and were divided into groups of between 14 and 46 children. The tendency was for relatively fewer children to get much out of the story with the increasing size of the groups. There was a clear tendency for relatively more of the children to be outside any discussion in the bigger groups. The closer a child sat to the teacher, the more it took part in conversation, and thus the physical distance from the teacher played its part in keeping the child outside. Such factors were more important than the child's social position, which seemed to be unconnected with its role in the group.

A Russian study (Ginsberg, 1960) compared a group of 15 with a group of 30 five and six-year-olds learning to speak English, French and German. There seemed to be no difference in what the two groups got out of the teaching, but the larger group was quicker to repeat words and in general more lively. However, these results were achieved after earlier experiments had shown the necessity of discarding traditional methods of teaching and of, instead, basing language teaching on play activities, so it is possible that there was a spontaneous division into groups of a suitable size in both these main groups.

Murphy, Murphy and Newcomb (1937) suggest that if there is too large a group which at the same time is too homogeneous in composition, tensions can be reduced by dividing it into smaller groups.

An American dissertation (Mould, 1958) on the significance of the group's size for the development of personality has unfortunately been unobtainable.

A Swedish study (Bendz-Sandell, 1964) of the incidence of symptoms of tiredness in nursery school children considered the question of whether this had any connection with the size of the group. In the first report, published in 1964 and only concerned with three-year-olds, there appeared to be no connection. A later report (Sandels et al., 1967) used the adult-child ratio as its basis rather than the size of the group. This study also found it impossible to find any relationship between symptoms of tiredness and the number of children per adult. However, it gives no clear indication of the significance of the group's size for tiredness in the child, as the concept of tiredness with which it operates is composed of very disparate factors which cannot really be considered as a whole. Some of the symptoms of tiredness registered might be the results of positive experiences and activities, while others may result from negative experiences or a lack of experiences or boredom etc. The number of symptoms can thus be the same in a little group of children who have spent a time full of exciting experiences as in a large group of children who have either been thoroughly bored or completely at loggerheads with one another.

Meanwhile there are some studies from which it is impossible indirectly to derive information on the importance of the group's size for the teaching. The bigger the group, the less space there will normally be for each member of it, and the studies of the significance of the amount of space have already shown that this can have a direct influence on the children. The same is true with respect to teaching material. The more children to share them, the more conflicts and other negative situations there are in the group. But in the latter instance, of course, it is easier to iron out the differences by giving large groups more material than it is to find more room for them.

Perhaps one of the most remarkable things is the effect of a large group on the teacher. There are many studies and experiments to cast light on this question. The larger the group concerned, the greater will be the tendency towards uniformity of treatment and the smaller the tendency to give the children individual treatment. A common objection to the composition of mixed groups is then that they are too difficult to work with if they are too large.

Numerous studies have indicated that the bigger the group becomes, the more the teacher is forced to formalise her work in order to keep things in check. It has even been possible to demonstrate that the same teacher behaves in a much more authoritarian manner when faced with a larger group. The voice is raised, and more orders are given, while questions are either not heard or simply ignored. The teacher spends more time on keeping control and less on stimulating, or else the reverse occurs and she gives up, at which the group life ends in chaos and conflict.

The number of children per teacher

In a way the optimal size of a group is the answer to the question of what is the optimal number of children per teacher. However, there is also the possibility of putting two or more teachers in charge of a larger group, a method to which a good deal of attention is being given at the moment. It can, however, be assumed that the system will lead to certain problems of identification for the children, especially if the two teachers are not given clearly defined roles. Meanwhile, no studies of this problem have yet been made. On the other hand the harmful effect of too many changes of staff in day nurseries has already been pointed out.

Bertoye and Dumorand (1957) studied 100 day nursery children and found plenty of evidence that constant changes of staff had a harmful effect on the children. The monthly changeover of students caused a temporary standstill on the children's weight charts.

At this age it seems that it is harmful to the children to introduce a system of dividing out various functions among the adults, so that each has her own task with the child, instead of one person looking after all the child's needs. No studies of this problem have been made at nursery school age, and so it is not known whether it is more advantageous to make use of individual teachers' special gifts with a large number of children than to let one teacher look after one group in all respects, irrespective of how well she does it.

The children's age must presumably be the most important factor in deciding how many children there can be to each adult. In general terms it can be said that the older the children are, the more there can be to one adult, although a fall in the optimal number occurs when the children are aged between five and six—c.f. the studies dealing with the significance of stimulation from adults at this age. However, there are no real studies of this question.

Apart from various remarks to the effect that there must be a suitable number of teachers, there are only three studies pointing directly to the unfortunate effect of too small a staff: Simonsen (1947) concluded that the principal reason for a poorer development in children from residential homes was to be found in a milieu with too little stimulation and where there was too small a staff for it to be possible to give the children individual attention. Jersild and Markey (1935), in their comprehensive study of the cause of conflict, found them to be much more common in nursery schools with too few teachers as distinct from nursery schools with more teachers. Sandels et al. (1967) certainly found no relationship between the incidence of symptoms of tiredness and the number of children per adult, but as has already been remarked, this result is of dubious validity. Roudinesco and Appell (1950) found that by increasing the staff so as to be able to give the children more personal attention, it was possible to register progress in social adjustment six months later.

The duration of attendance at nursery school

The question of the optimal duration of attendance at nursery school has not been answered in any study, although some consider certain aspects of the problem. It is obvious that a child must have attended nursery school for a certain period of time if there is to be any effect from it; some of the studies already reviewed which have been unable to discover any effects of nursery school attendance, can in their turn be criticised for having studied children who had spent too short a time attending, either per day or altogether.

Wellmann and Pegram (1944), commenting on Skeels' work on the significance of nursery school for children from residential homes (Skeels et al., 1938), point out that every bit of intellectual progress in these children depended on the extent and regularity of their attendance at nursery school.

Some of the studies of the effect of nursery school attendance on the development of intelligence (e.g. Borum and Livson, 1965) do, however, find that there is no connection between the duration of nursery school attendance and increase in intelligence.

On the other hand there are also studies, such as Sandels (1964) and Erasmie (1964 a and b), demonstrating that retardation can be caused by too protracted a period spent attending nursery school, during which the child becomes tired of going. Sandels notes that some six-year-olds, especially the more intelligent, grew tired of nursery school when they no longer could find material there which could present them with problems. So experiments are called for to try new materials and teaching methods with the aim of offering something new to this age group.

One aspect of the problem is the question of how early a child should start nursery school attendance so as to be able to benefit from it. No studies have been found which deal with this problem systematically enough, but several of those referred to have related the age at which attendance begins to the effect of nursery school.

Borum and Livson (1965) found that the earlier a start was made at nursery school, the greater was the mental development achieved. However, this result can only be true of the age group concerned, which in this case was kindergarten. In other words this study really tells more of how late the optimal development can be achieved. A couple of studies of younger children come to the opposite conclusion in other areas.

Moore (1963), comparing nursery school children who had begun before they were two years old with others who were over three on starting, found a tendency for the first group to be dependent and lacking in self-confidence, while the others showed greater independence than the control group.

Hansson et al. (1967) came to the same conclusion in their Swedish study. While nursery school children as a whole were more independent and self-confident and better adjusted to reality than children brought up at home, this was not true of children who had started nursery school before reaching the age of three.

An American study (Tyler and Whisenhunt, 1962) of two groups of different ages starting with the same teacher finds that the children who are older on starting develop more independence, while those who are younger seem to become more dependent on adults, to need protection and to seek their approval.

As has already been pointed out, studies of day nurseries do not point to similar negative effects at an even earlier age. If these apparently contradictory results are reliable, it might be that the period from two to three years of age is a particularly critical period for the transition from home to nursery school, at least as far as the development of independence is concerned (cf. Erikson, 1950 a and b).

There may be a certain danger that the independence a child achieves in relation to its parents will be replaced by a new dependence on its playmates if it is not supported in its efforts to achieve self-sufficiency. A couple of Russian studies touch on this. Volkova (1950) sees it as a specific problem for children of this age; the transition from the protective atmosphere of the home must be accompanied by the development of self-sufficiency and confidence in being able to look after itself.

Nikol'skia (1948) mentions that a three-year-old child who is only used to the home atmosphere has great difficulty in adjusting to nursery school. The pattern of behaviour which the child has developed at home influences the way in which it adjusts. The problems, it is suggested, can best be solved by careful grouping, a close knowledge of the child's background, close cooperation with the home and a fulfilling of the child's needs, all in a relaxed atmosphere in which the adjustment gradually takes place.

Some French studies believe these difficulties to be only a short transitional phenomenon. Lebovici (1964) points out that the only dangerous time is when the child starts. Once the separation has been accepted, it will no longer be painful. Lévy-Bruhl (1956) finds it quite natural that a child who has never been away from home before should show signs of nervousness at first.

An American study (Slater, 1939) of 40 beginners in a nursery school with high standards found pronounced nervous symptoms such as muscular tension, face ague, timidity or reticence. These all disappeared within the first week as the children became accustomed to the nursery school.

Then comes the question of how long the child should spend there each day or every other day. Two hours spent at nursery school every day or every other day might well provide the child with two hours of pleasant occupation, but it may well be that the period is not long enough for the child as a whole to be influenced by it. Conversely it may be thought that attendance from early morning until late in the evening will have an unfortunate influence. This will be true especially in cases when the actual nursery school programme is only intended to last between six and seven hours, while the remaining hours simply become a sort of waiting time for the few children remaining behind. A superficial comparison of the effect of half-day nursery school and full-time nursery school seems to indicate that the first of these produces predominently positive effects, while the effects of the whole time nursery school are more uncertain. There are however such great differences both in the teaching methods of half-day nursery school as opposed to full-time nursery schools and in the milieus of the two that results of this kind cannot be compared without further ado. The attempts made in some experiments to iron out differences in milieu also show that with this the differences in results also disappear.

In connection with half-day nursery schools the question also rises of whether morning or afternoon attendance is preferable. One study, Dawe and Foster (1935), looked at this question and found that children attending in the mornings showed more signs of fatigue than those attending in the afternoons. The most common symptoms were noise and restlessness. However, as no reference is made to differences in milieu, it is not easy to say whether this factor was of significance or not.

One important factor which certainly is of significance is the presence of symptoms of fatigue in the teacher, at least according to a Swedish study of the role played by nursery school teachers (Askling, 1967). This finds far more fatigue symptoms in the afternoons than in the mornings, and these tend to affect the teaching (see the section on the significance of the teacher). So if the same teacher has classes both morning and afternoon, this must be expected to have an indirect effect on the children.

In Australia (Ferguson, 1957) two groups of three to five-year-olds, with twenty-eight in each group matched in pairs with regard to background and adjustment to nursery school, were compared in order to study the difference resulting from attending every day or every other day. An attempt was made to see whether there were differences in the two groups with respect to play, social contacts, physical development and behaviour and development at home. A difference was only found in one sphere; sociometric testing and parental reports indicated differences in social contacts with their playmates, though these were not observed in the nursery school itself. The study concludes that it appears to be of little consequence whether the children attend every day or every other day, but as there were some differences in 'social interaction' in favour of the children attending every day, this appears to be a somewhat hasty conclusion. As has already been shown, social interaction is an important guide to a child's subsequent adjustment.

Finally there is the question of whether attendance at nursery school should be by the day or by the week. Only one study, undertaken in East Germany (Schmith-Kolmer, 1964), has directly touched on this question, and comes to the conclusion that weekly boarders develop far less to their advantage than the children who go home every day. Similar conclusions are drawn in some Czech studies. Studies carried out in Israeli kibbutzes have, however, reached the opposite conclusion, but it has not been possible there to drawn direct comparisons between children attending daily and weekly boarders. Faigin (1958) studied two groups of nursery school children aged between two and three years in kibbutzes and compared them with American nursery school children. The study concluded that the kibbutz children were at least as well adjusted as the control group, but there are, of course, very great differences of milieu in this study.

All in all, it is impossible on the basis of present research to say anything definite about the optimal duration of nursery school attendance, either with regard to the amount of time spent there each day or particular hours during each day, or, indeed, of the duration of nursery school attendance as a whole.

16 Teaching in Nursery Schools

The significance of the teacher in the child's development

Many general studies of the effect of nursery school emphasise the importance of the teacher. On the one hand it has been pointed out that a precondition for a positive effect resulting from nursery school attendance is the presence of the necessary teaching staff, and on the other that the personality, qualifications and attitude of the teachers is of decisive importance if a positive effect is to be achieved.

In connection with the training of nursery school teachers it is impossible to avoid committing onself to defining what such a training should entail, 'what a nursery school teacher ought to be like'. In training nursery school teachers it is not possible to avoid the problem by insisting solely on the acquisition of knowledge, as is the case in training for some other careers. Many textbooks do in fact devote attention to what a nursery school teacher ought to be like. The demands are based partly on experience and partly also on a subjective understanding of what things should be like. This leads to the very difficult question of the extent to which nursery school teaching and its aims can be given a scientific basis. If the aims of a nursery school can be expressed in precise terms, it will also be possible to define the ultimate aim of training courses, both with respect to what functions a teacher is to carry out in nursery school, and to enable the teacher to carry them out. In other words there are two questions: what personal attributes are desirable, and what professional training is desirable.

Irrespective of the answers to these questions, many studies have been made of the effect which nursery school teachers have on the children in their care. There are many emphasising that there are enormous differences between individual teachers, and also others pointing to more general differences between them resulting from the extent of their training and experience, and to some extent dependent on their age. Then there are differences from one nursery school to another in the general teaching pattern, in what might be called the psychological climate. Irrespective of general and individual differences between teachers, this climate will affect them all, and to a great extent it will be dictated by the principal.

Then comes the question of what significance these differences between teachers and climates of individual nursery schools have upon the child's development. A number of studies relate these differences to various effects on the child, sometimes of a general nature, such as positive or negative, sometimes much more specific.

Apart from these observations of differences, experiments have been carried out to discover whether a specific effect will always result from a specific form of influence. They have studied the differences between teachers, between the teaching climates of nursery schools, and between entire institutions, and it has been their aim to discover whether these differences had any effect on the child's general behaviour and adjustment, or whether they had any on specific aspects of the child's process of adjustment.

Differences between teachers

Moore (1938) studied three nursery school groups and three kindergarten groups to discover the relationship between the group and the teacher. Among other things, observations were made of the teacher's verbal communication with the children. This was classified as commands, reasoned commands, negative commands, suggestions and requests. There was no particular difference between teachers from the two types of institution, but there were differences between individual teachers. Moreover, there were variations in the behaviour of single individuals; suggestions and requests were used more in the mornings, and commands were more common in the afternoons. The children were quicker to react to suggestions than to commands.

Landreth et al. (1943) compared the contact between teachers and children in university nursery schools on the one hand and nursery schools for children from a poor social background on the other. The contacts were divided according to type, method, aim and situation. In the schools for children with a poor social background there were far fewer contacts, less than half as many as in the case of university children; on the other hand three times as many commands were given. More use was made of physical methods and physical force, and disapproval, punishments and taking away the children's rights were more common; there were fewer attempts to enlighten the children, to encourage them and to guide them than in the university nursery school. The aim of the nursery schools for children from a poor milieu was much more to persuade them to adjust to a rather inflexible routine than to develop their individuality. The teachers in these nursery schools were on the whole less well qualified

224

than those in the university nursery schools.

Wilensky (1966) carried out a study of four nursery school teachers in order to compare their performance in the following fields: the amount of information passed on; their willingness to engage with the children in answering questions and giving encouragement; their answers and guidance; and disciplinary actions. The overall relationship between the four was: 53 per cent information; 26 per cent questions aimed at engaging the children; 12 per cent answers and guidance; and 9 per cent disciplinary actions. The differences between the individual teachers were, however, very great, and they were significant on all points. The study has not yet related this to the children's behaviour.

Prescott and Harris (1964), in their extensive comparative survey of nursery schools in California, found that besides noticeable individual differences between the teachers, there were group differences between them. For instance, if they were divided up according to whether they were employed in public or private nursery schools, it emerged that those in private institutions were on the whole stricter than the others, and that on the whole they were less well trained.

Dawe et al. (1949) compared two kinds of contact between teachers and children. In the first category, the dominative, they were restrictive, aimed at directing and controlling, while in the second, the integrative, they sought to encourage and to satisfy needs. On this basis trained teachers were compared with student teachers. On the one hand differences were observed in the same person in the course of the day, corresponding to the symptoms of fatigue already referred to: the more tired the teacher was the more she resorted to orders instead of encouragement. On the other hand there were group differences between teachers and student teachers in that the latter showed less ability to encourage and satisfy needs.

Rigney (1952) compared differences in practice between experienced and inexperienced nursery school teachers. The inexperienced were more concerned with external aspects of behaviour and surroundings than with understanding either others or themselves, and they did more to satisfy physical and material needs than deeper psychological needs.

Nesbitt (1943) found that student teachers were more inclined either to go to extremes in helping a child, or to leave it alone, and they had difficulty in helping a child to solve a problem itself without providing it with the final answer. On the whole the student teachers were more integrative than dominative, and with increasing experience they became more and more integrative and less and less dominative, and made use of progressively better techniques.

A corresponding improvement in the attitudes of student teachers has been noted in an unpublished study. By means of a questionnaire on attitudes (Sjølund, 1963) a comparison was made between student teachers at the beginning and end of their training and nursery school teachers of several years' standing. The attitudes of parents and a group of psychologists were included in the study. A comparison of the five groups' replies showed that student teachers at the beginning of their course had roughly the same attitude as mothers towards discipline, but were still not as disciplinarian as the fathers. Discipline was measured as authoritarian as opposed to democratic attitudes, which on the whole corresponded to dominative and integrative behaviour. At the end of their courses, student teachers were more democratic in their methods, the most extreme in this direction being experienced nursery school teachers and psychologists.

A Swedish study (Askling, 1967) sets out to analyse the work of nursery school teachers. A comparison is made between teachers in whole day nursery school and *lekskola*. The *lekskola* teacher instructs and guides the child's activities more, and gives it more direct help with what it is doing; moreover she has to adapt her wishes to fit the child's abilities. The teacher in the whole-day nursery school, on the other hand, showed more affection for the children and was more often forced to adapt her behaviour to the situation; in other words more flexibility was called for in which consideration for the child's needs and moods was decisive. As a whole the study gives the impression that the *lekskola* teacher is more likely to adjust her demands to the child's abilities, while the whole-day nursery school teacher is more inclined to show gentleness, kindness and understanding. As the teachers in whole-day institutions look after relatively more younger children, it could be that this explains the differences between them and the *lekskola* teachers. However, grouping the teachers according to whether they were in charge of five to seven-year-olds or two to four-year-olds did not support this conclusion. A division according to the age of the teachers indicates certain differences. The younger ones are more likely to allow the children to get on with individual activities, while the older ones tend to guide them and occupy them more. The younger ones are also more inclined to teach the child to be tolerant and considerate. There is, however, no indication of whether the differences are due to training or experience.

Differences in the psychological climate of nursery schools

In the study of Californian nursery schools (Prescott, 1965; Prescott and

Harris, 1964) it was pointed out that there were enormous variations in atmosphere from one nursery school to another. In some there was a great deal of activity with very little obvious direction; in others there was a lot of directing, but still with a pleasant, cooperative atmosphere. Some institutions placed great emphasis on rules and regulations, while in others there appeared to be hardly any at all. At first an attempt was made to categorise nursery schools according to the presence or lack of emotional warmth, but it was soon discovered that irrespective of whether the climate was warm or cold there might well be differences in the manner of running the nursery school. In some there was a great deal of independence, while in others everything was controlled. At the same time it appeared as though the principal of the nursery school was ultimately responsible for these differences; certainly, the teachers and the children's backgrounds played their part, as did the actual physical surroundings, but it was first and foremost the principal who gave the nursery school its special character, and a distribution according to size showed that the smaller the nursery school, the more obvious this was. On the basis of these observations an attempt was made to divide nursery schools according to emotional climate on the basis of the principal's attitude to authority on the one hand and to emotional aspects on the other, i.e. cold or warm. On the basis of a combination of these two features the nursery schools were divided into four groups:

(1) Warm, non-authoritarian climate; here there was a fair amount of contact between children and adults, the teaching was flexible, and an attempt was made to satisfy the children's needs. 11 nursery schools were included in this category.

(2) Warm, authoritarian climate; here it was the teachers who controlled activities and guided the children in their behaviour; little was left to the child's own initiative. There were six nursery schools in this group.

(3) Cold, non-authoritarian climate; the teaching was little more than supervision; there was a certain distance between adults and children, and the programme was usually very routine. The teachers were content to provide children with materials, but did little to either stimulate or guide. There were four nursery schools in this group.

(4) Cold, authoritarian climate; it was characteristic of these institutions that there was usually a distance between adults and children, and that the programmes were very rigidly structured; it was left almost exclusively to the adults to guide the children's activities; everything was extremely orderly, and usually the nursery schools were well equipped. There were six in this category.

As an example of the differences an incident is taken when two children quarrelled over the same toy. In the warm, non-authoritarian school the teachers would allow the quarrel to take its course until she saw that the children themselves could not solve it, when she would intervene by asking questions and making suggestions, until the children found a solution. In the warm, authoritarian nursery school the teacher would be quicker to intervene and would take more initiative in solving the problem; she would remind the children that they should share things and draw their attention to the consequences of quarrelling and make it plain that adults wanted them to work and play together in harmony. In the cold, non-authoritarian nursery school the teacher would intervene before it was strictly speaking necessary, either by separating the children or removing the toy. In the cold, authoritarian climate the teacher would intervene and stop the quarrel as soon as it was noticed.

The psychological climate, judged on the basis of the attitude of the principal of the nursery school, had an obvious influence on the teachers. Those in types (3) and (4) (cold climates) expected better manners and behaviour and care of things; of these the authoritarian ones, category (4), were stricter than the non-authoritarian ones, category (3). In the non-authoritarian nursery schools the teachers did more to encourage the children to become independent, while the cold authoritarian type came lowest and the warm, authoritarian one second lowest. The teachers in the warm, authoritarian nursery schools made most use of training methods, while the others made most use of compulsion. In the non-authoritarian climates there was a difference in the use of praise, in that the warm, non-authoritarian ones made little use of it, pointing out that it interfered with the child's own ability to learn, while the teachers in the cold, non-authoritarian climates often made use of praise, as they considered that the children needed it. In the authoritarian nursery schools there was a difference in the amount of absolute obedience expected, in that the teachers in the warm, authoritarian schools did not demand such instant obedience as those in the cold authoritarian ones. There were also differences in methods of maintaining discipline in that teachers in institutions with cold atmospheres were more inclined to use punishments than those in institutions with warm atmospheres, and there was the additional difference that teachers in the cold non-authoritarian nursery schools were most inclined to isolate children as a punishment, while those in the cold authoritarian ones tended to take away their privileges.

An examination of the principals' own training indicated a connection between this and the division into warm and cold, but there was no apparent link between training and the degree of authority. Three-quarters of the principals with at least three years' training had nursery schools with a warm atmosphere, while all those with an inferior training were in charge of institutions classed as cold.

Similarly there was a link between psychological climate and the activities carried out in the institution. The nursery schools with warm non-authoritarian climates had the most varied programmes. Moreover the extent of cooperation with the parents was connected with the nursery school atmosphere. Mothers were less inclined to visit the schools with cold climates than those with a warm climate, and there were differences in what they discussed with the principals. Those in nursery schools with warm, non-authoritarian climates said that they were particularly concerned with the children's emotional adjustment, while teachers in cold, authoritarian climates said that they usually discussed the child's physical care and development.

The effect which these differences have on children's behaviour has not yet been studied.

The effect of the teacher's behaviour on the children

Murphy (1937), in his study of sympathy and conflicts among children, noted that the incidence of conflicts was greatest in a group with a stern, unfriendly teacher and least in groups with warm and understanding teachers who had a natural liking for children. In addition she discovered a correlation between the incidence of conflict and the extent of interference by the teacher. This indicates that an evaluation of individual teachers on the basis of warmth and coldness and the amount of interference might also be relevant.

Jersild and Markey (1935) studied 54 nursery school children, aged between two and four years and coming from two different nursery schools, to discover the incidence of social conflicts during play. Most of the children were observed again a year later, when they had started kindergarten. In the first of the nursery schools the teachers intervened more often than in the other, and at the same time there were more adults in the group intervening most. In the year studied there were far fewer conflicts between the children when there were plenty of teachers and where efforts were made to prevent them, but when the children were at kindergarten the following year, when teachers intervened less, the incidence of conflict was reversed. The children who had previously shown little tendency to conflict due to the presence of many teachers now caused twice as many quarrels, while the children who had been left more to their own devices in nursery school quarrelled less. Jersild concludes that teachers too often interfere in quarrels which the children can and should sort out for themselves. In the material as a whole he found that teachers had intervened in every third quarrel. In most cases they solved it to the advantage of the less aggressive of the two children, which is only a reasonable solution on the surface, as the less aggressive is not necessarily the less guilty.

Fite (1940) noted that teachers often clamped down on an aggressive child without finding out the reason for its aggressive actions. For instance, he argues, what might look like a quarrel over a toy might well only be an attempt to get even for something which has happened before.

Appel (1942) studied 232 nursery school children and collected descriptions of 641 periods of aggression. She studied both the children's motives for the quarrels and the way in which adults dealt with them. Conflicts arising from the urge to possess were the commonest in the smaller children, and were more common in underprivileged groups, but aggressive tendencies were not only dependent on social background, but also on the individual child's own experiences. The most successful technique for dealing with these episodes was to part those quarrelling and occupy them in other ways; next in efficiency came attempts to explain one child's point of view to the other, to explain rights of possession and suggest a solution; least successful was disapproval or moralising. Appel distinguished between direct and indirect methods. The direct methods were didactic and tended to produce defensive attitudes and either opposition or sulking, while the indirect methods consisted in getting the child to understand aims and feelings without personally feeling it was being attacked.

Body (1955) found what appeared to be a close connection between the forms and directions taken by children's aggressiveness and the way in which the teacher dealt with the situation, and he concluded that a closer study should be made of the composition of groups.

Jersild and Fite (1939) found that the attitude of the teacher affected children's quarrels both directly and indirectly, directly through personal contact and the technique adopted in dealing with the child, and indirectly through the organisation of the school and the arrangement of the materials used.

Dragan (1935) studying 2,000 nursery school children, found that the nursery school and the personality of the teacher, along with the child's home background were of great importance for the way in which the child developed.

Markey (1935), in his study of the development of nursery school children's imagination, found that creativity was increased if the adults took an active part in children's games so as to help them to form clear concepts in their imaginative play and to develop methods for adjusting themselves socially and emotionally to other members of the group.

Reichenberg-Hackett (1962, 1964), who studied the significance of the nursery school milieu for children's potential creativity, found in his study that the nursery school milieu varied greatly in teaching practice and the teachers' attitudes. They used routine actions and activities to pass on and emphasise the attitudes and values which they themselves represented. The atmosphere of the nursery school group, he found, was mainly decided by the teacher in charge of the group. An evaluation of children's creativity based on their drawings indicated that it was more pronounced where the teaching methods were not too restrictive. The children were exposed to very varied experiences, not all of which were likely to further a healthy and happy development. The study, one of the most recent and comprehensive of its kind, stresses the need for further investigation of the subject.

Bendz-Sandell (1964), in his study of symptoms of fatigue in children, found that the signs were most apparent in the morning before nine o'clock and late in the afternoon, but that they depended mainly on what was going on; the standard of teaching was decisive. The situation is presumably that at the beginning and end of the day there is less of interest to keep them alert. Despite the reservations already expressed due to the many various causes of symptoms of fatigue, it is interesting to compare this study with that of Moore (1938), which demonstrates that in the mornings the teacher is more inclined to explain or treat a subject in depth, while in the afternoons she is more likely to give orders and use more direct methods, which presumably are symptoms of fatigue in the teacher herself.

Dawe (1934 a) studied verbal contacts between teachers and children in nursery schools in three different situations: (1) when the children came up to show what they had been doing; (2) when they came up for help; and (3) when they came up to complain of others. The teachers' reactions were categorised as commentary or criticism, approval, specific praise, instruction, direct help or mechanical agreement. The study confirmed the connection between the use of the various methods and the effect they had in improving the children's behaviour. There were certain differences between the sexes.

It is apparent from general studies that the extent to which the teacher intervenes in life in the nursery school is of significance, as are the direct or indirect methods which she uses and the warm or cold feelings to which she gives expression. Attempts have been made to produce an acceptable scale for measuring these forms of behaviour, and so far the most successful seems to be H. H. Anderson's division into dominative and integrative behaviour (Anderson, 1937 a; 1937 b; 1939 a; 1939 b; 1945). Dominative behaviour includes attempts to force one's own wishes, methods and aims upon others without taking the other person's wishes etc. into consideration. Integrative behaviour consists of taking the other person's wishes and aims into serious consideration in working out common aims or solutions. In general terms integrative behaviour is a democratic way of working with others, and dominative behaviour an autocratic method. Anderson's extensive studies started with nursery school children's behaviour towards each other, as is reported in the papers from 1937, but it soon became obvious that the question of the extent to which a child behaved in an integrative or dominative manner depended to some extent on the teacher's manner. This connection is the subject of the papers from 1939. Anderson indentified 26 categories into which the teacher's influence on the child could be divided. He distinguished between teachers on the basis of the relative incidence of integrative contacts (in which they showed sympathy or encouraged) and dominative contacts (expressing disapproval or authoritarian attitudes) between them and the children. The dominative behaviour of teachers is characterised by intransigence and rigidity, by unwillingness and inability to understand and act as others would like or as they judge best, an inability to see the inevitability of individual differences. Integrative behaviour is characterised by the opposite: the ability to cooperate, to change one's plans on being confronted with new views and situations and to put one's own wishes aside for the sake of the general good of the group. Differences in the children's behaviour corresponding to this could be traced (Brewer and Anderson, 1940). It was demonstrated that children whose teacher behaved in an integrative manner were less likely to be disturbed or badly adjusted in their own behaviour, and there was a significantly higher frequency of spontaneous, cooperative and independent behaviour. Dominative behaviour on the part of the teacher appeared to have the opposite effect.

The dominative behaviour of the teacher becomes apparent whether a given form of activity is started by the child itself or by the teacher. Between teachers' dominative behaviour during activities which they themselves had set in motion and dominative behaviour in activities started by the child there was a correlation of 0.57, which indicates that the children who were set going in a dominative manner by the teacher were also treated in a dominative manner when they themselves turned to her.

Moreover it was shown that the children who themselves had been dominative were very seldom treated integratively by their teachers, from which the author concluded that it was difficult for the teacher to break out of the vicious circle of dominative behaviour on the part of the teacher and resistance on the part of the child.

Against the background of these studies Anderson established the theory of circular effect, arguing that dominative behaviour produces resistance, that this resistance provokes more dominative behaviour, which in turn gives rise to more resistance, and so on. This is a psychological parallel to the physical phenomenon that pressure produces counter-pressure. The teacher's problem is to break the circle. Conversely, integrative behaviour in the teacher helps to produce integrative behaviour in the child both in its reactions to the teacher and its attitude to other children.

Basing himself on this theory, Anderson has since studied various quite specific cases, and in the 1945 paper there is a section on the incidence of dominative behaviour emanating from teachers themselves. Two contacts out of three behaved in a dominative manner; there was a greater tendency to be dominative towards boys, and the incidence of dominative behaviour was greater in the afternoons than in the mornings (cf. what has already been said about symptoms of fatigue). The teachers were inclined to be more dominative in their behaviour when children gave them cause, instead of compensating for it. When the teacher was addressing herself to groups instead of individual children the tendency towards dominative behaviour was even more pronounced (which has an even greater effect, as it directly affects the climate of the group).

Whether the concepts of dominative and integrative behaviour are sufficient to describe teachers' approaches is not certain, despite the close relationship (already demonstrated) between this and the children's behaviour. It may well be that the dimensions of authority and warmth in the Californian studies (Prescott, 1964, 1965) are more varied and fruitful than a single dimension.

The effect of nursery school's psychological climate on the child's development

Apart from the Californian studies mentioned earlier (Prescott, 1964, 1965), in which a comprehensive survey seeks to relate the psychological climate of nursery school to the child's development, there are few studies of this sort.

Henry and Sharpe (1947) compared the behaviour of children from two different nursery school milieus. One was directly connected with a school, which gave rise to the placing of numerous restrictions on the children's activities, together with a rigid programme without much play, but with a great deal of guidance and organising on the part of the adults. The other nursery school was connected with a university. Here the teaching was principally aimed at encouraging the children's spontaneous social activities. In the first of the two the children showed less social interaction of any kind, and when they were invited to join in a game organised for experimental purposes there were many who felt their security threatened and refused to participate.

Faigin (1958) studied the relationship between the psychological climate of two kibbutz nursery schools and its effect on three groups of children aged between two and three years in the two institutions. Systematic observations both of the individual children and of their group activities were carried out for a period of six months. One of the kibbutzes allowed the children a great deal of freedom, while the other was much more rigid in its teaching methods. Various differences in effect were discernible according to the children's ages. In the nursery school with the most rigid programme the younger children were more dependent, but they also developed more quickly in some fields, for instance linguistically. These differences were evened out among the older children. There, where neither group was more dependent than the other, there was the difference that the children from the school with the liberal programme were instrumentally independent (they only sought help when they needed it), while those in the stricter one were more independent emotionally.

Ziv (1967), in a French study, compared the development of 180 children from six different institutions, the psychological climates of which were divided into three types: authoritarian, democratic and *laissez faire*, corresponding to the categorisation given by Lewin et al., to which reference will be made later. There were two institutions of each type. In this very thorough and extensive study a close connection was found between the children's behaviour and the climate of the institution they were attending. The democratic climate allowed them to develop best. The authoritarian climate led to an inhibited development, while the *laissez faire* climate led to restlessness and insecurity. The study concludes that the climate is largely decided by the principal of the institution, but also to some extent by the teacher in charge of each group. It is of decisive importance for the teacher whether her attitude is centred on the children or not.

Another French study (Lézine and Spionek, 1958) of the climate in day nurseries indicated the importance of checking it against the home atmosphere. To begin with, the study demonstrates that the climate in the day nursery depends on the principal and her ideas on teaching. The various climates can be described as anarchistic, rigorous, anarchistic-rigorous and liberal-active, which corresponds more or less to the categories in Ziv's study, except that here a fourth category is added in which the climate alternates between the anarchistic and the rigorous, i.e. an attitude alternating between *laissez faire* and authoritarian. The study notes that these climates appear to produce different results in the home and in the day nursery, and that much depends on whether the climates in the home and institution are similar or in contrast to each other.

The theoretical foundation for the idea of psychological climate was laid in the research centre for group dynamics at Michigan University (Lewin et al., 1939). Here a series of ambitious experiments was conducted to study the effect which the teaching staff had on the climate of individual groups, through which the members were influenced. These experiments were carried out with groups of 11-year-old boys taking part in leisure club activities, building various things, including model aeroplanes, which they were to be allowed to keep. The groups were composed so as not to differ from each other in age, intelligence or social background. The groups were under the leadership of Lewin's colleagues who in turn behaved in the manner of the various leadership roles: the autocratic, democratic and *laissez faire*. This resulted in the partial removal of personal differences, so that they were no longer statistically significant. Thus each group experienced each type of leadership in turn. The democratic groups reached a common decision on what to do. The authoritarian groups were told to do the same things as the first group chose. In the *laissez faire* groups the same potential kinds of occupation were available as in the groups under democratic leadership.

The leaders behaved in the following manner: the autocratic leader was to lead the group on the basis of power; he had to dominate and decide everything; all activities were directed step by step without any explanation as to why, and so the group was given no insight into the leader's plans; it was he alone who was responsible for carrying out the work, and it was up to him to maintain a certain distance between the group and himself. He maintained order in a friendly but dictatorial manner.

The democratic leader was to act in a group orientated manner and lead the group to common decisions by means of discussion. All tasks were viewed as efforts leading towards a common goal of which all the members of the group were to be aware. The leader sought to achieve independent cooperation on the part of the members, and to this end the group was to organise itself and discover the best way of working. The leader tried to become as one of the group, without taking too active a part in carrying out the work. He was factual and objective in his criticism.

The *laissez faire* leader was to lead in a passive manner. He was to be friendly, like the other leaders, but he was to keep outside the group activities. There was complete freedom both for the group and for the individuals in it. The leader saw to it that the necessary materials were available and gave information when asked, but he did not take part in group discussions or work and did nothing to organise or stimulate the group with regard to the project. Nor did he comment on the work or criticise it in any way.

During each of the experiments four observers were placed behind glass screens through which they could see without being seen. They undertook respectively a continuous assessment of the group's teamwork, a description of the group structure at minute intervals, a continuous description registering the effect of actions by dominant members of the group, and a continuous shorthand record of all conversation and use of language. The four sets of data were divided into minutes so that they could be synchronised and thereby reproduce a continuous picture of the group's life as a whole.

During the course of the experiment observations for control purposes were made of the relationship between the various forms of behaviour exhibited by the leaders. About 60 per cent of the authoritarian leader's actions consisted of orders, interruptions and negative criticism, while behaviour of this kind only accounted for some 5 per cent of the other leaders' actions. The main difference between these two, the democratic and *laissez faire*, was that the former made more suggestions and did more to stimulate thought, while the latter spent more time giving information when asked, which was taken as an expression of irresoluteness in the group arising from the *laissez faire* type of leadership.

The effects of the various kinds of leadership were measured both in the achievements and the group teamwork. The achievements were lowest under the passive leadership, as there was no one to organise and keep things going. As a result of the slow progress there was a good deal of dissatisfaction, and there were numerous quarrels resulting from the lack of organisation. The difference between the democratic and authoritarian groups was that the latter worked the quickest, while the former achieved the highest standard. However, the psychological climate was completely different under these two kinds of leadership. Under the democratic leader the climate was characterised by friendliness, content and quiet. Cooperation and helpfulness towards each other were the dominant attitudes. Under the authoritarian leader two different climates were produced: one was characterised by open bursts of aggressiveness and expressions of rebelliousness and criticism, of quarrels and aggressive acts towards each other; the other was characterised by apathy and inhibited aggressiveness, indifference and suppressed discontent.

The precise form of aggression resulting from authoritarian leadership depends, according to this study, on the psychological field: (1) the actual kinds of tension between the members of the group; (2) restrictions in freedom of action; (3) rigidity of the group structure (for instance, a firmly established 'pecking order'); (4) the reaction pattern on the basis of the cultural background, in which the home background and attitude of the parents was of prime importance in determining how the children reacted to the authoritarian kind of leadership.

In both the authoritarian climates the members were clearly more dependent on the leader than in the two other climates. There was the greatest amount of dissatisfaction with the leader in the aggressive-authoritarian climate, while the greatest satisfaction with the leader was expressed by the group with the democratic climate. By registering the incidence of words such as 'we' and 'our' as opposed to 'I' and 'my' under the various forms of leadership it was possible to discover that the 'we' feeling was strongest in the democratic group and the 'I' feeling in the authoritarian group.

During the course of the experiments various 'test episodes' were contrived to see the effect of them on the different climates: (1) the leader arrived late; (2) the leader was called out to an imaginary telephone call; (3) a stranger, pretending to be an electrician about to attend to something in the room, came in while the leader was absent and started criticising the work both of individuals and of the group as a whole in an amateurish fashion.

Characteristic differences were noted in the groups' reactions to the provocative and negative criticism of this 'electrician'. The apathetic-authoritarian group put up with it and accepted his charges. The aggressive-authoritarian reacted to it by directing fresh charges at another group present. Thus frustration was canalised into an aggressive act aimed at another group. The other two groups put up with the electrician's criticisms, but the democratic group was more united in rejecting the real source of frustration, the electrician, and not reacting via aggressive attitudes towards 'the others'.

There were also characteristic differences in what happened in the various groups during the leaders' absence. When the authoritarian leaders left the room, the rate of work diminished noticeably when compared

237

with the group under democratic leadership, which shows that a group accustomed to working passively and always dependent on guidance grinds to a halt when the guidance is taken away from them. And when the pressure under which they normally labour is taken away, they abreact in a different manner. Under the group-orientated leadership the group is accustomed to independent activity and can continue during the leader's absence. As it does not work under pressure, there is no call to abreact. The reactions in the group with the *laissez faire* leadership were very striking indeed. Once the leader had gone the group's activity increased, as the conditions for a natural leader to emerge and begin to organise the group's activities were then created.

There were also characteristic differences in behaviour when the group changed from one form of leadership to another. If it changed from an authoritarian leader to a democratic one, there was a good deal of abreacting at first in the form of tomfoolery, a sign that there had been suppressed group tensions; this gradually diminished as more sessions were held in a freer atmosphere. If the change was from authoritarian to *laissez faire* leadership the tomfoolery was wilder and lasted longer.

This laboratory experiment was important because it demonstrated the relationship between many of the phenomena which teachers had noted in practice. Subsequently, as evolves from Ziv's study (1967), it is possible to observe a similar relationship between the form of leadership given by teachers in daycare institutions and the children's everyday behaviour.

Thompson (1944) carried out an experiment to test the significance of the psychological climate on two groups of nursery school children aged four years. The two groups were similar in the main. The experiment was carried out in the natural surroundings of the nursery school and was thus not a laboratory experiment. The groups were matched with regard to the social and financial status of the parents, the intelligence and mental age of the children and the children's social and emotional development.

Moreover the two groups were from the start alike in the personal characteristics upon which it was hoped to study the effect of the psychological climate:

(1) Constructiveness in a situation which might get out of hand. This was measured by presenting the child with a very difficult test situation and observing it for fifteen minutes to discover the incidence of the following forms of behaviour: attempts to solve the problem alone, no obvious attempt, asking someone else to do it, asking for help, giving up, destructive behaviour, rationalisation and varying kinds of emotional reaction.

238

(2)   Self-assertion, which was measured by putting the children in pairs into rooms with just a few toys. Each child was observed for five periods of five minutes, each time in the company of a different child. The measure of self assertion was the number of times a child tried to get a toy from its playmate, tried to order the other one about or criticise it, and the number of times it succeeded in ordering it about or altering the pattern of its behaviour or defending its own toys.

(3)   Social participation in group games, measured by a sort of sociometric observation.

(4)   The amount of leadership behaviour reckoned on the basis of the play situations in which the social behaviour was observed.

(5)   The incidence of nervous habits, noted according to an observation chart.

The two nursery school groups were to act in different group atmospheres. In group (A) the teachers were instructed to use an impersonal and disinterested attitude and only give information and help when directly asked for it by the child; they were to let the child work out and carry out its own ideas and only to interfere if there was real danger. In group (B) the teachers were instructed to help the child in its relations with other children and its use of toys as far as was appropriate for the child's social and emotional needs. The teacher should try to be a warm friend, to guide and take an active part in the child's play as an interested and helpful adult.

In both cases the teachers were to pay attention to the children and ensure their physical welfare. The fundamental differences between the two climates was that in (B) the teacher was to develop a particularly warm friendship with each child, while this was to be avoided in (A). In group (B) the teacher was to stimulate the child's activities by arranging its playthings in an appropriate manner and by giving help and information where appropriate or necessary when the child set about independent activities. In group (A) the extent of the teacher's participation in the children's games was to depend on how much the child asked for help or information.

In order to ensure that the external factors for the two groups were as nearly identical as possible, with the exception of the climates described, the following was done: the principal teachers were exchanged between the two groups and took it in turns to play both parts, so as to outweigh personal differences; the toys were identical for both groups; and the amount of time spent was the same for both groups.

By means of consultation and observation of the teachers' manner of behaving it was ensured that the experimental conditions conformed to the plan. At the end of the experiment the children were again tested as at the beginning. A number of significant differences was now discernible. In group (B) the children were more constructive when faced with difficulties than those in group (A); they were also better able to assert themselves, more sociable and more able to show leadership abilities. Conversely group (A) was more destructive. In both groups the children were more inclined to keep others out, reject them or ignore them; more inclined to hit or push, to threaten and to bully each other. On the other hand there was no difference between the groups with regard to nervous symptoms, intellectual development, the number of conflicts caused by possessiveness or the desire to grab as many toys as possible. This has to be seen against the fact that both groups were identically equipped and that the teachers in both groups were to look after the children when necessary.

The connection between the psychological climate created in the group by the teacher and the children's behaviour is thus proven both by observations in institutions, by teaching experiments and by laboratory experiments. Thus it is possible by means of a given form of behaviour on the part of the teacher to produce a specific form of behaviour on the part of the child. This does not mean that any teacher is capable of producing any form of behaviour in any one child. Personal characteristics and backgrounds play far too great a part for this, as will be seen in a later section.

17 Laboratory Studies of Teacher Effect

Dependence or independence

A study from the 1930s which has already been discussed indicated that although nursery school children's independence increased as they grew older, so did certain forms of dependence. A closer study showed that the increase in independence concerned a number of routine actions—'I can do it myself'—while the increasing dependence was at a more personal, emotional level. A subsequent study (from the 1940s) introduced a theoretical distinction between instrumental dependence and emotional dependence, in which the idea was that instrumental dependence meant that the children asked for help when in practical need of it, while the emotional dependence concerned situations in which the children turned to the adult for help, not for the sake of help, but for the sake of contact. Studies show clearly that the teacher's behaviour is very important to this sphere, both because it can made the child more independent and because it can modify such behaviour on the part of the child as has been brought about by background factors.

Hartup (1958) carried out an experiment to discover the extent to which the teacher's looking after the child led to the child's becoming dependent on her. The first stage of the experiment was to discover the degree of independence in the children beforehand, and this was done by means of observations in the nursery of how far the individual children: (1) sought praise and recognition; (2) sought unnecessary help; (3) sought necessary help; (4) sought physical contact; (5) sought to remain near the teacher; (6) sought positive attention; (7) sought negative attention. In addition to this, the children were assessed by their teachers, and finally by the leader of the experiment himself before the experiment began. The three modes of assessment produced results which agreed closely.

Then two groups were formed for the sake of the experiment, completely matched with regard to sex, age and degree of dependence. The children were all aged between four and five and a half years. To begin with the children in both groups played with the leaders of the experiment (both were nursery school teachers), who paid a great deal of obvious attention to the children. Then came a period during which one group again played with the leader in just the same way, while the other group received no attention at all. Then came the third period in the experiment, when the results were to be determined. Under play conditions the two groups were given various tasks to perform.

The result as a whole showed an increased degree of dependence in the experimental group, which was seen in their stronger desire to carry out the tasks the teacher gave them. A sub-division of the group according to sex showed that by and large the girls had become more dependent than the boys, whose degree of dependence had not increased. A fresh division, splitting the boys into those who had been very dependent beforehand and those who had not, however, brought two different trends to light. The particularly dependent boys, who were assumed to be particularly concerned with their relationship with adults, were even more dependent, while those who had been less dependent also turned out to be less dependent after the experiment.

In a later study (Hartup and Keller, 1960) attention was turned to the question of how far dependence in nursery school children might affect their inclination to look after other children, to protect them, sympathise with them, console them, praise them, help them and show affection to them. The categories of dependence were those previously described. The study showed that 'looking after' others by nursery school children was positively related to their own need for physical help and affection on the part of the adult and negatively to the kind of dependence which consisted in merely staying fairly close to the adult.

Hartup's forms of dependence thus seem to show certain similarities with the division into instrumental and emotional dependence to which reference was made earlier.

A later study (Hartup and Himeno, 1960) looked at the effect on a child's social behaviour when the adult stopped 'looking after' the child and paying attention to it. 48 nursery school children took part in this experiment. It showed that this led to frustration on the part of the child, which in some cases was accompanied by anger and aggressive acts and in others by increased efforts to establish contact with the teacher. The difference between boys and girls was that boys became more aggressive while girls made increased efforts to establish contact.

A number of studies by Gewirtz (1954, 1956), Gewirtz and Baer (1958 a, 1958 b) and Gewirtz, Baer and Roth (1958) have shown that children are more dependent on adults and more inclined to ask for attention and approval from their teacher if they have previously had limited or insufficient contact with an adult, due either to social isolation or intermittent 'looking after'. At nursery school age experiments have shown that dependence is expressed through an increased desire to ensure the approval of the adult; in day nurseries it is connected with the entire problem of deprivation.

Gewirtz' experiments have a direct significance for the question of the right teacher-child ratio, as one aspect touched on in the experiments was the importance of the teacher's presence and readiness to help. If the teacher's presence was limited there appeared to be more actions by the children indicative of dependence; the number of such actions was as great as in children who had previously been deprived.

Arsenian (1943) demonstrated the significance of the presence of an adult with a close personal relationship to the child for the child's ability to adjust to situations likely to give it a sense of insecurity. The children were aged between one and two-and-a-half years. The sudden disappearance of the adult in such a situation usually resulted in a high degree of insecurity which was reflected in obvious signs of insufficient adjustments such as crying, regression or withdrawal, while the continued presence of the adult enabled the child to examine its surroundings and work constructively with them. If, once the child was familiar with the new surroundings, the adult withdrew, there were no such signs of anxiety. The return of the adult after a period of isolation (and the disturbances arising from it) only removed the anxieties of the children whose insecurity has not been too extreme. The children who had been insecure from the start continued to show symptoms of increased insecurity even after the return of the adult.

This perhaps explains the apparent contradiction between Hartup's experiment (1958), which indicated that children who had been 'looked after' to a great extent by adults were less good at carrying out tasks, and a similar experiment carried out by Rosenblith (1959). She compared the significance which the presence of an adult and various degrees of attention by the adult had for a nursery school group's ability to carry out tasks. The experiment was similar to Hartup's, though in this case the children were not matched for their degree of dependence; they were, however, matched for their ability to carry out tasks. After the introductory phases the experiment entailed the two groups' carrying out a task on the one hand alone and on the other with an adult as a model who sometimes 'looked after' the children as a friendly adult who was interested in their play, and sometimes showed no interest in them at all. As a whole the groups who had an adult present carried out their tasks better than the others. Moreover, in the group where an adult was present it was seen that when she paid attention to the children they carried out their tasks better.

It looks as though the variable 'looking after' cannot simply be taken as a question of either-or, but rather as one of degree. It is possible to pay too much and too little attention to the children.

Bandura and Huston (1961) related the child's dependence on the adult to the way in which it learned relevant and irrelevant methods of working at a task and to the incidence of good and bad behaviour. In this experiment two nursery school groups took part; there were 20 children in each group, matched for sex and degree of dependence; the same teacher was in charge of both groups. In the first group, in which the teacher looked after the children, she sat on the floor with the child, promptly answered its requests for help and attention and by various means created a warm and emotionally satisfying degree of cooperation. In the other group the teacher placed the child in the experimental room and told it to play with the things it found there. Then she started to work at a desk in the corner of the room and avoided any sort of contact with the child during this period. The children had various tasks to carry out. In some variations of the experiment the adult undertook different actions, some of which were relevant, some irrelevant to the task in question. In other variations a doll was treated sometimes aggressively, sometimes gently.

The results indicated that the children who had been in a situation where the adult looked after them were far more inclined to copy the adult's behaviour, both where it was relevant and where it was not. There was a difference in the extent to which good and bad behaviour were copied. Aggressive behaviour was copied to the same extent whatever the situation, but non-aggressive behaviour was copied more in the situation where a warm 'looking after' relationship had been created by the grown up. According to the authors, the experiment gives striking evidence of the extent to which the behaviour of adults, both relevant and irrelevant and both good and bad, is copied by the child of nursery school age, and proves that the child is even more inclined to copy when a close relationship has been established as a result of the adult's looking after the child.

Ross (1966) studied the connection between children's dependence and the extent to which they acquired that part of the teacher's behaviour which was intentional and that part which was unintentional. In his experiment the children played post offices under the leadership of an adult whose behaviour was partly relevant and partly irrelevant to the experimental situation. The children taking part were chosen so as to represent a group of particularly dependent children and another group of children who were far less dependent. The result showed that the less dependent

244

children learned more behaviour relevant to the situation and the highly dependent ones more irrelevant behaviour. The author distinguished between 'intentional' and 'incidental' learning. The intentional learning takes place when the child copies what the teacher intends, and the incidental learning occurs when the child copies behaviour which was not intentional on the part of the teacher. The terms 'intentional' and 'unintentional' would probably have been better.

This distinction between intentional and unintentional learning corresponds to something discovered by the present author in experiments in communication, and which can be denoted as intentional and unintentional communication. This appears to be of great importance in teaching situations. If there is any conflict between intentional and unintentional communication, it will often be the latter which the child absorbs. (According to Ross's experiment, however, this happens more with children who are particularly dependent.) For instance, there is conflict between intentional and unintentional communication if a teacher gives a child an oral reprimand for something it has done, while her facial expression indicates that she thinks it was rather well done all the same. In such a case the unintentional communication is more likely to increase the child's inclination to behave in this manner than the intentional communication is likely to reduce it.

McCandles et al. (1961) studied the extent to which dependence on adults affects a child's popularity amongst the other children in nursery school. He concludes that popularity decreases as dependence increases.

Heathers (1955), distinguishing between instrumental and emotional dependence, concludes, however, that it is only the latter kind which is connected with low social status in the nursery school group.

Dependence in a child attending nursery school is presumably not nearly so much due to the teacher as due to conditions in the child's home, so the teacher's job is rather a modification of the child's dependence. A Danish study (Sjølund, 1967) took a look at the relationship between independence and dependence in nursery school children, and the parents' attitude to upbringing. The teachers of 41 different nursery school groups, basing themselves on clearly defined criteria, chose the most independent and the most dependent child in each group. Independently of this, the mothers were interviewed and asked about their attitudes towards bringing up children and about a number of social background factors. The result of the study was that, in social background factors, there was a difference between the mothers of the two groups in only one area: whether the mother went out to work or not. 50 per cent more of the mothers going out to work had children whom the teachers considered to be independent, while 50 per cent more of the mothers at home had children considered by their teachers to be dependent, a ratio which was also indicated by an earlier study (Sjølund, 1964).

The most significant difference between the mothers of the group of independent children and those whose children were more dependent was, however, their attitudes towards upbringing. The mothers of the dependent children consistently indicated a more protective or a cooler and more distant attitude than the mothers of the more independent children, attitudes which the research projects just reviewed point to as being particularly inclined to produce dependent behaviour patterns.

Aggression and conflicts

The teacher's role with regard to the incidence of conflicts between the children in the group is very complicated. The actual appearance or absence of conflicts is not in itself an indication of whether it is a well led nursery school group or not, which, it may be added, makes the value of studies based on the incidence of conflicts of just as doubtful validity as those working out the incidence of symptoms of fatigue. The absence of conflicts might mean that no conflicts arise, or that conflicts arising are solved, or that conflicts do arise but are suppressed. The presence of conflicts might on the other hand mean that the group is living in unfortunate conditions which produce conflict, or that it is living under conditions which allow the appearance and treatment of conflict.

Thus the teacher's actions can either create or prevent or inhibit conflict. Different studies indicate that the same is true of the mere presence of the teacher.

Bandura, Ross and Ross (1961) studied the incidence of aggression in children and its relationship to adult behaviour. The nursery school children were divided into three groups. The first group was able to observe an openly aggressive adult, the second an inhibited aggressive model, and the third group, the control group, had an adult model who showed neither of these symptoms. In the two experimental groups half of the children had an adult model of their own sex and half of the opposite sex. Then all the children were observed in new situations in which the adult was not present in order to test the incidence of imitative and non-imitative aggression. Those who had had an aggressive adult as their model, whether inhibited or open, clearly showed more signs of aggressive behaviour, open or inhibited according to the group in which they had been included, than the children in the control group. Those who had had the openly aggressive model were more inclined to be openly aggressive themselves and were in general less inhibited in their behaviour than those who had had an inhibitedly aggressive model. Those who had had an inhibited aggressive model were more inhibited than the children in the control group, and in later play situations when no adult was present it was noticed that these children sat passively without playing with the toys at their disposal for twice as long as the control group. The inhibited aggressive adult has, then, the effect on the children that not only are they more inhibited than usual, but they are also more inhibited in their play in general.

A Danish study carried out by teachers taking part in a one-year course in the Danish teachers' high school (discussed in Sjølund, 1964) compared the incidence of conflict in a group of children in a playground with that in a corresponding group of nursery school children in the same playground under the supervision of two teachers. The difference between the two groups was assessed by counting the number of serious conflict situations arising in the two groups over a period of time. The study showed that in the case of the nursery school children there were on average three major confrontations in the course of a day, while in the case of the others there were, on average, 11. At the same time the solution to the conflicts worked out by the children using the playground on their own showed a distinct tendency for the stronger child to have its way, while those between the nursery school children paid more attention to what was right and reasonable.

Jersild and Markey (1935) showed that the incidence of conflicts between children depended partly on the presence of an adult and partly on the extent to which the adult intervened. In the year relevant to the study the incidence of conflicts was much lower when the adult was quick to intervene, but the following year, when the two groups were moved to a nursery school for older children, where the teachers intervened less, it turned out that conflicts in the group with which adults had intervened now regularly increased, while those in the other group were reduced.

Roff and Roff (1940), examining children from a poorer milieu than those with which Jersild and Markeys were concerned, found a much lower incidence of conflict, which was attributed partly to the milieu and partly to the nursery school. The conclusion was that the incidence of conflict is heavily dependent on group factors in and between the groups.

Siegel and Kohn (1959) studied what happened when there was an adult present who did not intervene in a child's aggressive acts. The theory was that the child's aggression would increase if there was an adult there who did not intervene, as the child would conclude that its aggressiveness was not frowned upon, and then that inhibitions based on the fear of punishment would gradually diminish.

The experiment made use of boys from a nursery school, placed two at a time in two play situations at intervals of two days. The children were invited into the experimental room where the adult read a story for them, after which they were to be allowed to play with various toys. In the experimental situation in which the adult was to be present during the play period, she was to sit still and not interfere; she was to be friendly, receptive and interested, but not to take the initiative in conversation and only to reply briefly to anything the children said to her. The couples who were to play without the presence of an adult were told that she had to go because she had some work to do, and that they should carry on playing until she came back. Moreover she told them that she would knock on the door when she came back, so they would not be disturbed in the meantime. Throughout the entire play period the children were observed through an observation screen in the wall.

The result of the experiment confirmed the theory. Two thirds of the children who had had an adult present showed an increase in aggressiveness between the first and second occasions. The converse was found with the children who had been alone the first time: without exception they were less aggressive on the second occasion.

The result was explained as follows: the fact that the adult did not interfere with aggressive actions on the first occasion was not experienced as neutrality or non-intervention by the children, but on the contrary as approval of what they were doing, after which the tendency to act in this manner was naturally more pronounced on the next occasion. The reduction in the number of aggressive actions on the part of the children who had not had an adult present on the first occasion was explained as resulting from the fact that the children had been forced to adjust to each other and thereby evolved rules for their behaviour, which reduced the number of aggressive acts on the next occasion.

Kounin and Gump (1958) carried out an extensive study of the effect of the nursery school teacher's intervention in children's aggressiveness—not on the child directly affected, but on those who witnessed the event. The study covered groups of five or six children from 26 kindergartens. Altogether 406 situations were observed during the first few days. The observations were of the control technique adopted by the teacher, the behaviour of the children present before the episode and their behaviour after it. The children present when a teacher reprimanded or stopped another child reacted by attempting themselves to do what was demanded provided the teacher had made his objective plain. If the teacher was firm as well, the children present tried even harder. If the teacher used harsh methods the children present showed signs of disturbed behaviour, but did not attempt to do what the teacher said. If the children present had themselves done something undesirable, their reactions were stronger on the whole. It was of some importance whether the group was newly formed; as the children began to feel more at home in the nursery school and more relaxed with the teacher those present during reprimands reacted less strongly.

The effect of provoking aggressive behaviour in nursery school children emerges from a study by Sears (1961), which showed the relationship between various kinds of aggressive behaviour in children of 12 years of age and the reactions observed in the same children when they had been observed in nursery school at the age of five (Sears et al. 1957).

One theory has it that aggressive behaviour is often the result of frustration, for instance because a teacher has forbidden something which the child wishes to do. If the increased urge to be aggressive cannot be directed against the cause of the frustration, it might well be directed elsewhere, for instance towards some innocent party. Frustration can also be expressed through disorganised behaviour, so that creative and constructive abilities are not fully realised. The behaviour of a teacher who is continually forbidding and intervening will thus be particularly likely to produce frustrations which result in increased aggressiveness and reduced creativity and constructiveness in the child.

Various experiments have been carried out with nursery school children with the intention of studying frustration arising from interference by adults. The first experiment of this kind was carried out by Kurt Lewin and his colleagues (Barker, Dembo and Lewin, 1941), and the technique developed here has later been generally adopted in this kind of study. The object was to study the effects of frustration on constructive play. The experiment started with the observation of the children at free play with the material that was to be used in the study. Their behaviour was assessed on the basis of their constructiveness. The next step was to create a frustrating situation, and the third was to make a fresh observation of the children at play. The frustration was created by allowing the child into the experimental room, where the toys in question were placed. Apart from these toys, a large quantity of other very desirable toys was placed there. When the child had begun to play with the new toys, the teacher conducting the experiment took the toys the child had used previously to another part of the room and then asked the child to go over to them; a net was then placed over the highly desired new toys so that the child could see them but not get hold of them. Then the child was observed for as long a period as before, and its constructiveness was re-assessed with the same toys as it had played with earlier. The result was that the degree of constructiveness had diminished noticeably. Worked out in terms of mental age it meant a reduction of no less than eighteen months.

Wright (1942) made use of a similar technique to study the effect of frustration on a group situation. This time the children did not come to the experimental room singly, but in twos, sometimes accompanied by a good, close, reliable friend, and sometimes with a child chosen at random. All the children reacted in a less constructive manner after the frustration, but the children who were accompanied by a good friend showed less of a tendency in this direction than those accompanied by a random choice.

In a later study (Wright, 1943) using a similar experimental situation, it was discovered that when close friends found themselves in a frustrating situation their reaction was less likely to take the form of aggressiveness towards each other than it was in the case of a random pair; instead, the two friends cooperated more in expressing dislike of the adult who was the cause of their frustration.

Block and Martin (1958) studied the significance of a child's self-control in a frustrating situation of this kind. The actual experiment was similar to those already described. The child's self-control was defined and measured on the basis of how long it could wait for a delayed reward. The experimenter gave the child some sweets, one at a time, and a toy car called the 'candy car'. The child could have just as many sweets as it wanted, one at a time, but as soon as it tasted one, supplies stopped. In other words, the longer the child was able to wait, the more sweets it could collect. So the measurement used in the experiment was simply the number of sweets collected in the car.

The experiments confirmed the hypothesis that children with a low degree of self-control showed a particularly striking reduction in constructive play; nor could they control the feelings arising as a result of frustration, but reacted with constant and sometimes violent attacks on the net keeping them away from the toys. Children with a high degree of self-control, however, were able to continue their games after a frustration and to control the way in which they expressed their feelings. They played patiently and only made the occasional remark about the toys on the other side of the barrier.

Chasdi and Lawrence (1958) studied the aggression arising from previous frustration occasioned by reprimands. The child's home background was taken into consideration in this experiment as well as the experiment in the nursery school. On the basis of conversations with the mothers the children had already been divided into groups which had been severely punished and others which had only been mildly punished for aggressive acts, and who were liable to encounter many or few frustrations in the home. The experiment consisted in allowing the experimental group to play freely with dolls, but at certain predetermined times the leader of the experiment interrupted by saying, for instance, 'No, John, you know that nice boys don't do that sort of thing.' The result indicated that the children who had been punished in this way were significantly less aggressive in playing with dolls than the control group of children who had not been thus punished. In subsequent play situations, however, the children whose aggressiveness had been inhibited were much more inclined to be aggressive than the control children. The children who were used to a good deal of punishment and frustration at home showed the most extreme reactions in both situations. A reprimand reduced their aggressiveness in the short run, but it was later abreacted in other situations and with even greater force.

Yarrow (1948) studied three groups of nursery school children in free play, in situations in which they were to tell stories about the behaviour of their dolls. Each group had beforehand been in an experimental situation. The first group were given a task to perform which was too difficult for them. The second group were given a task which was very boring and which they were to go on with much longer than they wanted to. The third group was a control group and were not subjected to any sort of experimental influence. The game with dolls after the experimental situation showed clearly that both kinds of frustration, one resulting from a fiasco and the other from boredom, increased aggressive tendencies as compared with the children in the control group.

Modifying bad behaviour

As becomes apparent from the experiments just described, frustration is caused not only when the teacher prevents a child from attaining some objective, but also when the child finds itself incapable of attaining that objective. Keister (1943) tried to discover whether the teacher would be able to help a nursery school child in a frustrating situation. The experiment started with an examination of the children to discover how they reacted in situations which they found difficult. One of the tasks was to get hold of some toys in a box which was placed under another box weighing 100 pounds. The other task was to fit a jig-saw puzzle into a box so that the lid could be closed, a task which was also difficult for adults and which none of the children could manage. As a result of observations made of their behaviour during these tests the children were assessed for how soon they gave up, how often they asked for help, and for their aggressive or destructive behaviour, their inclination to explain things away, cry or grumble. Then the 12 children who had shown the greatest amount of immature and undesirable behaviour in this situation were chosen for the experiment. 12 other children were chosen to form a control group. The children in the experimental group, that is to say the weakest, were then given six weeks of special training aimed at increasing their determination when faced with a difficult task, making them less dependent on help from adults when a task is to be carried out and also less inclined to explain away a failure. This method of teaching had two aspects: to begin with there was to be gradual progress from one task to another, beginning with an easy one which the child would be quite certain to manage, and advancing gradually to more difficult ones as the child was able to cope with them. The other side of the training was the attitude of the teacher; the object was to let the child manage the tasks on its own, to encourage its independence and to praise it when it managed well. After this training period the two groups were again tested in situations with tasks similar to those used the first time round. The experimental group made a significantly better attempt to manage the task, and its reactions were more mature than had been the case in the previous test. The control group had not progressed significantly in either of these.

A field in which unfortunate behaviour can have far-reaching implications is the relationship with the group. A number of studies (discussed in Sjølund, 1965) have shown a connection between social status in the group and subsequent success at school or in a career, not least for those whose relationship with a group was insecure or who were isolated. Research has shown that a child's assurance and self-confidence are closely related to what the others in the group think of that child. Studies of what is particularly associated with a child's popularity in the group show that children whose group status is low are often dependent children lacking in self confidence. The opposite kind of behaviour towards the group, when the child forces its personality on the others through aggressive, domineering behaviour cannot unambiguously be related to social status, but from the teacher's point of view it is obviously just as unfortunate as the dependent behaviour of others. Experiments have been carried out to see to what extent it is possible for the teacher to modify both these behaviour forms.

Jack (1934) experimented to see whether it was possible by fostering special skills to improve a child's role and social status in the group. First he worked out a technique for discovering which children were not capable of asserting themselves with as much success as others in social situations. The children were set to play in twos, while they were observed to discover which were the leaders and which the followers. By combining all the children in twos it was possible to put them in order according to which were best at asserting themselves. Then the five at the bottom of the list were selected for special training. This was aimed at developing their understanding of and skill in three specific nursery school activities: making mosaics in coloured paper, doing jig-saw puzzles and telling stories. The children were given individual training in this. After several weeks of individual training of this sort they were again placed in experimental situations together with the children who had led on the previous occasion. A great change was to be seen in the behaviour of the five children after their special course of training: they were far more inclined to assert themselves, to lead and to do the deciding.

Page (1936) tested these results in practical teaching. Just under 100 children took part in the experiment; they were divided into two groups, a training group and a control group. The technique described by Jack (1934) was used. The children in the training group were trained individually in mastering certain playing skills, and this led to a considerable increase in their self confidence. The experiment clearly showed that the ability to assert themselves, carry out their own ideas and direct the behaviour of others could be built up even at the age of three years by training in skills which increased self-confidence.

However, not all the changes could be considered positive when viewed from the teacher's point of view. With this we come to the other side of the problem, the question of moderating the behaviour of children who are *too* self-assertive.

Mummery (1947) used a similar training procedure with the object of increasing self-assurance and self-confidence. After the experiment it turned out that the children had become much more self-assertive in various ways. Some of these were socially acceptable, while others were not. Together with constructive self-assertive behaviour there were also examples of selfish and hostile forms of behaviour.

Chittenden (1942) tried to discover whether domineering behaviour could be moderated and replaced by cooperation. On the basis of a situation in which the children played in pairs in a room containing only one toy, the most domineering and uncooperative children were selected to constitute the experimental group, while the others consituted the control group.

The children from the experimental group took part individually in a series of play situations in which two dolls were used. The teacher in charge of the experiment told the child a story in which the dolls quarrelled and refused to cooperate with each other. Then the child and the teachers discussed the situation and tried to find a good way of solving the problem. After a total of 11 play situations of this kind both the experimental group and the control group were put into their original situations again, i.e. in twos in a room with only one toy. The result was a clear improvement in the experimental group who were more cooperative and less inclined to domineer than they had been on the first occasion. Another control group who had also been domineering on the first occasion, but who had not been given any training, were also tested, and their behaviour was unchanged; they were as domineering as ever. The trained group was again tested a month later, and the improvement was seen to have been maintained. It was also noted that the children who were now more cooperative and less domineering showed no signs of being cowed, and they still took an active part in normal games with the other children in the school.

Boet (1943) repeated this experiment with a larger number of children from an ordinary nursery school and found that the improvement was statistically significant, which it had not been in the first experiment due to the small numbers taking part.

Various studies have been made of the different kinds of domineering behaviour found in groups of children (discussed at length in Sjølund, 1965). The different types can be divided into two categories, the 'ruler' and the 'genuine leader'. These two types are clearly distinguishable in nursery school children aged from three to four years. Their behaviour as leaders conforms entirely to Anderson's (1937, a, b) description of dominative and integrative behaviour. Both behaviour forms seek to achieve a personal objective through relations with others, but the domineering person tries to do so without consideration of the wishes and interests of others, and without considering other approaches, while the integrative child is more flexible in its approach and takes other methods into consideration as well as other people's interests, opinions and feelings. Whether a nursery school child behaves in either of these fashions or not is not merely a question of that child's own development, but of the entire group's development, as it will be remembered from Anderson's results that dominative behaviour leads to dominative behaviour in others, while integrative behaviour produces integrative behaviour.

In a Danish nursery school study (Sjølund, 1966) the most dominative and the most integrative children were selected from 50 different nursery schools (i.e. the child best fulfilling the conditions for the ruler type and the one best fulfilling conditions for the genuine leader type). Then, with the help of the questionnaire already referred to, a study was made of the parent's attitude to upbringing. There were very obvious differences in the replies from the parents of the ruler types and those of the genuine leader types. The parents of ruler types indicated attitudes which for the most part could best be described as authoritarian, though a minority were passive and weak. The parents of the children described as 'genuine leaders' were democratic in their attitudes to upbringing, and they were interested in their children's activities without being demanding.

Merei (1949) carried out an experiment showing how a nursery school can work with these problems via the group. For the first part of the nursery school year the children were observed in free and spontaneous play situations, after which those setting the tone were moved into other groups. Then the remainder continued for the rest of the year without the presence of the leaders. Finally the leaders were returned to their groups. The object of the experiment was to discover what would happen now. It emerged very clearly that only those 'leaders' who on coming back to their groups were able to live up to the traditions and the situation which had developed since their departure were in a position to assert themselves again. Those who made a new attempt at forcing their way forward found themselves rejected by the group. Only the 'genuine leader', the integrative leader, was able to come to prominence, while the 'ruler', the dominative leader, was incapable of asserting himself as he had done before.

The significance of a teacher's work with a child's personality development emerges from Brenner and Samelson's (1957) study, which indicated the personality factors in nursery school children which were connected with success or lack of success in the first form at school. Among the factors most closely associated with success in school were: personal confidence and a confident approach to others; intellectual curiosity and the ability to guide their own activities; and a pleasure in meeting up to others' expectations and doing the right thing. Among the personality factors connected with lack of success at school were: fear and anxiety of such strength as to make contact with reality difficult; disobedience and general immaturity in all fields; restlessness; aggressiveness and lack of ability to accept the rules necessary for social intercourse; and lack of ability to assert oneself or a tendency to avoid situations in which there was a risk of defeat.

Systematic use of social aspects of the teaching process

The role of the nursery school teacher is not only, as in the experiments discussed, either to be a model for the child's behaviour or to represent a set of norms. Through her acceptance or disapproval of the child's behaviour the teacher makes an active contribution to the social aspects of the teaching process. At the Chicago conference on nursery school teaching, held by the research council for social science in 1966, Donald Baer reported on experiments carried out by himself and his colleagues over a number of years (Baer, 1966) and making use of the theories on social aspects of the teaching process in planning the nursery school teacher's behaviour towards the children. This theory says, in short, that an individual's tendency to behave in a specific way will increase if it in some way is rewarded when employed in social relations, while, conversely, it will be diminished if it is leads to punitive action. Reward and punishment are not to be taken literally or concretely, but often merely as kindness or annoyance on the part of people who mean something to the child, e.g. its parents, teacher or group of playmates. However, the situation is made more complicated by the fact that some reactions in given social circumstances have a rewarding or punitive effect, as in the example cited above of the teacher giving a child a verbal reprimand while her face indicated that 'it was rather well done all the same'. Normally this latter kind of implied approval will have a more profound effect than the direct reprimand.

The same is true when different people react in different ways, some punitively, some rewardingly. For instance, a situation giving rise to a reprimand on the part of the teacher, but approval on the part of the group in general, might as a whole be taken as a rewarding situation, after which the tendency to repeat the action will be strengthened.

Baer (1966) carried out a series of experiments making use of these principles and aiming either at encouraging some desirable form of behaviour or discouraging undesirable forms by letting the nursery school teacher encourage the desirable form and ignore the undesirable ones. The experiments were fitted into the daily life of the nursery school. As they might have significance for future studies, the technique used must be described here in brief.

The first step was to notice some peculiarity of behaviour in the child and to observe the social consequences it produced in the teacher; usually it was either some form of behaviour which was undesirable and should be discouraged, or a form which was of value but not sufficiently well developed. The idea of the experiment was not merely to carry out a piece of theoretical research, but at the same time to do it in a field in which the child taking part in the experiment could benefit. The first stage continued until the observations provided a solid basis for understanding the child's behaviour and the teacher's reaction to it. Usually it was found that undesirable behaviour on the part of the child produced an attentive reaction from the teacher, while desirable behaviour normally did not. Since the attentive reaction easily strengthens the tendency, the child experiencing attention as a reward, the opposite is likely to weaken the tendency, the child experiencing an absence of reaction as a punishment, discouraging it from acting in this way. It will thus be seen that the usual practice of teachers militates against their real aims.

The next stage began with the teacher changing her manner of reacting to the child's behaviour. Where she had previously noticed undesirable behaviour, she now completely ignored it. She did not punish in the normal sense of the word, and neither did she show the child that its behaviour upset her; she merely ignored this special kind of behaviour on the part of the child. If she was in contact with the child when it acted in this way, she immediately found something else to occupy her attention. However, if she had previously been inclined to overlook some example of particularly good behaviour, she now made a point of seizing every opportunity to draw attention to it and thereby to strengthen this behaviour pattern. Assistants and colleagues present were as far as possible to help her in this. It was important that none of the adults present reacted in the opposite manner. This stage continued until the child began to improve (or until it became obvious that there was something which simply could not be changed, such as behaviour occasioned by the home background). Baer reported, however, that it was extremely rare for no result to be achieved.

The third stage consisted in the teacher's reverting to her original way of reacting; this continued until the child also reverted to its original behaviour. The object of this was not merely the usual experimental procedure, but also to help the teacher to understand the relationship existing between her behaviour and the child's reaction to it, an insight which was intended to have a strong and permanent effect in the fourth stage.

The fourth stage consisted in re-creating the situation in which the teacher selectively drew attention to good behaviour and consistently ignored bad. The problem was now to get the child to continue with its desirable behaviour without the help of the teacher, as she could not in practice devote all her efforts to a single child.

The fifth stage then took the form of a gradual change from a reward for every example of good behaviour to only an occasional reward. This had to be done by degrees, e.g. by only commenting on certain reactions: at first, for instance, it was every fourth time, but the numbers of examples overlooked grew gradually. If the child reverted to undesirable behaviour, it was possible to change the technique to a reward every second time, then every third time, and so on, until it could be seen that the desired behaviour form was maintained, and that the teacher only needed to encourage desirable behaviour to the extent to which she normally did for other children.

A number of experiments of this sort have already been carried out, and are described in professional journals. The first study (Harris et al., 1964) concerned a three-year-old girl who almost always crawled instead of walking. At first the teacher thought it was a form of regression, as the girl had recently been presented with a baby sister. So she showed her a good deal of sympathy, especially when she was crawling. However, as will be obvious from what has just been said, this merely reinforced the child's tendency to behave in this way. Next, the teacher was instructed to ignore her each time she crawled, and to show her a lot of attention whenever she got up and walked. Within a week the child had stopped crawling. The third stage, in which the original procedure was re-adopted, showed that it was only two days before the child was crawling again. In the third stage it took four days to re-establish the situation in which the child walked instead of crawled, at which the fifth stage was slowly introduced. Within a few weeks the teachers were able to leave this problem completely, as the reinforcement process had now been taken over by the group in which the child played.

The next experiment (Hart et al., 1964) concerned a four-year-old boy who reacted to mild frustrations by crying violently. On average there were eight such episodes every morning. In the second stage it took ten days to bring this down to, practically speaking, no episodes; this was done by the teacher's ignoring bouts of crying and showing interest in all the child's questions and remarks and all its efforts to manage on its own when it was in a frustrating situation. When, in the third stage, the teachers returned to their original way of dealing with the child, it only took three days for it to return to its former state. In the fourth stage the teachers returned to the experimental method, and this time it only took three days for them to weaken the tendency to weep and to reinforce the tendency for the child to manage on its own. In the fifth stage it was easy to maintain this behaviour, and it was soon possible for the teachers to relax their efforts.

Allen et al. (1964) used a similar method to help a four-year-old girl to fit into a group from which she was being excluded. The child was inclined to talk only to adults and to ignore her playmates. She knew a great deal about nature, which she was fond of demonstrating to the teacher. In the second stage the teacher ignored all attempts to attract attention, but praised the child every time she tried to establish contact with her play-mates. Within six days the frequency of her contacts with the other children rose from what had been 15 per cent of the time to 60 per cent. The next stages followed the pattern seen before, and the experiment resulted in the child's being completely absorbed into the group, speaking to the others on an equal footing and no more like an adult than usual. Subsequent observations showed that the child continued in the group after this without the teacher needing to take any special notice of it.

Foxwell et al. (1966) carried out a similar experiment with a child who was even more withdrawn and who did not have contact with adults either. The experiment meant not merely modifying the child's social activity, but creating it, which took considerably more time, but otherwise followed a similar pattern to that seen in the other experiments described, and with a similar positive result.

Hart et al. (1966) carried out an experiment in which the reinforcement process was not aimed at a child's social behaviour as a whole, but at a quite specific aspect. The child in the experiment was a five-year-old girl whose social behaviour was extremely unfortunate and usually resulted in her being rejected by children and adults alike. As a result of this her contacts with others, although many in number, were short in duration. Although at the beginning of the experiment she was in the company of the other children for about 50 per cent of the time, her cooperation with them was less than 5 per cent, which is very little for a five-year-old. The teachers were occupied with her for about 10 per cent of the time. The object of the experiment was to increase her cooperation with the other children. Before the experiment a normal training method was tried: a teacher stayed near the girl for a third of the time, talked to her, worked with her, observed her, gave her toys and materials and was friendly and encouraging. As a result of this the other children took an interest and made much greater efforts to establish contact, but despite these changes, the actual amount of time during which she cooperated with them was still down around 5 per cent. Then the experimental procedure was adopted: the teacher only showed the child interest and approval when she was cooperating with the others, and ignored all other forms of behaviour. Within 12 days the amount of time during which she cooperated with the other children had grown to 40 per cent, or eight times as much as before. After the third phase with the reversion to the old procedure it only took four days in stage four to re-create the cooperation between the girl and the group, and this result was maintained in the fifth phase, during which the reinforcement process by means of experimental attention stopped.

Johnston et al. (1965) demonstrated in the instance of a boy outside

259

the group that by increasing a child's skills in some respect which is attractive to the other children the child can be made more acceptable to them. In this case, one teacher thought that the behaviour of the boy was not due to his being asocial, but rather because he did not want to take part in the fairly vigorous activities which the others engaged in, such as running, climbing and so on. In the experiment climbing was chosen as the activity which was to be encouraged. At the beginning of the experiment the boy only spent 5 per cent of his time doing this. By means of the usual experimental procedure in which climbing was encouraged, it was only nine days before the boy was spending 60 per cent of his time at it. Then it took five days to revert to the original state by ignoring him, and then a further five days to restore to climbing. The result aimed at was not, of course, always to have the boy hanging on the climbing frame, but to get him accepted into the group, which was in fact achieved. The report on the experiment tells that he became a happy and extremely active member of various groups of boys in the playground and blossomed out in both physical and verbal social activities with his playmates.

Buell et al. (1966) undertook an experiment to discover the extent to which the establishment of positive behaviour in one field effected other aspects of behaviour. The child experimented on was a three-year-old girl who talked a good deal to adults and was extremely good at playing with materials provided indoors in the nursery school. However, she was not able to play with the other children, was inclined to use baby language, and did not take advantage of opportunities to play outdoors. In the experiment the idea was to increase her liking for playing outdoors, as it was felt that this might establish more contact between her and the other children and possibly persuade her to drop her baby language and speak like the others. When the experiment started she was using outdoor play equipment for less than 3 per cent of the time set aside for this kind of activity in the nursery school programme. The second phase consisted of 17 days' encouragement to play with the outdoor equipment. As there was hardly anything to start on, the teachers themselves had for the first nine days to arrange situations which could be rewarded, as, for instance, by giving the child a push on a swing, rewarding her by being near her, talking to her and so on, and then, when she withdrew from these activities, ignoring her. Under these conditions the child's use of outdoor equipment was raised to 50 per cent of the time allowed for this activity. For the next week the teachers continued to encourage the child's tendency to play with the outdoor equipment, but now without setting her going themselves. At first the frequency dropped to half of what it had been, but then it quickly rose to 50 per cent again. After the reversion period the frequency rose to about 60 per cent of the time, which was about normal for children in this situation. Parallel with this change of activity went a far greater contact with other children, resulting in far more verbal exchanges with them. Games requiring cooperation with others rose from almost nothing to a level the same as for other children. These parallel effects were not reduced in the periods when the tendency to play with the outdoor equipment was reduced by the teacher's ceasing to appear interested in it.

In his discussion of these experiments, Baer (1966) emphasises that it is the teacher's ordinary social reactions which stimulated the child's behaviour in these experiments. The teacher does not do anything unusual or unknown to her profession. She behaves towards these children in exactly the same way as she usually behaves to any child in the nursery school. What has been organised in these experiments is not what the teacher does, but when she does it. The conscious use of theories on the teaching process does not in any way change nursery school's normal and natural functions, but for the individual child who has his or her behaviour corrected it is of great significance, and through this it naturally also has a certain effect on the group life.

Systematic stimulation through play

Although there is not much in the studies reviewed to suggest that direct training of nursery school children with the object of furthering their development in one field or another is desirable, there are on the other hand numerous examples of the need for stimulation in the shape of opportunities and possibilities connected with either intellectual development (for instance, by linguistic stimulation or the possibility of going out and exploring the surroundings), or else the social and emotional sphere, with stimulating play situations and social contact with others.

This section will discuss a number of experiments to stimulate the child's development in the educational field. The results available come largely from Russian experiments. There appear to be three main reasons for the appearance of a large number of thorough studies during the past six or seven years.

To begin with, a special research institute for research into teaching at pre-school age has been established under the Academy of Pedagogical Sciences (Goncharof, 1961). This institute has been in a position to organise widespread research.

Secondly, there has been the reorganisation of various institutions for children below school age, including day nurseries, into one single institute under the Ministry of Education (Usova, 1961 a).

Thirdly, there is a completely new teaching programme for this combined nursery school, catering for children aged between one and seven years, which has been worked out by the Academy of Pedagogical Sciences in conjunction with the Academy of Medical Sciences (Usova, 1961 a; Zaporozhets, 1962). This programme denotes a decisive break in various ways with previous practice and its emphasis on training, and according to Zaporozhets it places its main emphasis on the child's physical and mental development. The aim is the development of the child's personality, with due consideration being given to age and individuality. Play is of special importance, not only as a teaching method for specific aims. It must not be viewed as a preparation for future activity, but as part of a child's life and something necessary for the development of its personality. The main emphasis must be placed on the development of personality, the development of an aesthetic sense, creativity and moral development (Usova, 1961 a).

At the same time the new programme affects the training of new nursery school teachers. Kistiakovskaia (1961) takes a look at the changes in a nursery school teacher's training arising from the fact that day nurseries are now a sub-division of the nursery school, and she also stresses the importance of sensory stimulation at first, which gradually evolves into play between different children.

Zaporozhets (1962) reports that under the old system day nursery children often had speech defects or suffered from mental retardation when they entered nursery school (cf. deprivation studies from other countries), and says that this will now be prevented by increased educational stimulation at this early age.

Solov'eva (1962) suggests that in training nursery school teachers it will be necessary to get away from the old formal methods, and argues that a changeover must be made to profound studies of the child through observing it and sharing its experiences.

Frolova (1963) also stresses that as the new nursery school programme is not merely a matter of training and instruction, but of upbringing, it will be necessary to get away from the old-fashioned kind of training and instead to acquaint oneself with nursery school life by taking part in it.

Baturina (1961), on the basis of a study of competitiveness in nursery school, concludes that tendencies to compete should not be encouraged as they have negative emotional and social effects.

Radina (1963) discusses a number of studies (carried out in the Research Institute for Pre-School Teaching) which indicate significance of language and of play for mental development, and in connection with this stresses the value of the right kind of educational programme for the child's development.

Mention has already been made of Ginsberg's (1960) experiments with teaching nursery school children a foreign language, in which positive results were achieved when the traditional form of teaching was abandoned in favour of a method based on play.

Usova (1961 b; 1961 c; 1963) has been particularly concerned with the significance of play for a child's development. The old system of didactic games taking place in a teaching atmosphere must, he says, be abolished. Play can have educational significance as a training factor by organising group life and individual activity; however, the group, not the individual, must be at the centre. No specific demands must be made on the child, but the teacher must organise play so that the right kind of development is stimulated; play loses its significance if it ceases to be free and active. A healthy development is impossible without an active and interesting life, which play can ensure, and free play never makes greater demands on the child than it can cope with. The teacher's duty is to arrange games in such a way that they produce positive feelings between those taking part and thus contribute to the individual child's development.

Zhukovskaya (1962) has made a close study of the significance of play for developing a child's imagination. In it she distinguishes between day-dreaming and a healthy, fertile imagination which helps the child to re-create situations from real life in its play, and thus develops its understanding of real life. The study started with two questions: what ought the imagination to be concerned with, and by what means can it be developed so as to help the child to arrange chance information into new concepts.

Various methods were employed in carrying out this project, one of which was a study of what highly qualified and experienced teachers did. The conclusion drawn was that only a few, really outstanding pre-school teachers were capable of stimulating the child's imagination in the right way. Most of them did not make sufficient systematic use of the child's primary play interests in order to stimulate its imagination and fantasy.

Then came a number of experiments with games of make-believe, half of which were based on spontaneous ideas while half came after some stimulation of the imagination in the form of a group discussion of the children's own earlier experiences. A game of this sort could, for instance, consist of an imaginary flight to the permanent exhibition in Moscow. The study showed that under spontaneous conditions it was difficult for the children to concentrate; their imagination was not strong enough, and the game broke down. In the experimental game there was an interaction between imagination and the discussion of realistic experiences, and so a creative imagination was fostered. The fantasies were on a more realistic level, and the experiment also showed how under the experimental conditions the children became more creative in constructing things connected with flying. The study concludes in short that creative activity on the part of a child is a result of the way in which it is taught.

Nechaieva (1948) carried out a similar experiment with constructive activities in nursery school. The emphasis here is placed particularly on the fact that the activities must be meaningful and expedient as well as being psychologically right for the child; they must correspond to its play or to its practical needs. Under these conditions constructive activity will develop a child's creative ability.

Conclusion

Stukat (1966) finishes his study of the influence which Swedish *lekskola* has on children's development with a discussion of the aims, programmes and methods of nursery school. He believes that a more precise formulation of the aims of nursery school is necessary, not least with regard to the question of development of personality. Although no objections can be raised to stressing social and emotional development as among the aims of nursery school, it would be a good thing to express more clearly and in more concrete terms just what the ultimate goal is in this respect. Closer coordination of aims and methods is necessary in choosing methods of attaining the goals, once they have been defined. Apart from aims in general terms, a more explicit and systematically constructed plan for nursery school must be evolved, for instance, a more consciously arranged introduction to nature study through different experimental play situations, or variety of concrete and manipulative exercises intended gradually to give the child a sense of space, time and number. It is important that the tasks and the materials should be such as will exercise the child's abilities to the right degree. One of the essential problems for groups of six and seven-year-olds in nursery schools is that the children are intellectually starved, often being forced to occupy themselves with the same materials they have used before, and which are perhaps more suited to younger children.

The demand for a definite teaching aim and conscious teaching efforts means that the learning as well as the maturation processes must be taken into consideration. This doubtless happens in practice, but in theoretical discussions of nursery school the maturation processes have been emphasised far more than the learning process as being of importance for the child's development. This can presumably be explained (and defended) as a reaction against older teaching methods with their drill-like approach and complete indifference to the child's level of attainment. By asserting the principle that every aspect of teaching must pay attention to the child's level of maturity nursery school has without doubt been, and still is, of inestimable value for theories of teaching at all stages. At the same time it is important that this fundamental view should not turn into a dogma, so that the nursery school teacher comes to rely entirely on 'spontaneous' development and is therefore inclined to adopt a passive-attitude to the question of development.

So far the assumption has been that developmental psychology was fundamental to nursery school teaching theory, while learning psychology only comes into the picture with the start of school proper. But upbringing presupposes some sort of learning, and the problem for nursery school is to bring about a balance between maturing and learning so that the two together can result in the best possible development. Even in fields where spontaneous creative activity is usually thought to be the only right thing, as for instance in artistic activities, there might well be a need for a degree of limited guidance. Even something as fundamental as fitting into a group is a manner of behaviour which can be learnt. The teacher can and should guide this learning process, not by means of formal exercises, but by devising situations in which it will seem natural and satisfying to the child to be of help to the other children and to give them pleasure. Emotional reactions can likewise be modified by learning; for instance when the teacher tries to help a child to overcome its anxiety and shyness *vis-à-vis* other children by putting it into friendly play groups and by letting it do things which result in the approbation of the others and thereby increase the child's own self-confidence, she is making use of reinforcement principles, in other words a principle of learning psychology. The more clearly a teacher understands this, the greater are her chances of bringing her efforts to a successful conclusion.

Thus it is desirable that a clear definition of aims should go hand in hand with a carefully made choice of the ways of influencing a child, and this is true even of aspects of nursery school aimed at developing personality in a wider sense.

Bibliography

Ackerly, S. and R. Meller, 'The value of a nursery school in a psychiatric set-up' *American Journal of Psychiatry* 11, 1941, pp. 172-5.

Ainsworth, Mary D., R. G. Andry, R. G. Harlow, S. Lebovici, M. Mead, D. G. Prough and D. Wobton, *Deprivation of maternal care: a reassessment of its effects*, World Health Organisation, Geneva 1962.

Ainsworth, M. D. and J. Bowlby, 'Research strategy in the study of mother-child separation' *Courrier* 4, no. 3, 1954.

Allegato, R., *Preschool training program is partial success*, Detroit Free Press, 1966.

Allen, Gregory B. and Joseph Masling, 'An evaluation of the effects of nursery school training on children in the kindergarten, first and second grades' *Journal of Educational Research* 51, 1957, pp. 285-96.

Allen, K. E., Betty Hart, Joan S. Buell, Florence R. Harris and M. M. Wolf, 'Effects of social reinforcement on isolate behavior of a nursery school child' *Child Development* 35, 1964, pp. 511-18.

Alper, T. G., H. T. Blane and B. K. Abrams, 'Reactions of middle- and lower-class children to fingerpaints as a function of class differences in child training practices' *Journal of Abnormal and Social Psychology* 51, 1955, pp. 439-48.

Alpern, G. D., 'The failure of a nursery school enrichment program for culturally deprived children.' Paper presented at the 1966 meeting of the American Orthopsychiatric Association, San Francisco, Calif.

Alpert, Augusta, 'The treatment of emotionally disturbed children in a therapeutic nursery' *American Journal of Orthopsychiatry* 25, 1955, pp. 826-34.

Anderson, H. H., 'An experimental study of dominative and integrative behavior in children of preschool age' *Journal of Social Psychology* 8, 1937 (a), pp. 335-45.

Anderson, H. H., 'Domination and integration in the social behavior of young children in an experimental play situation' *Genetic Psychological Monograph* 19, 1937 (b), pp. 343-408.

Anderson, H. H., 'Domination and social integration in the behavior of kindergarten children and teachers' *Genetic Psychology Monograph* 21, 1939 (a), pp. 287-385.

Anderson, H. H., 'The measurement of domination and socially integrative behavior in teachers' contacts with children' *Child Development* 10, 1939 (b), pp. 73-89.

Anderson, L. D., 'A longitudinal study of the effects of nursery school training on successive intelligence test ratings' *Yearbook of the National Society for the Study of Education* 39 (2), 1940, pp. 3-10.

Anderson, H. H. and H. M. Brewer, 'Studies of teachers' classroom personalities' in *Dominative and socially integrative behavior of kindergarten teachers*, Applied Psychology Monograph no. 6, 1945.

Andrus, R. and E. L. Horowitz, 'The effect of nursery school training: insecurity feelings' *Child Development* 9, 1938, pp. 169-84.

Angell, D. B., 'Differences in social behavior between elementary school children who have attended nursery school' (Master's Thesis), North Texas State College, Denfon 1954.

Appel, M. H., 'Aggressive behavior of nursery school children and adult procedures in dealing with such behavior' *Journal of Experimental Education* 11, 1942, pp. 185-99.

Argy, W. P., 'Montessori versus orthodox: a study to determine the relative improvement of the preschool child with brain damage trained by one of two methods' *Rehabilitation Literature* 26, 1965, pp. 294-304.

Arsenian, J. M., 'Young children in an insecure situation' *Journal of Abnormal'Psychology* 38, 1943, pp. 225-49.

Askling, Berit, *Arbetsanalys av förskolläraryrket*, Göteborg 1967.

Asprea, Annamaria and M. C. Barbiero, 'Aspects of socialization in the first years of life in the family environment and in the child community' *Atti del XIV Congresso degli Psicologi Italiani*, Naples, 27 September – 3 October 1962.

Axtell, Joy B. and Mary M. Edmunds, 'The effect of preschool experience on fathers, mothers and children' *California Journal of Educational Research* 11, 1960, pp. 195-203.

Baer, Donald M., *Some remedial uses of the reinforcement contingency*, Mannship, Chicago 1966.

Baldwin, Alfred L., 'The effect of home environment on nursery school behavior' *Child Development* 20, 1949, pp. 49-62.

Baldwin, B. T. and L. L. Stecher, *The psychology of the preschool child*, Appleton, New York 1924.

Baltimore Public Schools, 'An early school admission project progress report. Home and school (culturally deprived children). Educational experiment during three years' in *Children* vol. 11, no. 2, 1964.

Bandura, A. and A. C. Huston, 'Identification as a process of incidental learning' *Journal of Abnormal and Social Psychology* 63, 1961, pp. 311-18.

Bandura, A., D. Ross and S. A. Ross, 'Transmission of aggression through imitation of aggressive models' *Journal of Abnormal and Social Psychology* 63, 1961, pp. 575-82.

Barbiero, M. C. and G. Villone Betocchi, 'Observations preliminary to a study of the ecological factors in developmental psychology' in *Atti del XIV Congresso degli Psicologi Italiani*, Naples, 27 September – 3 October 1962.

Barbiero, M. C. and A. M. Galdo, 'Premises for a study of "semi-boarding" ' *Infanzia anormale* vol. 39, 1960, pp. 401-17.

Barker, R. G., T. Dembo and K. Lewin, 'Frustration and regression: an experiment with young children' *University of Iowa Studies in Child Welfare* 18, 1941, pp. 1-134.

Barrett, H. E. and H. L. Koch, 'The effect of nursery school training upon the mental-test performance of a group of orphanage children' *Journal of Genetic Psychology* 37, 1930, pp. 102-22.

Baruch, D. W., 'A study of reported tensions in interparental relationships as coexistent with behavior adjustment in young children' *Journal of Experimental Child Psychology* 6, 1937, pp. 187-204.

Baturina, E. G., 'Competition at the kindergarten level' *Soviet Education* vol. 3, no. 9, 1961, pp. 33-5.

Bayley, N., 'Factors influencing the growth of intelligence in young children' *Yearbook of the National Society for the Study of Education* 39, 1940, pp. 49-79.

Beer, E. S., 'Social psychiatry in the day nursery' *Journal of Educational Sociology* 10, 1936, pp. 207-14.

Beller, E. K., 'Annual report of research in Philadelphia experimental nursery school project' (stencil) Philadelphia Council for Community Advancement, 1965.

Bender, L. and H. Yarnell, 'An observation nursery' *American Journal of Psychiatry* 97, 1941, pp. 1158-74.

Bendz-Sandell, Margareta, ' "Trötthetssymtom" hos treåringer på daghem. Orienterande utredning' *Sociale Meddelanden* 1-2, 1964, pp. 189-210.

Benning, O. B., 'Nursery schools for the deaf' *American Annals of the Deaf* 83, 1938, pp. 417-24.

Bentsen, P. V., *Pasning af gifte kvinders småbørn*, Socialforskningsinstituttet (Danish National Institute of Social Research) study no. 10, Copenhagen 1968.

Bereiter, C., et al., 'An academically-oriented preschool for culturally deprived children' in Hechinger, New York 1966.

Bergamini, Y. and W. Swanson, 'Does kindergarten make any difference?' *School Executive* vol. 74, 1954, pp. 54-5.

Bernstein, Lotte, Margaret Kirk, Mary Monk, Helen Noble and Elisabeth Westley, 'The use of a therapeutic nursery school in co-operation with clinical treatment of an acute separation problem' *American Journal of Orthopsychiatry* 24, 1954, pp. 291-306.

Bertoye, P. and C. Dumorand, 'Troubles de croissance du nourisson par choc affectif' *Revue de Hygiène et de Médicine Sociale* 5, Paris 1957, pp. 187-9.

Betænkning fra Børne og Ungdomsforsorgens pædagogiske nævn (Educational Committee for the Care of Children and Young People). *'Om børnehaveproblemer* (report no. 337) 1963.

Bird, G. E., 'The effect of nursery school attendance upon mental growth of children' *Yearbook of the National Society for the Study of Education* 39 (2), 1940, pp. 81-4.

Black, I. S., 'The use of the Stanford-Binet (1937 revision) in a group of nursery school children' *Child Development* 10, 1939, pp. 157-71.

Blackhurst, D. J., *The value of play apparatus for developing motor control in preschool children*, Iowa City State University, 1929.

Block, J. and B. Martin, 'Predicting the behavior of children under frustration' in J. Seidmann (ed.), *The child: a book of readings*, New York 1958.

Blomart, J., 'Attitudes maternelles et réactions à l'entrée au jardin d'enfants' *Acta Psychologica* 21 (2), 1963, pp. 75-97.

Bloom, B. S., *Stability and change in human characteristics*, Wiley, New York 1964.

Body, Margaret K., 'Patterns of aggression in the nursery school' *Child Development* 26, 1955, pp. 3-11.

Boet, J., 'A further study in the modification of assertive behavior in young children' (Thesis), University of Iowa, 1943.

Borum, Elisabeth A. and Norman Livson, 'Mental test score changes at kindergarten entry' *Journal of Experimental Education* 34 (1), 1965, pp. 89-92.

Boulding, Elise, 'The cooperative nursery and the young mother's role conflict' *Marriage and Family Living* 17, 1955, pp. 303-9.

Bowlby, J., *Maternal care and mental health*, World Health Organisation Monograph no. 2, Geneva 1951.

Brenner, A. and Nancy M. Samelson, 'Kindergarten behavior and first grade achievement: a case study exploration' *Merrill-Palmer Quarterly* 3, 1957, pp. 114-35.

Brewer, H. M. and H. H. Anderson, 'The measurement of the behavior of kindergarten children in relation to the teacher's dominative and socially integrative contacts' *Psychological Bulletin* 37, 1940, p. 583.

Brown, Ann Wilson, and Raymond G. Hunt, 'Relations between nursery school attendance and teachers' ratings of some aspects of children's adjustment in kindergarten' *Child Development* 32, 1961, pp. 585-96.

Brueckner, L. J., 'The changing elementary school' *The Regent's Inquiry*, Inor Publishing Co., New York 1939, pp. 80-1.

Buell, J. S., et al., 'Patterns of social development collateral to social reinforcement of one form of play in an isolate nursery school child' in Baer, 1966.

Burchinal, L. G. and J. E. Rossman, 'Relations among maternal employment indices and development characteristics of children' *Marriage and Family Living* vol. 23, 1961, p. 334.

Böttcher, H. F., 'Trainingsverfahren zur Entwicklung des Zahlbegriffs im Vorschulalter' *Problem und Ergebnisse der Psychologie* 19, 1966, pp.7-43.

Caille, R. K., *Resistant behavior in young children*, Child Development Monograph no. 11, 1933.

Caldwell, Bettye M., Julius B. Honig, S. Alice, Stanley E. Moldovan, Charlene Mozell and Mary B. Kawash, 'A daycare program for disadvantaged infants and young children. Observations after one year' (stencil) 1965.

Caldwell, Bettye M. and J. B. Richmond, 'Programmed daycare for the very young child. A preliminary report' *Journal of Marriage and the Family*, November 1964, pp. 481-8.

Campbell, E. H., 'The effect of nursery school training upon the later food habits of the child' *Child Development* 4, 1933, pp. 329-45.

Care of children in day-centres, *World Health Organisation Public Health Paper no. 24, Geneva 1964.*

Carr, V. S., 'The social and emotional changes in a group of children of high intelligence during a program of increased educational stimulation' (unpublished Master's Thesis), University of Iowa, 1938.

Casler, Lawrence, *Maternal deprivation: a critical review of the literature*, Society for Research in Child Development, Monograph no. 26, 1961.

Chadwick, M., 'Six months' experiment at a nursery school' *Psychoanalytic Review* 15, 1928, pp. 27-36.

Chasdi, E. H. and M. S. Lawrence, 'Some antecedents of aggression and effects of frustration in doll play' in Seidman (ed.) *The child: a book of readings*, New York 1958.

Chittenden, G. E., *An experimental study in measuring and modifying assertive behavior in young children,* Society for Research in Child Development, Monograph 7, no. 1, 1942.

Church, Marilyn, 'Kindergarten–education or babysitting?' *Elementary School Journal* 64, no. 1, 1963.

Coffey, H. S. and B. L. Wellman, 'The role of cultural status in intelligence changes of preschool children' *Journal of Experimental Education* 5, 1936, pp. 191-202.

Colby, M. G., 'Instrumental reproduction of melody by preschool children' *Journal of Genetic Psychology* 47, 1935, pp. 413-30.

Conrad, H. S. and M. C. Jones, 'A two-year record of attendance and colds in a nursery school' *Child Development* 3, 1932, pp. 43-52.

Corcoran, A. L., 'Color usage in nursery school painting' *Child Development* 25, 1954, pp. 107-13.

Craig, W. N., 'Effects of preschool training on the development of reading and lip-reading skills of children' *American Annals of the Deaf* 109, 1964, pp. 280-96.

Crissey, O. L., 'The mental development of children of the same IQ in differing institutional environments' *Child Development* 8, 1937, pp. 217-20.

Cummings, Jean D., 'The incidence of emotional symptoms in school children' *British Journal of Educational Psychology* 14, 1944, pp. 151-61.

Cushing, H. M., 'A tentative report on the influence of nursery school training upon kindergarten adjustments as reported by kindergarten teachers' *Child Development* 5, 1934, pp. 304-14.

Daghem och förskolor: Betänkande om barnstugor och barntillsyn, SOU no. 15, Stockholm 1951.

David, Myriam, and Genevieve Appell, 'A study of nursing care and nurse-infant interaction' in B. M. Foss (ed.) *Determinants of infant behavior,* London 1961.

David, Myriam, and Genevieve Appell, 'Etude des facteurs de carence affective dans une pouponnière' *Psychiatrie de l'Enfant,* Paris 1962.

Davidson, F., 'Daycare centres in Paris and its suburbs' in *Care of children in day centres,* World Health Organisation Public Health Paper no. 24, 1964.

Dawe, Helen C., 'Raising standards of behavior in the kindergarten' *Elementary School Journal* 35, 1934 (a), pp. 267-80.

Dawe, Helen C., 'The influence of size of kindergarten group upon performance' *Child Development* 5, 1934 (b), pp. 295-303.

Dawe, Helen C., 'A study of the effect of an educational program upon language development and related mental functions in young children' *Journal of Experimental Education* 11, 1942, pp. 200-9.

Dawe, Helen C., Dorothy Ekern and Harriet Berger, 'Differences in adult contacts with children' *Journal of Home Economy* 41, 1949, pp. 85-7.

Dawe, Helen C. and Josephine C. Foster, 'Fatigue and rest in the kindergarten' *Childhood Education* 11, 1935, pp. 211-15.

Denhoff, Eric, 'The physically handicapped child and the nursery school' *Exceptional Children* 20, 1954, pp. 202-8.

Deutch, M., *Institute for Developmental Studies. Annual Report*, New York 1965.

Diehl, Isabelle, 'The prevalence of colds in nursery school children and non-nursery school children' *Journal of Pediatrics* 34, 1949, pp. 52-62.

Douglas, J. W. B. and J. M. Blomfield, *Children under five*, London 1958.

Douglas, J. W. B. and J. M. Ross, 'The later educational progress and emotional adjustment of children who went to nursery school or classes' *Educational Research* 7, 1964, pp. 73-80.

Dragan, H., 'Medical and social researches on preschool children' *Rev. Igienä Soc.* (Romanian journal) 5, 1935, pp. 353-9.

Dreyer, A. S. and D. Haupt, 'The assertion of authority: differences between teachers, student-teachers, and mothers of young children' *Journal of Educational Research* no. 2, 1960, pp. 63-6.

Drillien, 'A longitudinal study of the growth and development of prematurely and maturely born children' *Archives of Disease in Childhood* 36, 1961, p. 515.

Dubin, Elisabeth R., 'The effect of training on the tempo of development of graphic representation in preschool children' *Journal of Experimental Education* 15, 1946, pp. 166-73.

Durkin, Dolores, 'Children who read before the first grade' in W. Cutts (ed.) *Teaching young children to read*, US Office of Education, US Government Printing Office, Washington 1964.

Erasmie, Thord, 'II Språkutvecklingen under förskolåldern' *Sociale Meddelanden*, 1963, pp. 697-722.

Erasmie, Thord, *Studier rörande språkutvecklingen hos barn i åldern 4-6½ år*, Göteborg 1964 (a).

Erasmie, Thord, 'Undersökning av språkutvecklingen hos förskolbarn' *Barnträdgården* no. 4, 1964(b).

Erikson, E. H., *Childhood and society*, New York 1950 (a).

Erikson E. H., 'Growth and crises of the "Healthy Personality"' in Senn, M. J. E. (ed.) *Transactions of the fourth conference on infancy and childhood*, 1950 (b).

Ezekiel, L. F., 'Changes in egocentricity of nursery school children' *Child Development* 2, 1931, pp. 74-5.

Faigin, H., 'Social behavior of young children in the kibbutz' *Journal of Abnormal Psychology* 56, 1958, pp. 117-29.

Farquhar, T., 'The school adjustment of the members of a kindergarten class four years later' *Smith College Studies in Social Work* 13, 1942, pp. 91-146.

Fast, Irene, 'Kindergarten training and grade 1 reading' *Journal of Educational Psychology* 48, 1957, pp. 52-7.

Feldmann, Shirley, 'A preschool enrichment program for disadvantaged children' *New Era* vol. 45, no. 3, 1964, pp. 79-82.

Ferguson, Eva Dreikurs, 'An evaluation of two types of kindergarten attendance programs' *Journal of Educational Psychology* 48, 1957, pp. 287-301.

Fite, Mary D., 'Aggressive behavior in young children and children's attitudes towards aggression' *Genetic Psychology Monograph* 22, 1940, pp. 153-319.

Fouracre, M. H., 'Effect of group training on four and five year-old children who are mentally retarded' *Exceptional Children* 24, 1958, pp. 326-8 (report of research in progress).

Fowler, William, 'Cognitive learning in infancy and early childhood' *Psychological Bulletin* 59, 1962, pp. 116-52.

Fowler, William, *Longitudinal study of early stimulation in the emergence of cognitive processes*, Conference on Preschool Education, February 1966.

Fox, R. B. and M. Powell, 'Evaluating kindergarten experiences' *The Reading Teacher* 18, 1964, pp. 118-20.

Foxwell, H. R., et al., 'The development of social responsiveness to other children in a nursery school child through experimental use of social reinforcement' in Baer, 1966.

Frandsen, A. and F. P. Barlow, 'Influence of the nursery school on mental growth' *Yearbook of the National Society for the Study of Education* 39 (2), 1940, pp. 143-8.

Fredsted, Gudrun, Er 40% af vore børnehavemødre hjemmegående?' *Forebyggende børneværn*, May 1967.

Freud, Anna, 'Nursery school education; its uses and dangers' *Child Study*, 1949, pp. 35-7.

Freud, Anna, and S. Dann, 'An experiment in group upbringing' in W. E. Martin and C. B. Stendler (eds.) *Reading in child development*, Harcourt Brace, New York 1954.

Frolova, O., 'Methods leadership' *Soviet Education* vol. 5, no. 5, 1963, pp. 35-9.

Fuller, L., 'The effect of kindergarten speech training on primary grade progress and achievement of children with foreign language handicaps' *California Journal of Elementary Education* 4, 1936, pp. 165-73.

Gard, W. L., 'The influence of kindergarten on achievement in reading' *Educational Research Bulletin* 3, 1924, pp. 135-8.

Gardner, D. E. M., *The education of young children*, Philosophical Library Inc., New York 1957, p. 118.

Gardner, D. E. M., *Modern research with children, other than the under-privileged, on the effects of attending nursery schools*, The Institute of Education, London 1967 (a).

Gardner, D. E. M., *Effects of nursery school attendance on intelligence. Disadvantaged children*, The Institute of Education, London 1967 (b).

Gates, A. I. and G. L. Bond, 'Reading readiness. A study of factors determining success and failure in beginning reading' *Teachers College Record*, 1936, p. 681 ff.

Getzels, J. W., 'Preschool education' *Contemporary Issues in American Education*, July 1965, pp. 105-14.

Getzels, J. W. C. and P. W. Jackson, *Creativity and Intelligence*, Wiley, New York 1962.

Gewirtz, J. L., 'Three determinants of attention seeking in young children' *Society for Research in Child Development Monograph* 19 (2), 1954, pp. 1-48.

Gewirtz, J. L., 'Factor analysis of some attention seeking behavior of young children' *Child Development* 27, 1956, pp. 17-36.

Gewirtz, J. L. and D. M. Baer, 'The effect of brief social deprivation on behavior for a social reinforcer' *Journal of Abnormal Psychology* 56, 1958 (a), pp. 49-56.

Gewirtz, J. L. and D. M. Baer, 'Deprivation and satiation of social reinforcers as drive conditions' *Journal of Abnormal and Social Psychology* 57, 1958 (b), pp. 165-172.

Gewirtz, J. L., D. M. Baer and C. H. Roth, 'A note on the similar effects of low social availability of an adult and brief social deprivation on young children's behavior' *Child Development* 29, 1958, pp. 149-52.

Ginsberg, V. S., 'An experiment in teaching preschool children a foreign language' *Soviet Education* vol. 2, no. 11, 1960, pp. 18-26.

Girolami-Boulinier, A., 'Comment prévenir ou atténuer les premières difficultés scolaires. Essai de mise au point suivi d'une série d'exercices destinés aux grandes sections des écoles maternelles' *Bulletin Société A. Binet* 63, 1963, pp. 65-190.

Glass, Netta, 'Eating, sleeping, and elimination habits in children attending day nurseries and children cared for at home by mothers' *American Journal of Orthopsychiatry* 19, 1949, pp. 697-711.

Goetch, Edward W., 'The kindergarten as a factor in elementary school achievement and progress' *University of Iowa Studies in Education* vol. 3, no. 4, University of Iowa 1926.

Goldstein, K. M. and S. B. Chorost, 'A preliminary evaluation of nursery school experience of the later school adjustment of culturally disadvantaged children' (stencil, unpublished), Wakoff Research Center, Staten Island, New York 1966.

Goldstein, Leo S., 'Evaluation of an enrichment program for disadvantaged children' (stencil), New York 1965.

Goncharof, N. K., 'Concerning the 1961 research plan for the academy of pedagogical sciences of the RSFSR' *Soviet Education* 3, no. 10, 1961, pp. 50-8.

Goodenough, F. L., 'A preliminary report on the effect of nursery school training upon the intelligence test scores of young children' *Yearbook of the National Society for the Study of Education* 27, 1928, pp. 361-9.

Goodenough, F. L., 'Look to the evidence: A critique of recent experiments on raising the I.Q.' *Educational Methods* 19, 1939, pp. 73-9. In *Yearbook of the National Society for the Study of Education* 39 (2) 1940.

Goodenough, F. L., 'New evidence on environmental influence on intelligence' *Yearbook of the National Society for the Study of Education* 39, 1940, pp. 307-65.

Goodenough, F. L. and K. M. Maurer, 'The mental development of nursery school children compared with that of non-nursery school children' *Yearbook of the National Society for the Study of Education* 39 (2), 1940 (a), pp. 161-78.

Goodenough, F. L. and K. M. Maurer, 'The relative potency of the nursery school and the statistical laboratory in boosting the I.Q.' *Journal of Educational Psychology* 31, 1940 (b), pp. 541-9.

Gordon, Ronnie, 'A nursery school in a rehabilitation centre' *Children* vol. 13, no. 4, 1966.

Gornicki, B., 'The development of children in the family and in daycare centres in Poland' in *Care of children in day centres*, World Health Organisation Public Health Paper no. 24, 1964.

Gottemoller, R., 'The influence of certain aspects of the home environment on the adjustment of children to kindergarten' *Smith College Studies in Social Work* 9, 1939, pp. 303-59.

Gottsdanker, Josephine S., 'Contributions of a cooperative parent nursery school to parent education' *Quarterly Journal of Child Behavior* 4, 1952, pp. 17-23.

Grant, Eva, 'The effect of certain factors in the home environment upon child behavior' *University of Iowa Studies in Child Welfare* 15, 1939, pp. 61-94.

Gray, Susan W. and Rupert A. Klaus, 'An experimental preschool program for culturally deprived children' *Child Development* 36 (4), 1965, pp. 887-98.

Green, E. H., 'Friendship and quarrels among preschool children' *Child Development* 4, 1933 (a), pp. 237-52.

Green, E. H., 'Group play and quarreling among preschool children' *Child Development* 4, 1933 (b), pp. 302-7.

Greene, Katharine D., 'Relations between kindergartens and nursery schools' *Childhood Education* 8, no. 7, 1931, pp. 352-5.

Griffiths, Anita N., 'Intelligence and certain personality traits of twenty-four children who have attended the Iowa State College Nursery School' (abstract of Master's Thesis), Iowa State College, Ames, Iowa, 1939.

Grue-Sørenson, K., *Pædagogik mellem videnskab og filosofi,* Copenhagen 1965.

Gutteridge, Mary V., 'A study of motor achievements of young children' *Archives of Psychology* 34, no. 244, New York 1939.

Hagen, E. and R. L. Thorndike, 'Evaluation' in *Encyclopedia of educational research*, McMillan, New York 1960.

Hahn, E., 'Analyses of the content and form of the speech of first grade children' *Quarterly Journal of Speech* 34, 1948, pp. 361-6.

Hammond, S. L., 'What about kindergarten?' *Childhood Education* 33, 1957, pp. 314-15.

Hammond, Sarah Lou, and Dora S. Skipper, 'Factors involved in the adjustment of children entering first grade' *Journal of Educational Research* 56, 2, 1957, pp. 89-95.

Hansson, Kjell, Tiit Saarmann and Paul Åkerstrom, *Daghem barn och hemuppfostrade barn. En komparativ studie i beroende*, Psykologiska Institutionen, Lund University, 1967.

Harris, F. R., et al., 'Effects of positive social reinforcement on regressed crawling of a nursery school child' *Journal of Educational Psychology* 55, 1964, pp. 35-41.

Hart, B. M., N. J. Reynolds, E. Brawley, F. R. Harris and M. M. Wolf, 'Effects of social reinforcement on operant crying' *Journal of Experimental Child Psychology* 1, 1964, pp. 145-53.

Hart, B. M., et al., 'Effects of contingent and non-contingent social reinforcement on the isolate behavior of a nursery school girl' in Baer, 1966.

Hartup, Willard W., 'Nurturance and nurturance-withdrawal in relation to the dependency behavior of preschool children' *Child Development* 29, 1958, pp. 191-201.

Hartup, Willard W., 'An evaluation of the Highberger Early-Adjustment-to-School-Scale' *Child Development* 30, 1959, pp. 421-32.

Hartup, Willard W. and Yayoi Himeno, 'Social isolation *vs.* interaction with adults in relation to aggression in preschool children' *Journal of Abnormal and Social Psychology* 59, 1, 1960, pp. 17-22.

Hartup, W. W. and E. D. Keller, 'Nurturance in preschool children and its relation to dependency' *Child Development* 31, 1960, pp. 681-9.

Hattwick, B. W., 'The influence of nursery school attendance upon the behavior and personality of the preschool child' *Journal of Experimental Psychology* 5, 1936 (a), pp. 180-90.

Hattwick, B. W., 'Interrelations between the preschool child's behavior and certain factors in the home' *Child Development* 7, 1936, pp. 200-26.

Hattwick, B. W. and M. Stowell, 'The relation of parental over-attentiveness to children's work habits and social adjustment in kindergarten and the first six grades in school' *Journal of Educational Research* 30, 1936, pp. 169-76.

Health Report of the London County Council, 1927' *Nursery School Education* 23, 51, London 1928, p. 317.

Heathers, G., 'Emotional dependence and independence needs in nursery school play' *Journal of Genetic Psychology* 87, 1955, pp. 37-57.

Hechinger, Fred M. (ed.), *Preschool education today. New approaches to teaching 3-, 4-, and 5-year-olds*, New York 1966.

Heinicke, C. M., 'Some effects of separating two-year-old children from their parents. A comparative study' *Human Relations* 9, 1956, pp. 105-76.

Heinicke, C. and I. Westheimer, *Brief separations*, London 1965.

Henderson, A. S., *1964-65 annual progress report to the Ford Foundation on the preschool and primary education project*, Council for Human Services, Harrisburg Pa., 1965.

Henry, M. M. and D. F. Sharpe, 'Some influential factors in the determination of aggressive behavior in preschool children *Child Development* 18, 1947, pp. 11-28.

Herr, Selma E., 'The effects of pre-first-grade training upon reading readiness and reading achievement among Spanish-American children' *Journal of Educational Psychology* 37, 1946, pp. 87-102.

Hesselvik, L., 'Respiratory infections among children in day nurseries' *Acta paediatrica* supplement 74, Uppsala 1949. Contained in Sjφlin 1964.

Hetzer, H. and G. Noelle, 'Die Funktion verschiedengearteter Kinder in der Kindergarten-Gemeinschaft' *Zeitschrift für pädagogische Psychologie* 37, 1936, pp. 15-34.

Highberger, Ruth, 'The relationship between maternal behavior and the child's early adjustment to nursery school' *Child Development* 26, 1955, pp. 49-61.

Hildreth, G., 'The effect of school environment upon Stanford-Binet tests of young children' *Yearbook of the National Society for the Study of Education* 27 (1), 1928, pp. 355-9.

Hilgard, J. R., 'Learning and maturation in preschool children' *Journal of Genetic Psychology* 41, 1932, pp. 36-56.

Hobson, J. R., 'High school performance of underage pupils initially admitted to kindergarten on the basis of physical and psychological examinations' *Educational and Psychological Measurement* 23 (1), 1963, pp. 159-70.

Hofmann, Helmut, 'Behavioral patterns in kindergarten and first grade. An evaluation of consistency and change by parents and teachers' *Merril-Palmer Quarterly* 3, 1957, pp. 136-44.

Horowitz, E. L., 'Child-adult relationship in the preschool years' *Journal of Social Psychology* 11, 1940, pp. 41-58.

Horowitz, E. L. and R. B. Smith, 'Social relations and personality patterning in preschool children' *Journal of Genetic Psychology* 54, 1939, pp. 337-52.

Hunt, J. McV., *Intelligence and experience*, Ronald Press, New York 1961.

Hunt, J. McV., 'The psychological basis for using preschool enrichment as an antidote for cultural deprivation' *Merril-Palmer Quarterly* 10, 1964 (a), pp. 210-48.

Hunt, J. McV., 'How children develop intellectually' *Children* vol. 11, no. 3, 1964 (b).

Ikeda, Hannah, 'Adapting the nursery school program for the mentally retarded child' *Exceptional Children* 21, 1955, pp. 171-3, 196.

Irvine, E. Elisabeth, 'Observations on the aims and methods of child rearing in communal settlements in Israel' *Human Relations* 5, 1952, pp. 247-75.

Isaacs, Susan, *The educational value of the nursery school. Childhood and after*, International Universities' Press Inc., New York 1949.

Isaacs, Susan, *The educational value of the nursery school*, University of London Press Ltd. for the Nursery School Association of Great Britain, 1952.

Jack, L. M., 'An experimental study of ascendant behavior in preschool children' *University of Iowa Studies in Child Welfare* 9, 1934, pp. 7-65.

Jersild, A. T. and S. F. Bienstock, 'The influence of training on the vocal ability of three-year-old children' *Child Development* 2, 1931, pp. 272-91.

Jersild, A. T. and S. F. Bienstock, 'A study of the development of children's ability to sing' *Journal of Educational Psychology*, 1934. Cited in *Daghem och Förskolor*, SOU no. 15, Stockholm 1951.

Jersild, A. T. and S. F. Bienstock, *Development of rhythm in young children*, Society for Research in Child Development, Monograph no. 22, 1935.

Jersild, A. T. and M. D. Fite, 'Children's social adjustments in nursery school' *Journal of Experimental Education* 6, 1937, pp. 161-6.

Jersild, A. T. and M. D. Fite, 'The influence of nursery school experience on children's social adjustment', *Child Development Monograph* no. 25, 1939.

Jersild, A. T. and F. V. Markey, 'Conflicts between preschool children' *Child Development Monograph* no. 21, 9, 1935, p. 181.

Joel, W., 'The influence of nursery school education upon behavior maturity' *Journal of Experimental Education* 8, 1939, pp. 164-5.

Johansson, B. A., *Criteria of school readiness*, Stockholm 1965.

Johnson, M. W., 'The effects on behavior of variation in amount of play equipment' *Child Development* 6, 1935, pp. 56-68.

Johnston, M. K., et al., 'Application of reinforcement principles to the development of motor skills of a young child' in Baer, 1966.

Jones, Betty and Elizabeth Prescott, *Day care and nursery education in Los Angeles County*, Los Angeles 1964.

Jones, Harold E., 'Seasonal variations in I.Q.' *Journal of Experimental Education* 10, 1941, pp. 91-9.

Jones, Harold E., 'The environment and mental development' in L. Carmichael, *Manual of Child Psychology*, 2nd edn., New York 1965.

Jones, H. E. and A. P. Jorgensen, 'Mental growth as related to nursery school attendance' *Yearbook of the National Society for the Study of Education* 39 (2), 1940, pp. 207-22.

Kaffman, M., 'Evaluation of emotional disturbance in 403 Israeli kibbutz children' *American Journal of Psychiatry* 117, 1961, pp. 732-8.

Kalinina, Z. A. and L. A. Chepeleuts., 'Capricious children' *Soviet Education* 4, no. 3, 1962, pp. 53-6. In *Doshkol'noe Vospitanie* no. 11, 1961.

Kawin, E. and C. Hoefer, *A comparative study of a nursery school versus a non-nursery school group*, University of Chicago Press, Chicago 1931.

Keister, M. E., 'The behavior of young children in failure' in R. G. Barker, J. Kounin and H. F. Wright (eds) *Child behavior and development*, New York 1943.

Kihlblom, Birgit, 'Daghem och familiedaghem—en jämförande psykologisk undersökning' *Barnavård och Ungdomsskydd* vol. 28, no. 4 and 5, 1953.

Kirk, S. A., *Early education of the mentally retarded: an experimental study*, University of Illinois Press, Urbana 1958.

Kistakovskaia, M., 'The work of the teacher with children of nursery age' *Soviet Education* vol. 3, no. 8, 1961, pp. 3-6.

Kitano, H. H., *The childcare center. A study of the interaction among one-parent children, parents and school*, University of California Press, Berkeley 1964.

Koch, Fremont P., 'A nursery school for children with cerebral palsy: five-year follow-up study of thirteen children' *Pediatrics* 22, 1958, pp. 401-8.

Koenher, R. H., 'Arithmetic readiness at the kindergarten level' *Journal of Educational Research* 42, 1948, pp. 218-23.

Kohlberg, Lawrence, 'Montessori with the culturally disadvantaged: a cognitive-developmental interpretation and some research findings' (stencil) 1966.

Koshuk, Ruth Pearson, 'Developmental records of 500 nursery school children' *Journal of Experimental Education* 16, 1947, pp. 134-48.

Kounin, I., 'The effect of preschool attendance upon later school achievement' (unpublished Master's Thesis), State University of Iowa, 1939.

Kounin, I. S. and P. V. Gump, 'The ripple effect in discipline' *Elementary School Journal* 59, 1958, pp. 158-62.

Lafore, G. G., 'Practices of parents in dealing with preschool children' *Child Development Monograph* no. 31, pp. 14, 150.

Lamson, E. E., 'A follow-up study of a group of nursery school children'

Yearbook of the National Society for the Study of Education 39 (2), 1940, pp. 231-6.

Landreth, C., 'Factors associated with crying in young children in the nursery school and the home' *Child Development* 12, 1941, pp. 81-97.

Landreth, C., G. M. Gardner, B. C. Eckhardt and A. D. Prugh, 'Teacher-child contacts in nursery schools' *Journal of Experimental Education* 12, 1943 pp. 65-91.

Lane, H. S., 'Influence of nursery school education on school achievement' *Volta Review* 44, 1942, pp. 677-80.

Langmeier, I. and Zdenek Matejĕck, *Psychicka deprivace u deti* (Psychological deprivation in childhood), State Health Publ., Prague 1963.

Larson, R. G. and J. L. Olson, 'A pilot project for culturally deprived kindergarten children. Final report' (stencil), Unified School District no. 1, Racine Wis., July 1965.

Lebovici, S., 'A child psychiatrist on children in daycare centres' in *Care of children in day centres*, World Health Organisation Public Health Paper no. 24, 1964.

Leont'eva, E. V. (ed.), 'Opyt obucheniia detel shestiletnego voxrasta' *Izvestiga Akademiya Pedagogischeskikh Nauk. RSFSR* no. 108, 1960, p. 179.

Lévy-Bruhl, Odile, 'L'adaptation à l'école maternelle' *Enfance* 9, 1956, pp. 57-64.

Lewin, Kurt, Ronald Lippitt, and Ralph K. White, 'Patterns of aggressive behavior in experimentally created "social climates" ' *Journal of Social Psychology* 10, 1939 pp. 271-99.

Lézine, Irène, in M. Cohen (ed.), *Études sur le language de l'enfant*, Paris 1962.

Lézine, Irène, 'The role of toys and games in the daycare centre' in *Care of Children in Day Centre*, World Health Organisation Public Health Paper no. 24, 1964.

Lézine, Irène, and Halina Spionek, 'Quelques problèmes de dévelopment psychomoteur et d'éducation des enfants dans les crèches' *Enfance* no. 3, 1958, pp. 245-67.

Lie, H. and B. Egge, 'Behovet for daginstitusjoner for barn' *Socialt Arbeit* no. 10, 1965 and no. 1, 1966.

Lithauer, D. B., 'An experimental kindergarten for children of primary school age' *Journal of Juvenile Research* 16, 1932, pp. 153-60.

Lithauer, D. B., 'A follow-up report of the later school progress of children of primary school age trained in an experimental kindergarten' *Journal of Juvenile Research* 17, 1933, pp. 175-8.

Little, H. H., 'The relationship between nursery school training and the intelligence and social maturity of preschool children' *Pennsylvania State College for the Study of Education* no. 22, 1940, pp. 43-4.

Löfström, S., 'Smittriskerne på daghem' in *Daghem och Förskolor*, Statens offentliga utredningar no. 15, Stockholm 1951.

Mallay, H., 'Growth in social behavior and mental activity after six months in nursery school' *Child Development* 6, 1935, pp. 303-9.

Mallet, L., 'La jardinière de crèche' *Ecole Nouvelle Francaise* no. 114, 1964, pp. 2-6.

Markey, F. V., *Imaginative behavior of preschool children*, Society for Research in Child Development, Monograph no. 18, 1935.

Marshall, H. R., 'Relations between home experiences and children's use of language in play interactions with peers' *Psychological Monographs* 75, 1961, pp. 1-76.

Marshall, William H., 'An evaluation study of a group of cooperative pre-schools' *Family Life Coordinator* 9, 1961, pp. 3-4.

Maslow, A. H., 'A dynamic theory of human motivation' *Psychological Review* 50, 1943, pp. 370-96.

Maslow, A. H., *Motivation and personality*, New York 1954.

McCandles, B. R., 'The effect of enriched educational experiences upon the growth of intelligence of very superior children' (unpublished Master's Thesis), State University of Iowa 1938.

McCandles, B. R., C. B. Bilons and H. L. Bennet, 'Peer popularity and dependence on adults in preschool age socialization' *Child Development* 32, 1961, pp. 511-18.

McCarthy, Dorothea, 'Language development of the preschool child' in Barker, Kounin and Wright, *Child behavior and development*, New York 1943, pp. 107-28.

McCarthy, Dorothea, 'Language development in children' in L. Carmichael (ed.), *Manual of child psychology*, New York 1954.

McCay, Jeannette B., Ethel B. Waring and Helen D. Bull, 'Health and development of a group of nursery school children' *Child Development* 11, 1940, pp. 127-41.

McConnon, K., *The situation factor in the language responses of nursery school children* (Ph. D. Dissertation), University of Minnesota 1935.

McDavid, John W., 'Imitative behavior in preschool children' *Psychological Monographs* vol. 73, no. 16, American Psychological Association, Washington 1959.

McHugh, G., 'Changes in Goodenough I.Q. at the public school kindergarten level' *Journal of Educational Psychology* 36, 1945, pp. 17-30.

McLatchy, J., 'The influence of kindergarten attendance on progress in grade 1' *Educational Research Bulletin* 3, 1924, p. 361.

McLatchy, Josephine H., (ed.), 'Studies in childhood' *Research Bulletin of the International Kindergarten Union* (stencil), Washington DC, 1929.

McNemar, Q., 'A critical examination of the University of Iowa studies of environmental influences upon the I.Q.' *Psychological Bulletin* 37, 1940, pp. 63-92.

McNemar, Q., 'Not on Wellman's reanalysis of I.Q. changes of orphanage preschool children' *Journal of Genetic Psychology* 67, 1945, pp. 215-9.

Mead, Margaret, 'Some theoretical considerations on the problem of mother-child separation' *American Journal of Orthopsychiatry* 24, 1954, p. 477.

Mehringer, Andreas, *Geschützte Kleinkindzeit.—Noch immer Hospitalismus—das Bild, die Bedeutung, die weiteren Folgen.—Möglichkeiten einer Lösung*, Munich 1966.

Menzies, Hilda F., 'Children in day nurseries with special reference to the child under two years old' *Lancet* 251, 1946, pp. 499-501.

Merei, F., 'Group leadership and institutionalization' *Human Relations* 2, 1949, pp. 23-9.

Messenger, Virginia M., *A longitudinal comparative study of nursery school and non-nursery school children* University of Iowa, Iowa City 1940.

Moore, S. B., 'The use of commands, suggestions, and requests by nursery school and kindergarten teachers' *Child Development* 9, 1938, pp. 185-201.

Moore, T. W., 'Studying the growth of personality. A discussion on the uses of psychological data obtained in a longitudinal study of child development' *Vita Humana* 2, 1959.

Moore, Terence W., 'Effects on the children. A report from the Child Study Centre' in Simon Yudkin and Anthea Holme, *Working mothers and their children*, London 1963.

Moore, Terence, 'Children of full and part time mothers' *International Journal of Social Psychiatry* vol. 1, 1964.

Moore, Terence, 'Language and Intelligence: a longitudinal study of the first eight years. Part 2: Environmental correlates of mental growth' *Human Development* end 1966/beginning 1967.

Moore, T. W., C. B. Hindley and F. Falkner, 'A longitudinal research in child development' *British Medical Journal* 2, 1954.

Morrison, J. Cayce, *The influence of kindergarten on the age-grade progress of pupils in New York's elementary schools*, University of the State of New York Press, New York, 1938.

Mott, S. and M. E. Martin, 'Do first graders retain number concepts learned in kindergarten?' *Mathematics Teacher* vol. 60, 1947, pp. 75-8.

Mould, Lillian J., 'Class size and personality development: a study of the effect of class size on personality development of the kindergarten level' *Dissertation Abstract* 18, 1958, pp. 1108-9.

Moustakas, Clark E., 'Personality studies conducted in nursery schools' *Journal of Educational Research* 46, 1952, pp. 161-77.

Mummery, D. V., 'An analytical study of ascendant behavior of preschool children' *Child Development* 18, 1947, pp. 40-81.

Murphy, G., L. B. Murphy and T. M. Newcomb, *Experimental social psychology*, New York 1937.

Murphy, L. B., *Social behavior and child personality. An exploratory study of some roots of sympathy* Columbia University Press, New York 1937.

Nechaieva, V. G., 'Konstruierovanie v diet skom sadoo' (Construction activities in the kindergarten) *Doshkol'noe Vospitanie* 3, 1948, pp. 19-27.

Nechaieva, V. G., 'Contact between children of different ages in the joint preschool institution' *Sovietskaya Pedagogika* no. 9, 1963.

Nesbitt, M., 'Student and child relationships in the nursery school' *Child Development* 19, 1943, pp. 143-66.

Nikol'skia A. V., 'I z semi v dietskiu sad' (From the home to the nursery) *Doshkol'noe Vospitanie* 10, 1948, pp. 17-24.

Nicholson, E. L., 'The relative social development of children with preschool background as opposed to those who lack such experiences' (Master's Thesis), North Texas State College, Denton 1957.

Nye, F. I. and Lois W. Hoffman, *The employed mother in America*, Rand McNally, Chicago 1963.

Nye, F. I., J. P. Perry Jun., and R. H. Ogles, 'Anxiety and anti-social behavior in preschool children' in Nye and Hoffman, 1963.

O'Connor, N., 'The evidence for the permanently disturbing effects of mother-child separation' *Acta Psychologica* 12, 1956, pp. 174-91.

Olson, J. and R. Larson, 'A pilot study evaluating one method of teaching culturally deprived kindergarten children' (stencil), Racine Wis., August 1962.

Olson, W. C. and B. O. Hughes, 'Subsequent growth of children with and without nursery school experience' *Yearbook of the National Society for the Study of Education* 39 (2), 1940, pp. 237-44.

Page, J. D., 'The effect of nursery school attendance upon the I.Q.' *Psychological Bulletin* 36, 1939, p. 551.

Page, J. D., 'The effects of nursery school attendance upon subsequent I.Q.' *Journal of Psychology* 10, 1940, pp. 221-30.

Page, M. L., 'The modification of ascendant behavior in preschool children' *Studies in Child Welfare* 12, University of Iowa 1936, p. 69.

Painter, G., 'The effect of a rhythmic and sensory motor activity program on perceptual motor spatial abilities of kindergarten children' *Exceptional Children* 33, 1966, pp. 113-16.

Parten, M. B., 'Social participation among preschool children' *Journal of Abnormal and Social Psychology* 27, 1932, pp. 243-69.

Parten, M. B., 'Social play among preschool children', *Journal of Abnormal and Social Psychology* 28, 1933, pp. 136-47.

Pease, D. and B. D. Gardner, *Non-continuous mothering and the development of children. Progress Report no. 3*, Department of Child Development, Iowa State College, August 1958.

Pendergast, Katheen et al., 'An articulation study of 15.255 Seattle first grade children with and without kindergarten' *Exceptional Children* 32 (8), 1966, pp. 541-7.

Peters, W. J., 'The progress of kindergarten pupils in elementary grades' *Journal of Educational Research* 7, 1923, pp. 117-26.

Peterson, Theresa J., 'A preliminary study of the effect of previous nursery school attendance upon five-year-old children entering kindergarten' *University of Iowa Studies in Child Welfare* 14, no. 1, pp. 197-248.

Philips, G. I., 'Kindergarten training as a factor in social adjustment of a selected group of young children' (Master's Thesis), Eastern New Mexico University, Portalas 1953.

Piaget, I., *Introduction à l'épistémologie génétique*, Paris 1950.

Pinnau, S. R., 'The infantile disorders of hospitalism and anaclitic depression' *Psychological Bulletin* 52, 1955, pp. 429-59.

'Plan and research problems of the RSFSR, Academy of Pedagogical Sciences for 1962' *Sovietskaya Pedagogika* no. 3, 1962. See also *Soviet Education* vol. 4, 1961-62.

Plowden Report, *Children and their primary schools. Plowden Report on Primary Education*, 2 vols. (1: Report; 2: Research and Surveys), Department of Education and Science, HMSO, London 1967.

Plowmann, Gisela Julia, 'Daynursery care for two-year-olds' in G. Meyer, *Studies of Children*, 1948, pp. 147-56.

Pratt, Willis E., 'A study of the differences in the prediction of reading success of kindergarten and non-kindergarten children' *Journal of Educational Research* 2, 1949, pp. 525-33.

Prescott, Elisabeth, *A pilot study of daycare centers and their clientel*, Welfare Administration, Children's Bureau, US Department of Health, Education and Welfare, 1965.

Prescott, Elisabeth, and Joan Harris, *Children in group daycare. The effect of a dual child-rearing environment*, Los Angeles 1964.

Prescott, E. and J. R. Harris, 'An observational study of daycare program progress report' (stencil, unpublished), Pacific Oaks College, Pasadena Calif., 1965.

Pringle, K. L., *Deprivation and education*, London 1965.

Pringle, K. and V. Bossio, 'Intellectual emotional and social development of deprived children' *Vita Humana* 1, 1958 (a), pp. 65-92.

Pringle, K. and V. Bossio, 'Language development and reading attainment of deprived children' *Vita Humana* 1, 1958 (b), pp. 142-70.

Pringle, K. and V. Bossio, 'Early prolonged separation and emotional maladjustment' *Child Psychology and Psychiatry* 1, 1960, pp. 37-48.

Pringle, K. and M. Tanner, 'The effects of early deprivation on speech development. A comparative study of four-year-olds in a nursery school and in residential nurseries' *Language and Speech* 1, 1958, pp. 269-87.

Rabin, A. I., 'Personality maturity of kibbutz (Israel collective settlement) and non-kibbutz children as reflected in Rorschach findings' *Journal of Projective Techniques and Personality Assessment* 21, 1957, pp. 148-53.

Rabin, A. I., 'Behavior research in collective settlements in Israel: 6 infants and children under conditions of "Intermittent" mothering in the kibbutz' *American Journal of Orthopsychiatry* 28, 1958 (a), pp. 577-86.

Rabin, A. I., 'Some psychosexual differences between kibbutz and non-kibbutz Israeli boys' *Journal of Projective Techniques and Personality Assessment* 22, 1958 (b), pp. 328-32.

Rabin, A. I., (Michigan State University, East Lansing) 'Kibbutz children. Research findings to date' *Children* 5, 1958 (c), pp. 179-85.

Radina, E., 'Early childhood pedagogy' (La pédagogie de l'enfant en bas âge) *Soviet Education* 5, no. 10, 1963, pp. 22-5.

Raleigh, N. C., *A healthy personality for every child*, Health Publications Institute Inc., 1951.

Rasborg, F. and J. Florander, *Forskningsmetodologi. Pædagogisk-psykologiske tekster* vol. 2, Copenhagen 1966.

Reeves, K., 'Who goes to nursery school?' *Mental Hygiene* 25, New York 1941, pp. 458-61.

Reichenberg-Hackett, W., 'Practices, attitudes and values in nursery group education' *Psychological Reports* 10, 1962, pp. 151-72.

Reichenberg-Hackett, W., 'Influence of nursery group experience on children's drawings' *Psychological Reports* 14, 1964, pp. 433-4.

Rexford, Eveoleen N., 'The role of the nursery school in a child guidance clinic' *American Journal of Orthopsychiatry* 19, 1949, pp. 517-24.

Reyment, M. L. and R. T. Hinton, 'The effect of a change to a relative superior environment upon the I.Q.'s of one hundred children' *Yearbook of the National Society for the Study of Education* 39 (2), 1940, pp. 255-68.

Rhinehart, J. B., 'Some effects of a nursery school parent education program on a group of three-year-olds' *Journal of Genetic Psychology* 61, 1942, pp. 153-61.

Rhinehart, J. B., 'A comparative evaluation of two nursery school parent education programs' *Journal of Educational Psychology* 36, 1945, pp. 309-17.

Rifbjerg, Sofie, 'Underudviklede børn. "Head-start"-bevægelsen i U.S.A.' *Dansk pædagogisk tidsskrift* 15, 1967, pp. 256-61.

Rigney, M. G., 'Practices of teachers in dealing with preschool children' (unpublished Doctoral Dissertation) Columbia University 1952.

Ripin, R., 'A comparative study of the development of infants in an institution with those in homes of low socio-economic status' *Psychological Bulletin* 30, 1933, pp. 680-1.

Roff, M. and L. Roff, 'An analysis of the variance of conflict behavior in preschool children' *Child Development* 11, 1940, pp. 43-60.

Rosenblith, J. F., 'Learning by imitation in kindergarten children' *Child Development* 30, 1959, pp. 69-80.

Ross, D., 'Relationship between dependency, intentional learning and incidental learning in preschool children' *Journal of Personality and Social Psychology* 4, 1966, pp. 374-81.

Roudinesco, J. and G. Appell, 'Les répercussions de la stabulation hospitalière sur le développement psychomoteur des jeunes enfants' *Semaine des Hôpitaux de Paris* 26, 1950, pp. 2271-3.

Ryan, Mary E., 'Social adjustment of kindergarten children ten years later' *Smith College Studies in Social Work* 19, 1949, pp. 138-9

Saguisag, B. V., 'The effect of kindergarten and non-kindergarten education on the achievement of pupils in the primary department of the Philippine Women's University' *Education Abstract: Preschool Education* vol. 12, no. 1, 1960, p. 19.

Saksena, Shakuntala, 'Effects of preschool training upon educational attainment and personality traits of children' *Shiksha* 14 (2), 1961, pp. 106-17.

Salusky, A. S., 'Collective behavior of children at a preschool age' *Journal of Social Psychology* 1, 1930, pp. 367-78.

Sandels, Stina, *Drag ur förskolålderns psykologi och pedagogik,* Stockholm 1952.

Sandels, Stina, *Utvecklingspsychologiska beteende studier,* Stockholm 1952.

Sandels, Stina, 'Försummade aspekter på utvecklingen i den tidiga barnåldern' in 'Barn i barnstugor: motorik, kroppsmått, möbler' *Sociale Meddelanden,* 1963, pp. 661-696.

Sandels, Stina, 'Utvecklingspsykologiska forskninginstituttet vid Stockholms universitet–Lärarhögskolan. Översikt över virksomheten 1958-64' *Sociale Meddelanden* 1-2, 1964, pp. 149-68.

Sandels, Stina, M. Bendz-Sandell and Y. Krook, *Rapport om undersökning rörende "trötthetssymtom" hos barn på daghem,* Stockholm 1967.

Schmidt-Kolmer, Eva, *Der Einfluss der Lebensbedingungen auf die Entwicklung der Kinder im Vorschulalter,* Berlin 1963.

Schmidt-Kolmer, Eva, 'Organization of living and educational conditions for infants and small children in children's institutions' in *Care of children in day centres,* World Health Organisation Public Health Paper no. 24, 1964.

Schorr, R., 'Die Erkrankungshäufigkeit im Vorschulalter' in Schmidt-Kolmer, 1963.

Schultz Jørgensen, P., 'Forskolens indflydelse på børns udvikling' (stencil), Birkerød 1968.

Schütter-Janikulla, K. and H. Krohne, 'Transferprobleme und Schulreifetraining' *Zeitschrift für experimentelle und angewandte Psychologie* 13, 1966, pp. 632-44.

Sears, R. R., 'Relation of early socialization experiences to aggression in middle childhood' *Journal of Abnormal and Social Psychology* 63, 1961, pp. 466-92.

Sears, P. S. and E. M. Dowley, 'Research on teaching in the nursery school' in N. L. Gage (ed.) *Handbook of research on teaching,* Rand McNally, Chicago 1963.

Sears, R. R., Eleanor E. Maccoby and H. Levin, *Patterns of child rearing,* Evanston 1957.

Séminaire sur les crèches, Centre Internationale de l'Enfance, 5-7 December 1960, Paris 1961.

Shaw, Martha Luelle, 'The subsequent adjustment of first grade children in relation to age at entrance, socioeconomic status, and type of preschool experiences' *Dissertation Abstract* 17, 1957, p. 1014.

Sherman, Mandel, 'Growing children are studied at Washington child research center' *School Life* 14, 1929, pp. 184-7.

Siegel, A. E., 'Aggressive behavior of young children in the absence of an adult' *Child Development* 28, 1957, pp. 371-8.

Siegel, A. E., et al., 'Dependence and independence in children of working mothers' *Child Development* 30, 1959, pp. 533-47.

Siegel, A. E. and L. G. Kohn, 'Permissiveness, permission and aggression: the effect of adult presence on aggression in children's play' *Child Development* 30, 1959, pp. 131-41.

Simonsen, K. M., *Examination of children from children's homes and day nurseries*, Copenhagen 1947.

Sjölin, Stig, 'Care of well children in daycare centres' in *Care of children in day centres*, World Health Organisation Public Health Paper no. 24, 1964.

Sjølund, Arne, 'Den sociale tilpasningsproces i børnegrupper' *Dansk Psykologforenings Meddelelser* 14, 1961, pp. 121-5.

Sjølund, Arne, 'En sammenligning af indstilling til opdragelsesspørgsmål hos mødre og børnehavepædagoger' (stencil), Copenhagen 1962.

Sjølund, Arne, 'En undersøgelse af sammenhængen mellem moderne indstilling til opdragelse og barnets sociale adfærd' (manuscript), Copenhagen 1963.

Sjølund, Arne, 'Er der sammenhaeng mellem moderens udearbejde og børnenes sociale og arbejdsmæssige tilpasning i skolen' *Socialt Tidsskrift* 40, 1964, pp. 95-122.

Sjølund, Arne, *Gruppepsykologi*, Copenhagen 1965.

Sjølund, Arne, 'Dominans hos børnehavebørn og sammenhæng med forældrenes indstilling til opdragelse' (stencil), Copenhagen 1966.

Sjølund, Arne, 'En sammenligning af konforme og selvstændige børnehavebørns opvækst- og opdragelsessituation' (stencil), Copenhagen 1967 (a).

Sjølund, Arne, 'Kreativ adfærd hos børnehavebarnet og forældrenes indstilling til opdragelsesspørgsmål' (stencil), Copenhagen 1967 (b).

Skeels, H. M., 'Some Iowa studies of the mental growth of children in relation to differentials of the environment. A summary' *Yearbook of the National Society for the Study of Education* 39, 1940, pp. 281-308.

Skeels, H. M., 'Effects of adoption on children from institutions' *Children* 12, 1965, pp. 33-4.

Skeels, H. M. and H. B. Dye, 'A study of the effect of differential simulation on mentally retarded children' *Proceedings of American Associa-*

tion of Mental Deficiency 44, 1939, pp. 114-36.

Skeels, H. M. and E. A. Fillimore, 'The mental development of children from underprivileged homes' *Journal of Genetic Psychology* 50, 1937, pp. 427-39.

Skeels, H. M., R. Updegraff, B. L. Wellmann and H. M. Williams, 'A study of environmental stimulation: an orphanage preschool project' *University of Iowa Studies in Child Welfare* 15, no. 4, 1938.

Skeels, H. M., B. L. Wellmann and M. Skodak, 'Review of McNemar's critical examination of Iowa studies' *Psychological Bulletin* vol. 37, 1940, pp. 93-111.

Skodak, M., 'Children in foster homes: a study of mental development' *University of Iowa Studies in Child Welfare* 16, no. 1, 1939.

Slater, E. H., 'Types, levels and irregularities of response to a nursery school situation of forty children observed with special reference to the home environment' *Studies in Child Health and Development* 9, no. 2, Harvard University, 1939.

Smilansky, 'Gan hova keëmtsai lekidum hahitpathut haintelektualit' *Megamot* 9, 1958, pp. 163-80.

Smilansky, M., *Experiments in promoting intellectual development in preschoolers from socio-culturally underdeveloped strata*, Henrietta Szold Institute for Child and Youth Welfare, 1967.

Smith, M. E., A study of some factors influencing the development of the sentence in preschool children' *Journal of Genetic Psychology* 46, 1935, pp. 182-212.

Smith, R. B., 'Effect of group vocal training on the singing ability of nursery school children' *Journal of Research in Music Education* 19, 1964, pp. 194-7.

Solov'eva, O., 'Child care' *Soviet Education* vol. 5, no. 2, 1962, pp. 6-11.

Sommer, Agnes T., 'The effect of group training upon the correction articulatory defects in preschool children' *Child Development* 3, no. 2, 1932, pp. 91-103.

Spiro, M. E., 'Education in a communal village in Israel' *American Journal of Orthopsychiatry* 114, 1957, pp. 357-63.

Spiro, M. E., *Children of the kibbutz*, Harvard University Press, Cambridge Mass. 1958.

Spitz, R. A., 'Hospitalism: an inquiry into the genesis of psychiatric conditions in early childhood' *Psychoanalytic Study of the Child* 1, 1945, pp. 53-74.

Spitz, R. A., 'Analytic depression' *Psychoanalytic Study of the Child* 2, 1946 (a), pp. 313-42.

Spitz, R. A., 'Hospitalism: A follow-up report' *Psychoanalytic Study of the Child* 2, 1946 (b), pp. 113-17.

Sprinkle, Clemmie B., 'A comparison of reading abilities of kindergarten and non-kindergarten trained children in the first grade' in *University of North Carolina Record. Research in progress*, 1948.

Starkweather, E. K. and K. E. Roberts, 'IQ changes occurring during nursery school attendance at the Merril-Palmer school' *Yearbook of the National Society for the Study of Education* 39, 1940, pp. 315-35.

Stendler, Celia B., 'How well do elementary-school teachers understand child behavior?' *Journal of Educational Psychology* 40, 1949, pp. 489-98.

Stith, M. and R. Connor, 'Dependency and helpfulness in young children' *Child Development* 33, 1962, pp. 15-20.

Stoddard, G. D., 'Intelligence: Its nature and nurture' (Part 1: Comparative and critical expositions; Part 2: Original studies and experiments) *Yearbook of the National Society for the Study of Education* 39, 1940.

Stoddard, G. D. and B. L. Wellmann, 'Environment and the IQ' *Yearbook of the National Society for the Study of Education* 39, 1940, pp. 405-42.

Stolz, L. M., 'Effects of maternal employment on children: Evidence from research' *Child Development* 31 no. 4, 1960, pp. 749-82.

Stone, L. Joseph, Miriam Foster Fiedler and Carol Gabrielson Fine, 'Pre-school education of deaf children' *Journal of Speech and Hearing Disorders* 26, 1961, pp. 45-60.

Strodtbeck, F. L., *Progress report: the reading readiness nursery*, University of Chicago 1963.

Stukat, K. G., *Lekskolans inverkan på barns utveckling*, Stockholm 1966.

Svalastoga, Kaare, *Prestige, Class and Mobility*, (Part 2, chapter 3, p. 4), Copenhagen 1959.

Swift, J. W., 'Effects of early group experience: The nursery school and day nursery' in Hoffmann, M. L.,, and L. W. (eds.), *Review of child development research*, New York 1964.

Taylor, I. A., 'The nature of the creative process' in P. Smith, *Creativity. An examination of the creative process*, Hartings, New York 1959.

Taylor, Katharine W., 'A community-wide program of parent education (co-operative behavior)' *Children* vol. 9, no. 1, 1962.

Taylor, Marian W. and G. Frank, 'An experiment in nursery school follow-up' *Childhood Education* 7, no. 9, 1931, pp. 474-81.

Teegarden, L., 'The kindergarten and reading reversals' *Childhood Education* vol. 9, 1932, pp. 82-3.

Theisen, W. W., 'Factors affecting results in primary reading' *Yearbook of the National Society for the Study of Education* 20, 1925.

Thompson, G. G., *The social emotional development of preschool children under two separate types of educational program*, Psychological Monograph 56, no. 5, 1944.

Thorsell, Siv, 'Kvinnan i samhället' *Studieförbundet Näringsliv och Sämhälle Orientering* 3, 1966, pp. 2-6.

Tizard, Professor, *Meddeler om sine erfaringer fra undersøgelser*, Unesco, 1967.

Tjellström, Sylvia, 'Förskollärares och småskollärares bedömning av fyra aspekter på 6-7 åriga barns emotionella och sociale beteende' (stencil), Stockholm 1967.

Tordrup, S. A., *Alder-skolestandpunkt*, Copenhagen 1961.

Torrance, E. P. (ed.) *Creativity*, Minnesota 1960.

Torrance, E. P. (ed.) *Guiding creative talent*, Englewood Cliffs N.J., 1962.

Trautmann, J., cited in Sjölin 1964.

Trumbo, C., 'Relation of parent behavior to assertive behavior of children' (Thesis), Iowa State College 1945.

Trusal, M., 'The effect of kindergarten experience on social readiness and total readiness for first grade achievement in reading and numbers in the Williamsport, Pennsylvania, public schools' (Doctoral Dissertation), University Park, Pennsylvania State University, 1955.

Tyler, Forrest B. and James W. Whisenhunt, 'Motivational changes during preschool attendance' *Child Development* 33, 1962, pp. 427-42.

Unesco, *World survey of education*, 1955.

Unesco, 'Preschool education' *Education Abstract* vol. 12, no. 1, 1960.

Unesco, *Organization of pre-primary education*, publication 230, Paris 1961 (a).

Unesco, *Preschool education in 114 countries. Quant. Development from 1950-1958*, Paris 1961 (b).

Updegraff, R., 'Comparative frequency of certain communicable diseases of childhood in nursery school and non-nursery school children' *Child Development* 4, 1933, pp. 298-301.

Updegraff, R., L. Heiliger and J. Learned, 'The effect of training upon singing ability and musical interest of three-, four-, and five-year-old children' *University of Iowa Studies in Child Welfare* 14, 1938, pp. 85-131.

Updegraff, R. and E. K. Herbst, 'An experimental study of the social behavior stimulated in young children by certain play materials' *Journal of Genetic Psychology* 42, 1933, pp. 372-91.

US Children's Bureau, *Research relating to children: Studies in progress on research programs, physical and motor development, intelligence, behavior, personality, education, health services, and social services*, Clearing-house for Research on Child Life, Washington D.C., 1953.

Usova, A. P., 'Draft program of education in the kindergarten' *Soviet Education* 3, 1961 (a), pp. 3-8.

Usova, A. P., 'Draft program of education in the kindergarten' *Soviet Education*, 1961 (a), *Pedagogischeskikh Nauk. RSFSR* no. 118, 1961 (c), p. 132.

Usova, A. P., 'Play as a form of organizing the life and activity of children' *Soviet Education* vol. 3, no. 6, 1961 (b), pp. 19-21.

Usova, A. P., 'The pedagogy of games and its urgent problems' *Soviet Education* vol. 5, no. 5, 1963, pp. 29-35.

Van Alstyne, *Play behavior and choice of play material of preschool children*, Chicago 1932.

Van Alstyne, D. and Hattwick, L. A., 'A follow-up study of the behavior of nursery school children' *Child Development* 10, 1939, pp. 43-70.

Vitz, P., 'Some changes in behavior of nursery school children over a period of seven weeks' *Journal of Nursery Education* 16, 1961, pp. 62-5.

Voas, W. H., 'Does attendance at the Winnetka nursery school tend to raise the IQ?' *Yearbook of the National Society for the Study of Education* 39, 2, 1940, pp. 363-76.

Volkova, A. A., 'Vospitatel'naia rabota s det'mi trekh let' (Educational work with three-year-old children) *Doshkol'noe Vespitanie* no. 3, 1950, pp. 8-15.

Waddell, Charles W., Barbara Greenwood, and staff, *A six year experiment with a nursery school*, University of California Press, Berkeley 1931.

Wagner, M. A., 'The experimental preschool group of Clarke school' *American Annals of the Deaf* 80, 1935, pp. 391-4.

Walsh, M. E., 'The relation of nursery school training to the development of certain personality traits' *Child Development* 2, 1931, pp. 72-3.

Wann, Kenneth D., et al., *Fostering intellectual development in young children*, N.Y. Bureau of Publications, Teachers College, Columbia University, New York 1962.

Washburn, Ruth W., 'Re-education in a nursery group: A study in clinical psychology' *Monograph of the Society for Research in Child Development* vol. 9, no. 2, serial no. 38, 1944.

Weikart, D. P., *Preschool intervention: A preliminary report of the Perry preschool project*, Ann Arbor 1967 (a).

Weikart, D. P., 'Preschool programs: Preliminary findings' *Journal of Special Education* vol. 1, no. 2, 1967 (b), pp. 163-81.

Weikart, D. P., 'Preliminary results from a longitudinal study of disadvantaged children' (stencil), Michigan 1967 (c).

Weiss, R. G., 'The validity of early entrance into kindergarten' *Journal of Educational Research* 56, 1962, pp. 53-4.

Wellmann, B. L., *An evaluation of existing scales for measuring general intelligence*, Iowa Child Welfare Research Station, State University of Iowa, 1932 (a).

Wellmann, B. L., *Studies on growth in intelligence*, Iowa Child Welfare Research Station, State University of Iowa, 1932 (b).

Wellmann, B. L., 'The effect of preschool attendance upon the IQ' *Journal of Experimental Education* 1, 1933, pp. 48-69.

Wellmann, B. L., 'Growth in intelligence under differing school environments' *Journal of Experimental Education* 3, 1934, pp. 59-83.

Wellmann, B. L., 'The intelligence of preschool children as measured by the Merril-Palmer scale of performance tests' *University of Iowa Studies in Child Welfare, New Series* no. 361, vol. 15, no. 3, 1938.

Wellmann, B. L., 'The meaning of environment' *Yearbook of the National Society for the Study of Education* 39 (2), 1940 (a), pp. 21-40.

Wellmann, B. L., 'Iowa studies on the effects of schooling' *Yearbook of the National Society for the Study of Education* 39 (2), 1940 (b), pp. 377-99.

Wellmann, B. L., 'The effects of preschool attendance upon intellectual development' in Barker R. G., I. S. Kronin and H. F. Wright, *Child behavior and development*, New York 1943, pp. 229-43.

Wellmann, B. L., 'IQ changes of preschool and non-preschool groups during the preschool years. A summary of literature' *Journal of Psychology* no. 20, 1945, pp. 347-68.

Wellmann, B. L. and B. McCandles, *Factors associated with Binet IQ changes of preschool children*, Psychology Monograph 60, no. 2, 1946.

Wellmann, B. L. and Edna Lee Pegram, 'Binet IQ changes of orphanage preschool children. A re-analysis' *Journal of Genetic Psychology* 65, 1944, pp. 239-63.

Wilderson, D. A., 'Programs and practices in compensatory education for disadvantaged children' *Review of Educational Research* 35, 1965, pp. 426-40.

Wilensky, Harold, 'Teaching styles in the nursery' (stencil), 1966.

Williams, R. and M. L. Mattson, 'The effect of social groupings upon the language of preschool children' *Child Development* 13, 1942, pp. 233-45.

Williamson, Helen Charity, 'Self-dependence and responsibility of kindergarten children' (unpublished Master's Thesis), University of Chicago, 1932.

Wilson, Betty Ann, 'The development and evaluation of a speech improvement program for kindergarten children' *Journal of Speech and Hearing Disorders* 19, 1954, pp. 4-13.

Witmer, H., 'The influence of parental attitudes on the social adjustment of the individual' *American Sociological Review*, 1937, pp. 756-63.

Woolfolk, A. S., 'Social adjustment through kindergarten training' *Child Education* 5, 1929, pp. 264-8.

Woolley, H. T., 'The validity of standards of mental measurement' *School and Society* 21, 1925, pp. 476-82.

Wright, M. E., 'Constructiveness of play as affected by group organization and frustration' *Character and Personality* 11, 1942, pp. 40-9.

Wright, M. E., 'The influence of frustration upon social relations of young children' *Character & Personality* 12, 1943, pp. 111-22.

Yakubovskaya, K. L., 'Quelques particularités dans le développement de la compréhension de la parole dans des maisons d'enfants âgés de deux ans (en russe)' *Pediatria* 42, no. 6, 1963, pp. 30-5.

Yarrow, Leon, 'The effect of antecedent frustration on projective play' *Psychological Monographs* 62, no. 6, 1948.

Yarrow, Leon, 'Maternal deprivation: Toward an empirical and conceptual re-evaluation' *Psychological Bulletin* 58, 1961, pp. 459-90.

Yarrow, Leon, 'Research in dimensions of early maternal care' *Merril-Palmer Quarterly* 9, 1963, p. 101.

Yarrow, Leon, 'Measurement and specification of the early infant environment' in *Care of children in day centres*, World Health Organization Public Health Paper no. 24, 1964.

Yarrow, Leon, 'Separations from parents during early childhood' in M. and L. Hoffmann (eds.) *Review of Child Development Research* vol. 1, 1965, pp. 89-136.

Young, Florence M., 'An analysis of certain variables in a developmental study of language' *Genetic Psychology Monographs* vol. 23, 1941, pp. 3-141.

Yudkin, Simon, and Anthea Holme, *Working mothers and their children. A study for the council for children's welfare*, London 1963.

Yum, Louise, 'A nursery school for cerebral-palsied children' *Children* 1, 1954, pp. 138-42.

Yum, Louise, 'Adapting the nursery school for the mentally handicapped cerebral-palsied child' *Exceptional Children* 22 (1), 1955, pp. 7-9 and pp. 45-6

Zaluzhskaya, M., 'More concern for preschool education' *Soviet Education* vol. 2, no. 3, 1960, pp. 51-3.

Zaporozhets, A., 'New educational curriculum in the kindergarten' *Soviet Education* vol. 5, no. 2, 1962, pp. 3-6.

Zhukovskaya, R. J., 'Development of the child's imagination in the process of play' *Soviet Education* vol. 6, no. 4, 1962, pp. 44-53.

Ziv, Avner, 'Les maisons d'enfants-atmosphère, adaption' *Informations Sociales* 21, 1967, pp. 6-112.

Östlyngen, L. H., 'Er det skadelig for barn under 2-3 år å väre i daginstitusjon' *Norsk Pedagogisk Tidsskrift* vol. 6, 1956.

Ås, Dagfinn, *En spörreskemaundersögelse om barnehager. Lånborg i Bergen*, Oslo 1966.

Index